CRITICAL INSIGHTS

Salman Rushdie

CRITICAL INSIGHTS

Salman Rushdie

Editor
Bernard F. Rodgers, Jr.
Bard College at Simon's Rock

SALEM PRESS
A Division of EBSCO Publishing
Ipswich, Massachusetts

Cover Photo: UK - Edinburgh - 2008 International Book Festival - Salmon Rushdie © Colin McPherson/Corbis

Editor's text © 2013 by Bernard F. Rodgers, Jr.

Copyright © 2013, by Salem Press, A Division of EBSCO Publishing, Inc. All rights reserved. No part of this work may be used or reproduced in any manner whatsoever or transmitted in any form or by any means, electronic or mechanical, including photocopy, recording, or any information storage and retrieval system, without written permission from the copyright owner. For permissions requests, contact proprietarypublishing@ebscohost.com.

∞ The paper used in these volumes conforms to the American National Standard for Permanence of Paper for Printed Library Materials, Z39.48-1992 (R1997).

Library of Congress Cataloging-in-Publication Data
Salman Rushdie / editor, Bernard F. Rodgers, Jr.
 p. cm. -- (Critical insights)
 Includes bibliographical references and index.
 ISBN 978-1-4298-3729-3 (hardcover) -- ISBN 978-1-4298-3777-4 (ebook) 1. Rushdie, Salman--Criticism and interpretation. I. Rodgers, Bernard F., 1947-
 PR6068.U757Z8444 2012
 823'.914--dc23
                         2012019663

PRINTED IN THE UNITED STATES OF AMERICA

Contents

About This Volume, Bernard F. Rodgers, Jr.   vii

Career, Life, and Influence

On Salman Rushdie, Bernard F. Rodgers, Jr.   3
Biography of Salman Rushdie, R. S. Krishnan   16

Critical Contexts

Critical Reception, Joel Kuortti   25
History and Myth: Rewinding the Past in "The Prophet's Hair"
    and *The Moor's Last Sigh*, Mona Narain   44
Hybridity and the Chutnification of History, Nicole Weickgenannt Thiara   61
Salman Rushdie and Philip Roth: Parallels and Departures,
    David J. Zucker   77

Critical Readings

Rushdie's Other Worlds, Roger Y. Clark   97
History as Trope and Atrophying History in *Midnight's Children*,
    R. S. Krishnan   115
On Reading *Midnight's Children* Politically, Asma Abbas   131
Shame: "A Sort of Modern Fairytale," Harold Branam   150
Shilling Postcolonial Identity: Acting, Advertising, and the Capitalist
    Economy in *The Satanic Verses*, Lynn Wells   168
From Multiculturalism to Pop Cosmopolitanism: Transcultural
    Exchanges in Salman Rushdie's Children's Books,
    Justyna Deszcz-Tryhubczak   182
Rushdie as Artist, Migrant, and Humanist in *Imaginary Homelands*
    and *Step Across This Line*, Lydia Forssander-Song   198
One and Many in *The Moor's Last Sigh*, Dohra Ahmad   213
Disorientation and Double Vision in *The Ground Beneath Her Feet*,
    Bernard F. Rodgers, Jr.   233
Repetition and Listing in *Fury*, Robert C. Evans   247
Shalimar the Clown: Love, Betrayal, and the Myths of Colonialism,
    Patrick Colm Hogan   264

Resources

Chronology of Salman Rushdie	283
Works by Salman Rushdie	288
Bibliography	289
About the Editor	293
Contributors	295
Index	299

About This Volume

Bernard F. Rodgers, Jr.

For reasons both literary and political, Salman Rushdie is probably the most famous and the most infamous novelist of our time. Although he has only been publishing since 1975 and only began to draw serious attention with the 1981 publication of *Midnight's Children*, his work has already elicited a large and diverse international reaction from scholars and critics, including forty-six books and hundreds of essays and reviews. This volume in the Critical Insights series, however, is one of the first to treat nearly all of Rushdie's fiction from *Grimus* to *The Enchantress of Florence*, as well as his major essay collections, and is designed to offer a variety of views on both his work and the critical responses to it. (Since nearly a dozen books have already appeared about *The Satanic Verses* controversy, it is intentionally *not* the focus of this collection, although it is discussed in a number of the essays.) The book is divided into sections containing essays by scholars with roots in the United States, Canada, Britain, Poland, India, and Pakistan. It offers an overview of Rushdie's career, life, and influence; examinations of the critical reception of his writing as well as its cultural, political, and historical contexts; a series of readings from diverse critical perspectives that explore his major books, themes, characters, motifs, and concerns; and, finally, resources for further study.

My introduction draws on his essays and novels to offer a perspective on Rushdie's style, subjects, and persistent concerns. R. S. Krishnan's biographical sketch then surveys Rushdie's life and career, tracing his roots to the Bombay that he has continually returned to and immortalized in writing that has often been strongly autobiographical, outlining his influences and the influence he has had on others, and describing the evolution of his work.

The Critical Contexts section begins with Joel Kuortti, whose *The Salman Rushdie Bibliography* is the most thorough record of our subject's publications and the critical responses to it through 1997. He provides a survey of what he sees as the three phases of popular and scholarly reaction to the books through *The Enchantress of Florence*, along with an extensive bibliography. Mona Narain focuses on the short story "The Prophet's Hair" and the novel *The Moor's Last Sigh*, considering both how they are shaped by and how they fictionally reshape real events in recent Indian history. Among the events she considers are the violent religious conflict between Hindus and Muslims over the sacred Babri Masjid in the city of Ayodhya, the rise of the right-wing political party Shiv Sena in Bombay, and the 1963 theft of a relic of the Prophet from the Hazratbal mosque in Srinagar, Kashmir. Developing ideas she treats in her 2009 study *Salman Rushdie and Indian Historiography*, Nicole Weickgenannt Thiara also considers Rushdie's uses of history by examining one of the essential ideals in all of his work: the concept of cultural hybridity. This mixing of cultures, histories, ideas, and stories, she shows, is something that Rushdie consistently expresses in his language, style, and subjects—both through truthfully including actual historical examples and through trying to "write hybridity into being imaginatively" by improving on the historical record. This combination of factual accuracy and imagination, and its implications for storytelling, is exactly what Rushdie means when he refers to the "chutnification of history" in *Midnight's Children*, Thiara reminds us; one of its purposes in his work is to create a yearning in his readers for such cultural hybridity—embodied for him in 1940s Bombay and pre-Partition Kashmir—to be made real again. While the reaction of some of Philip Roth's Jewish readers to *Portnoy's Complaint* was a largely American phenomenon and not exactly life threatening, Roth's description of his response to it in *The Facts*, published while Salman Rushdie was still underground in the wake of *The Satanic Verses*, unsurprisingly attracted the younger writer's attention. David J. Zucker reviews this and much more in his discussion of the similarities and differences he observes between the lives of these two writers and the reactions to both their most controversial books and their later novels *Sabbath's Theater* and *Fury*, from members of their faith communities and from critics.

Rushdie's books are then further explored in twelve Critical Readings. Roger Y. Clark revisits ideas in his groundbreaking *Stranger Gods: Salman Rushdie's Other Worlds* and shows how the treatment of the relationship between this world and "other worlds" in the seldom-discussed first novel, *Grimus*, begins an argument between secularism and religious belief. This argument, he explains, is central to the themes, references, and images of *Midnight's Children*, *Shame*, and *The Satanic Verses*, but less radically and confrontationally pursued in *Haroun and the Sea of Stories* and Rushdie's subsequent novels. Through exploring the connections between *Grimus* and works ranging from Farid ud-Din Attâr's twelfth-century epic poem *The Conference of the Birds* and William Shakespeare's tragedy *Othello* to the poetry of Walt Whitman, T. S. Eliot, and William B. Yeats, Clark also reveals that the book marks the first appearance of the multilayered, multilingual, and multicultural style that would define all of Rushdie's work. R. S. Krishnan also turns to the subject of Rushdie and history to describe how the novelist historicizes his fiction and fictionalizes his history in *Midnight's Children*, choosing to write history as autobiography and, in the process, mixing narrative forms. Asma Abbas sets out to explore how a novel like *Midnight's Children* endures and is read today—in the contemporary global context and in light of the history of the subcontinent in the decades since it first appeared—and argues that the true test of its endurance is how effectively it "can raise and engage the question of our current crisis as a crisis of politics itself." Drawing on the ideas of Karel Kosík, Hannah Arendt, Jacques Rancière, and Homi Bhabha, she argues that both "politics" and what it means to "read politically" need to be redefined before *Midnight's Children* can be evaluated from this perspective; she then offers a sketch of what such a reading might look like.

As Harold Branam accurately notes, Rushdie's third novel has not been as widely read or given as much critical attention as its predecessor and successor. Branam sees *Midnight's Children*, *Shame*, and *The Satanic Verses* as a postcolonial epic or trilogy and focuses his attention on *Shame* as a typically complex multilayered work—a modern fairy tale that he reads as part bildungsroman of its fictional characters, part roman à clef political history of Pakistan from 1947 to 1982, and part authorial commentary by Rushdie about Pakistan and the novel itself. Much has been written about *The Satanic Verses* as controversy and international incident; much less has been written about it as a work of art and exploration of what Lynn Wells calls "the postmodern subject's radical experience of perceptual vertigo and personal fragmentation" in the contemporary city. Disoriented both by what Frederic Jameson calls the "schizophrenia" of mass consumerism and by the effect of being torn between old and new cultures, she writes, the migrants whose story Rushdie set out to write often find themselves in a "hostile encounter with a culture that resists their integration and identification with it." Through the characters of Gibreel Farishta and Saladin Chamcha, Wells explains, *The Satanic Verses* presents the struggle for identity and coherent selfhood that this encounter produces.

Justyna Deszcz-Tryhubczak, author of *Rushdie in Wonderland: "Fairytaleness" in Salman Rushdie's Fiction*, discusses the postcolonial fairy tale *Haroun and the Sea of Stories* and its sequel *Luka and the Fire of Life* as examples of Rushdie's blending of Eastern and Western literary forms. *Haroun and the Sea of Stories*, she explains, is inspired by the cyclical, episodic, and digressive storytelling of the *Kathāsaritsāgara*, the largest collection of tales in Sanskrit verse, as well as by Rushdie's long fascination with Frank Baum's *The Wonderful Wizard of Oz*. But his multiculturalism takes on yet another form in *Luka*, she writes, where the utopian vision of Third World cosmopolitanism that underlies the resolution of *Haroun* is succeeded by Rushdie's references to a new "pop cosmopolitanism" that has grown with global networks of social interactions, particularly among children's and youth culture. Lydia Forssander-Song describes the contents of his two collections of nonfiction, *Imaginary Homelands* and *Step Across This Line*, and then examines how they reflect Rushdie's journey as an artist, a migrant, and a humanist.

Dohra Ahmad sees *The Moor's Last Sigh*, the first full-length novel that Salman Rushdie wrote after the *fatwā* (legal ruling), as his most effective and complex treatment of the clash between fundamentalism and hybridity. She suggests that the novel treats them as "not only competing modes of expression but competing forms of historiography." She also argues, however, that Rushdie reveals these apparent opposites to be "distorted versions of each other," since there are multiple versions of fundamentalism and hybridity can become its own version of fundamentalism. In my essay on *The Ground Beneath Her Feet*, I discuss Rushdie's rock 'n' roll novel as a transitional work—similar in many ways to the works that came before, yet different in a number of important respects. Its setting, for example, is divided between a Bombay and London that will be familiar to readers of his earlier books and scenes in South America and New York City; his use of other worlds is expressed this time through both doubles and the metaphor of double vision; and his focus on the alienation of the migrant expands in this novel to encompass a disorientation that Rushdie treats here as much more widespread and various. Robert C. Evans's essay, one of the few to carefully examine the 2001 novel *Fury*, offers the first close reading of the language of this text. His specific focus is on the purposes and effects of Rushdie's use of listing and repetition, a recurrent feature of his writing that Evans sees as especially prominent in this book.

By examining ancient and modern Kashmiri history, Patrick Colm Hogan demonstrates that Rushdie's Edenic vision of pre-Partition Kashmir is largely a myth, and he investigates how Rushdie treats the cycles of violence and reaction that have dominated the region. In *Shalimar the Clown*, Hogan believes, Rushdie has written a deeply tragic anticolonial novel that seeks to preserve the memory of a culture that may soon be destroyed forever and offers a complex analysis of both history and the process by which violence becomes an accepted form of behavior, justified in the name of religion and socially sanctioned.

Since even my colleagues' thought-provoking and insightful essays cannot cover Salman Rushdie's work completely, this volume concludes with resources for further study: a detailed chronology of Rushdie's life and work, a list of his publications, and a selected bibliography to aid readers in their continued exploration of this fascinating writer and his creations.

CAREER, LIFE, AND INFLUENCE

On Salman Rushdie
Bernard F. Rodgers, Jr.

Salman Rushdie set out to be an artist, not a symbol, but he quickly became both. The publication of *The Satanic Verses* in 1988 became an international incident—turning the novel into fuel for book burnings, riots, and political posturing, and transforming its author into an effigy hung in public squares, a target, an underground man, a blasphemer against Islam to some, and a martyr to the principle of freedom of expression to others. Even before this, however, his startlingly original second novel *Midnight's Children*, which appeared in 1981 and was awarded the Booker Prize, had led to his being widely discussed for nearly a decade as the harbinger of a new wave of writers from the margins.

One of Rushdie's first and most vocal defenders during *The Satanic Verses* controversy was Susan Sontag. In several of the speeches collected in *At the Same Time*, she makes observations about the nature and purposes of literature that help to explain why Rushdie's works immediately attracted so much attention. "Each work of literature that matters, that deserves the name of literature," she said in an acceptance speech for the Jerusalem Prize, "incarnates an idea of singularity, of the singular voice. But literature, which is an accumulation, incarnates an ideal of plurality, of multiplicity, of promiscuity" (149). Writers' imperative, Sontag added, is to "free us up, shake us up. Open avenues of compassion and new interests" (154). The role of literature, she argued, is "to extend our sympathies; to educate the heart and mind; to create inwardness; to secure and deepen the awareness (with all its consequences) that other people, people different from us, really do exist" (177). The combination of Rushdie's singular voice with a style and vision that grew out of and reflected the plurality and multiplicity of his experience is exactly what captured readers of his first novels and has continued to define all he has written since. From the beginning, he has shaken us up, while seeking to expand the sympathies and educate the hearts and minds of his readers in both the East and the West.

Throughout the 1980s, he also wrote essays, eloquently and often, in which he used his growing celebrity to do this by talking about his work as prompted and shaped by the migration and cultural hybridity that he views as the archetypal experiences of the twentieth century. "It may be that writers in my position, exiles or emigrants or expatriates, are haunted by some sense of loss, some urge to reclaim, to look back, even at the risk of being mutated into pillars of salt," he says in the title essay of his nonfiction collection *Imaginary Homelands* (*IH*). He goes on to add that perhaps "we will not be capable of reclaiming precisely the thing that was lost . . . we will, in short, create fictions, not actual cities or villages, but invisible ones, imaginary homelands, Indias of the mind" (10). Several of Rushdie's novels—*Midnight's Children, Shame, The Satanic Verses, The Ground Beneath Her Feet, Shalimar the Clown*—conjure other such imaginary homelands, from India and Pakistan to London, Bombay, Manhattan, and Kashmir. "It is the natural condition of exile," he writes in his debut novel, *Grimus*, "putting down roots in memories" (107). His novels, like those of James Joyce, Günter Grass, or Milan Kundera, are all rooted in memories of cultures and places concrete and imagined, cherished and abandoned, mythologized and mourned, and capture the essence of reality as seen through the eyes of characters who, like their author, face the challenge of straddling two (or more) worlds.

"How does newness come into the world? How is it born?" Rushdie asks in *The Satanic Verses*. "Of what fusions, translations, conjoining is it made?" (8). He addresses these same questions in his essays. The word "translation," he notes, comes from the Latin for "bearing across," and "having been borne across the world, we are translated men. It is normally supposed that something gets lost in the translation; I cling, obstinately, to the notion that something can also be gained." The migrant, he writes, "is not simply transformed by his act; he also transforms his new world. Migrants may become mutants, but it is out of such hybridization that newness can emerge" (*IH* 17, 210).

Rushdie's aspirations as an artist were inspired by a wide range of writers and works. One of the most important inspirations as he attempted to understand and convey the experience of migration in his fiction was Günter Grass, and he makes several observations in his essay on Grass that help to explain his own work's concerns, perspectives, and techniques. He writes,

> A full migrant suffers, traditionally, a triple disruption: he loses his place, he enters an alien language, and he finds himself surrounded by beings whose social behaviour and codes are very unlike, and sometimes even offensive to, his own. And this is what makes migrants such important figures: because roots, language and social norms have been three of the most important parts of the definition of what it is to be a human being. The migrant, denied all three, is obliged to find new ways of describing himself, new ways of being human. (*IH* 277–78)

He then elaborates, explaining what migrants learn from such disruption of reality:

> Reality is an artefact, that it does not exist until it is made, and that, like any other artefact, it can be made well or badly, and that it can also, of course, be unmade. What Grass learned on his journey across the frontiers of history was Doubt. Now he distrusts all those who claim to possess absolute forms of knowledge; he suspects all total explanations, all systems of thought which purport to be complete. Amongst the world's great writers, he is quintessentially the artist of uncertainty, whose symbol might easily have been the question mark if it were not the Snail. (280)

Like Grass's, all of Rushdie's work has been written in opposition to those whose claims to righteousness and absolute truth are used to justify their oppression, intolerance, and silencing of anyone who disagrees with them, an opposition that is most often expressed through his emphasis on the importance of hybridity to a culture. While

Midnight's Children is not about migration—it builds its fiction on, under, and around the actual (and, at times, fractured and imagined) history of India—its perspective and style are profoundly shaped by the fact that Rushdie wrote it as an émigré, from a distance, and migration has explicitly been a subject and provided the context for all of his novels since. Beginning with *Grimus*, in fact, he has sought to speak for all migrants, those who, like him, "have been torn from their place, their language, and their social norms, and forced to reshape and root themselves in a strange and estranging new world" (Rodgers 2225). The multiple names and uncertain parentage Rushdie frequently gives his major characters reinforce the fluidity of identity, while the novels' recurring theme of a traumatic fall speaks to the migrant's dislocation and alienation. Personal memory, subjective and malleable, acts as the cornerstone of storytelling in his fiction, such that the products are inevitably "flawed, unreliable, skewed by the obsessions and blind spots of their tellers" (Rodgers 2225). Thus, even though the narratives may feature actual persons, places, or occurrences, they exceed the bounds of realism.

Rushdie once told an interviewer that when he decided to call his collection of short stories *East, West* he felt that the comma was the most important part of the title because "it seems to me that I am that comma—or at least I live in that comma" ("Homeless" 163). Set down between East and West, now looking one way and now the other, always linked to both but never wholly a part of either, a small figure in the middle of larger forces, again and again he has written such "East, West" tales. Grass has his snail; the symbol Rushdie chooses for himself is that comma. To express the multiplicity of his experience living "in that comma" and remain faithful to his worldview, Rushdie had to invent his own language and literary form. As a result, his books are a fascinating, exuberant, and extravagant melding of genres, religions, histories, languages, and cultures, bringing together disparate concepts from realism and fantasy, humanism and fundamentalism, major world mythologies and theologies, Eastern and Western media, developed and developing nations, the legacies of empire and struggles of newly acquired independence. India's thoughts in *Shalimar the Clown* echo many of his own: "Everywhere was now a part of everywhere else. Russia, America, London, Kashmir. Our lives, our stories, flowed into one another's, were no longer our own, individual, discrete. This unsettled people. There were collisions and explosions" (47).

To relate the multicultural experience authentically, Rushdie relies on what he terms "stereoscopic vision," a perspective that enables the simultaneous examination of two societies from within and outside. Another émigré, the Polish American Nobel Prize–winner Czesław Miłosz, makes a similar point in his *Native Realm* when he speaks of a new organ: "the telescopic eye, that perceives simultaneously not only different points on the globe but also different moments in time . . . New images canceled out none of the old and, strictly speaking, I do not see them in chronological order as if on a strip of film, but in parallel, colliding with one another, overlapping" (2–3). Memory is "our force," Miłosz later explained in his *Nobel Lecture*, and the poet's role must be to see and to describe: "'To see' means not only to have before one's eyes. It may also mean to preserve in memory. 'To see and to describe' may also mean to reconstruct in imagination" (21–22).

Rushdie's stereoscopic or telescopic vision, his own effort to reconstruct in imagination, is buttressed by his "aesthetic of excess," his signature technique of heaping "episode on episode, character on character, plot on plot, pun on pun, comic name on comic name, digression on digression." It is also marked by erudition without pretension, allowing him to blend the narrative energy of *The Arabian Nights*, the playfulness of *Tristram Shandy*, and the political and psychological ambition of *The Tin Drum* into the formal space needed to treat the myriad subjects demanding to be written (Rodgers 2225).

In her introduction to the Everyman's Library edition of *Midnight's Children*, fellow novelist Anita Desai offers the best description I have read of just what this formal space reads and sounds like. Rushdie "turned his back on the Victorian/Indian tradition," she observes, "delightedly and insouciantly jumbling genres and employing postmodern techniques such as discontinuous narrative, cinematic images and metaphors, mirror games and linguistic blasphemies" (ix). This was linked by critics to the school of magic realism in Europe and Latin America; however, Desai remarks, "he had journeyed so far west that he had returned, curiously enough, to the older Indian traditions of story-telling . . . and proved the oral tradition not only alive but capable of versatility and invention" (ix). The "subversions" of his startlingly polyglot, hodgepodge language, she writes,

> belong more to the spoken mode, and in particular to gossip—highly subjective, the ever-present narrator commenting, judging, persuading, digressing and repeating—so that the narrative proceeds in a disjointed fashion, an episode or anecdote presented at a time, and with constant changes introduced of pace and tone, now comic, now ribald, now moralistic, now informative. . . . Yet the language itself belongs to the contemporary world—of comics and cartoons, newspapers and tabloids, of advertisements and posters, with capitals, exclamations, imprecations and the use of onomatopoeia. Babble, or Bombay-speak—that uncouth "chutney" made up of English, Hindi, Urdu, Konkani, Marathi, Gujarati and various dialects thereof—allows Rushdie to revel in interlingual puns. . . . (xviii–xix)

This blending of language Desai calls "a cacophony" that "defies nationality and the carving up of the world's geography into separate and sealed areas." She then goes on to parse his disruption of grammar and punctuation:

> Some passages are dense with punctuation marks—hyphens, dashes, ellipses, colons, semicolons and parentheses—so that they resemble teeming ant-hills (or crowded Bombay streets), and in other passages punctuation is altogether jettisoned, words and sentences running together with multiple force . . . as if the author can barely contain the creative energy

and its momentum.... While some of his sentences are as formal and correct as any grammarian could wish, in others he chooses to apply the rules of Indian grammar.... (xix)

Desai concludes that this "eclectic style belongs to a world that does not know purity of race or tongue" (xix).

These linguistic pyrotechnics are used in the service of his cross-cultural vision. Rushdie grew up in Bombay, which he has described as a place "in which the West was totally mixed up with the East." His family spoke Hindustani, "a colloquial mixture of Hindi and Urdu [that] isn't written," and "some mixture of Hindustani and English is what [they] spoke at home" ("The Art of Fiction" 110, 119). At Cambridge, he both studied Western literature and majored in Islamic history. Unsurprisingly, then, he has acknowledged a host of artistic touchstones from the literature of both East and West. In addition to those already mentioned, they include the Ramayana, Farid ud-Din Attâr's *The Conference of Birds*, Jorge Luis Borges, Giovanni Boccaccio, Jonathan Swift, François Rabelais, Nikolai Vasilievich Gogol, Italo Calvino, Charles Dickens, Joseph Conrad, Franz Kafka, James Joyce, Eugène Ionesco, G. V. Desani, Gabriel García Márquez, Saul Bellow, Milan Kundera, Vladimir Nabokov, Philip Roth, and Ted Hughes. His connections to any of them are fascinating to consider, as several of the essays in this volume demonstrate. Here, however, I want to look briefly at an example of the cross-cultural multivalence of one of his most famous images—Saleem Sinai's nose in *Midnight's Children*—which is representative of the literary method and layered perspective that characterize each of his works.

Above all, Saleem's nose serves as a comic device, linking him to the likes of Pinocchio, Gogol, Sterne, and Cyrano de Bergerac, as well as Ganesh, the elephant-headed Hindu god of literature. Such associations offer subtle implications about Saleem's character, namely, that he lies, may be insane, digresses frequently, and is unlucky in love. Like Ganesh, who, according to myth, belongs to both the gods Shiva and Parvati, Saleem's parentage is equally uncertain. Furthering the Ganesh connection is Rushdie's choice of naming other major characters Shiva and Parvati. This physical feature therefore simultaneously provides comic relief, alludes to the literary and religious traditions being combined in the narrative, and works as plot element. Such multifunctional, multidimensional elements are common throughout Rushdie's work. A reader need not recognize all of these reverberations, however, nor be familiar with both Eastern and Western traditions, to enjoy such images or feel at least some of their effects. This makes Rushdie's novels both multilayered and accessible, enjoyable to an audience that may not be aware of all of his intentions and references as well as to those readers who are.

Nonetheless, his writing is ambitious and can be demanding. In his essay on Günter Grass, Rushdie acknowledges another important influence that the elder writer had on his work and, in the process, helps to explain the impulses behind *Midnight's Children* and all of the books that have followed it. "A book is a kind of passport," he says, which gives readers who want to write "permission to become the sort of writers they have it in themselves to be" (*IH* 276). *The Tin Drum* was such a passport for him when he first read it in the summer of 1967:

> This is what Grass's great novel said to me in its drumbeats: Go for broke. Always try to do too much. Dispense with safety nets. Take a deep breath before you begin talking. Aim for the stars. Keep grinning. Be bloody-minded. Argue with the world. And never forget that writing is as close as we get to keeping a hold on the thousand and one things—childhood, certainties, cities, doubts, dreams, instants, phrases, parents, loves—that go on slipping, like sand, through our fingers. I have tried to learn the lessons of the midget drummer. And one more, which I got from that other, immense work, *Dog Years*: When you've done it once, start all over again and do it better. (*IH* 277)

Rushdie learned all of these lessons well, and used them to become the writer he had it in himself to be in *Midnight's Children.*

When he set out to "do it better" in *The Satanic Verses*—to go for broke, be bloody-minded, argue with the world—a large part of the world argued back with a violence and hatred he could not have imagined beforehand. He certainly did not expect his novel to be welcomed in places like Pakistan and Iran. After all, he had put many of the words he would hear as the controversy grew into the voice of the people of his imaginary Pakistan in *Shame*. "*Outsider! Trespasser! You have no right to this subject!*" he imagined them saying. "*Poacher! Pirate! We reject your authority. We know you, with your foreign language wrapped around you like a flag: speaking about us in your forked tongue, what do you tell but lies*" (23; italics in orig.). Nonetheless, it is one thing to expect vehement criticism, quite another to envision a *fatwā* (legal ruling), death threats, and a price on his head. He also seems not to have imagined that many Muslim migrants in Britain were not like him. Many of them had no intention of leaving their language, customs, culture, and religion behind simply because they had crossed the water; they did not think the Prophet was a fit subject for imaginative reinvention; and they had no desire to embrace the newness Rushdie valorized.

His shell-shocked comments as the furor grew make it clear that he thought he was speaking *for* these migrants, defending them against Thatcherite Britain as well as the oppressions of fundamentalist demagogues, and sympathetically exploring their existential condition. By contrast, they saw him as mocking and blaspheming *against* them and all they considered sacred. They were not interested in explanations of his authorial intentions. In fact, most of the people who rioted, threatened him and his publishers and translators, and burned his book in Britain and around the world had not *read* it. To read the book was considered a desecration, so it and its author were condemned by entire populations on the basis of politically and religiously based descriptions of it.

The novel and its author deserved and still deserve better. The story begins with its two heroes, both Indian actors, falling to earth on New Year's Day after terrorists blow up the plane in which they were traveling to London. When they miraculously land on the British coast alive, Gibreel Farishta and Saladin Chamcha are reborn, transfigured. As the story shifts from East to West and back and from the present day of Margaret Thatcher to the seventh century of Muhammad, the irreligious Gibreel experiences a crisis of faith and sanity, while the anglophile Chamcha experiences a crisis of cultural self-identity. In Gibreel's psychotic visions, he alternately plays the part of the archangel giving the Recitation to Muhammad (here given the pejorative name Mahound) and Salman, Mahound's scribe. Chamcha, meanwhile, loses all that is familiar and comforting—home, loved ones, sense of self—yet ultimately gains protection from those he reviled, taps into his rage against the racism he endures, reconciles with his father, and embraces a new sense of self. A variety of subplots interweave throughout the whole, maintaining a whirlwind pace for over five hundred pages. As critic Robert Irwin said, *The Satanic Verses* is "several of the best novels that [Rushdie] has written" (1067).

Depictions of the prophet Muhammad are forbidden in Islam, and Muslims consider the Recitation (Qur'an) to be holy. Tradition holds that, in the early days of Islam, Muhammad was briefly persuaded by the devil to acknowledge three goddesses as intercessors to or daughters of Allah, the one male god of Islam, to ameliorate relations with the local people. In this account, Muhammad was later set right by the archangel Gabriel, who informed him that Satan had tricked him. The incident, known as the Satanic Verses episode, was accepted in Muslim scholarship for a time but has become contentious over time. Thus, when Rushdie decided to feature the episode in his novel, he knew the faithful would not take kindly to it. Not only does Rushdie's version show the Prophet as fallible, but it calls him by a medieval Christian epithet and adds a character (named after the author no less) who intentionally distorts the Recitation, thereby calling the very legitimacy of the Qur'an into question. Adding insult to injury, the women of a fictional brothel in the novel adopt the names of Muhammad's wives as a business strategy. For all his disclaiming after the fact about fictional representation, Gibreel's psychosis, his own lack of faith, Rushdie's defenses were not taken seriously because surely he must have known what an insult these scenes would be to faithful Muslims. Moreover, the novel's subplot about a tyrannical imam, a thinly veiled reference to the ayatollah's rule in Iran, undoubtedly contributed to Khomeini's ire.

Despite the offense it has caused, *The Satanic Verses* ought to be examined according to its original intent: to explore "the deepest religious and personal conflicts within its author and many others," to "capture the sense of rootlessness and alienation that comes with displacement and migration," and to "encompass the extremes of contemporary experience in a form that would allow the freest possible range to its author's talent and imagination" (Rodgers 2227). It is also, ironically, a "dispute between different ideas of the text," as Rushdie told an interviewer, "between the sacred and profane ideas of what a book is. The book whose legitimization comes simply as an act of the imagination—and these other books that are supposed to be handed down from another place. . . . [an] argument about the status of the work of the imagination as opposed to so-called revealed texts" ("Salman Rushdie" 115). This argument described in a work of fiction created very real collisions and explosions in the world far beyond it.

When he was once again able to find enough concentration to write fiction, Rushdie created a fable, *Haroun and the Sea of Stories*, which is both an extraordinary children's story and a pointed allegory of his own situation that treats the suppression of the imagination and its consequences. Six years after the fatwā, he published his first full-length post–*Satanic Verses* novel, *The Moor's Last Sigh*, which critics have found to be one of his strongest and most important books. Like *Midnight's Children*, a multigenerational saga engages the politics of contemporary India. Three of the novels that followed—*The Ground Beneath Her Feet*, *The Enchantress of Florence*, and *Luka and the Fire of Life*—garnered mixed reviews and have so far not elicited much critical commentary. One of the later novels, *Fury*—which is based in New York City, where Rushdie resettled at the beginning of the millennium—received the worst reviews of his career; another, *Shalimar the Clown*, was widely praised. This volume offers fuller commentary on them all.

"Description is a political act," Rushdie asserts in one of his essays, and from the start, his work has been controversial because it has been both idiosyncratic and deeply engaged with the realities of the world he comes from and of the world to which he migrated (*IH* 13). He has engaged both parts of his experience in thought-provoking essays gathered in two valuable collections, but he has focused his efforts as an artist on representing that experience imaginatively in his fiction. In a single sentence ("Once upon a time—*it was and it was not so,* as the old stories used to say, *it happened and it never did*—maybe, then, or maybe not"), Rushdie succinctly illustrates the parallel between the Eastern storytelling tradition and Western magic realism, two major sources of inspiration for his own genre-defying stories (*Satanic Verses* 35). Seeking to convey the turbulence of his times through his art, Rushdie became its hostage. More than twenty years after his life turned upside down, however, he has been neither silenced nor cowed.

In a commencement address at Williams College in 1984, Joseph Brodsky, yet another Nobel Prize–winning émigré to America who knew firsthand the price of speaking truth to power, declared that "the surest defense against Evil is extreme individualism, originality of thinking, whimsicality, even—if you will—eccentricity" (Brodsky 385). Like Brodsky, Sontag, and Miłosz, Salman Rushdie clearly believes that there is evil in our world and that the artist can help us to recognize and defend ourselves against it. Like them, he has seen his work as nothing less than a confrontation with and conversation about our times. Not everything he has written has had the far-reaching significance of *Midnight's Children* or *The Satanic Verses*, but the voice and vision of all of his novels have surely been individual, original, entertaining, at times whimsical, and even eccentric. They have also been important contributions to the art and language of the novel, to cross-cultural understanding, to the emergence of postcolonial writing, and to the essential effort to understand the fundamental—and fundamentalist—conflicts that pervade contemporary culture in both the East and the West.

Works Cited

Brodsky, Joseph. *Less Than One: Selected Essays*. New York: Farrar, 1986.

Irwin, Robert. "Original Parables." *Times Literary Supplement* 4.461 (Sept. 1988): 1067.

Miłosz, Czesław. *Native Realm: A Search for Self-Definition*. New York: Doubleday, 1968.

_____. *Nobel Lecture*. New York: Farrar, 1981.

Rodgers, Bernard F. "Salman Rushdie." *Magill's Survey of World Literature*. Vol. 5. Ed. Stephen G. Kellman. Pasadena: Salem Press, 2009. 2223–29.

Rushdie, Salman. *Grimus*. London: Paladin, 1989.

_____. "Homeless Is Where the Art Is." *Conversations with Salman Rushdie*. Ed. Michael R. Reder. Jackson: UP of Mississippi, 2000. 162–65.

_____. *Imaginary Homelands: Essays and Criticism, 1981–1991*. London: Granta, 1991.

_____. *Midnight's Children*. New York: Knopf/Everyman's Library, 1995.

_____. "Salman Rushdie." *Conversations with Salman Rushdie*. Ed. Michael R. Reder. Jackson: UP of Mississippi, 2000. 110–122.

_____. "Salman Rushdie, The Art of Fiction No. 186." Interview with Jack Livings. *Paris Review* 174 (2005): 107–43.

_____. *The Satanic Verses*. New York: Viking Penguin, 1988.

_____. *Shalimar the Clown*. New York: Random, 2005.

_____. *Shame*. New York: Knopf, 1983.

Sontag, Susan. *At the Same Time: Essays & Speeches*. Ed. Paolo Dilonardo and Anne Jump. New York: Farrar, 2007.

Biography of Salman Rushdie

R. S. Krishnan

Ahmed Salman Rushdie was born on June 19, 1947, in Bombay (now Mumbai), in the Indian state of Maharashtra, to Anis Ahmed Rushdie and Negin Bhutt Rushdie. His Cambridge-educated father was a well-to-do businessman, and though Rushdie and his three sisters were born in a Muslim family, they were raised in a secular environment. Rushdie's early secular upbringing and outlook have shaped his works to a great extent, as shall become evident. Educated at the Cathedral and John Connon School in Bombay (originally established by the Anglo-Scottish Education Society), Rushdie left for England in 1961, where he completed his schooling at Rugby, after which he enrolled in King's College, Cambridge, which awarded him a master of arts degree in history in 1968. In 1964, his parents and sisters immigrated to Pakistan, and after graduation, Rushdie too went to Pakistan and briefly worked in television in that country. When his production of Edward Albee's *The Zoo Story* was censored by the authorities for inclusion of the word "pork," and his views on Pakistan, which he attempted to publish in a local magazine, met with a similar fate, Rushdie returned to England. There, he worked as an actor in a theater group until 1970 and as a freelance copywriter for advertising agencies in London until 1981.

Rushdie's first novel, *Grimus*, was published in 1975. A work of fantasy and science fiction based on the twelfth-century Sufi poem *The Conference of Birds* by Farid ud-Din Attâr, *Grimus* provides an early indication of Rushdie's delight in mythology and most especially his penchant for linguistic exuberance; indeed, the title of the novel is an anagram for Simurg, the wise bird in Attar's allegorical poem. In writing it, as Rushdie had stated, "I was trying to take a theme out of eastern philosophy or mythology and transpose it into a western convention" (Haffenden 245). If *Grimus* met with limited critical success, Rushdie's next novel, *Midnight's Children* (1981), which took him almost five years to write, was received with the kind of critical accolade seldom given to a contemporary work. Rushdie's epic retelling of India's postindependence history—a bravura performance of myth, history, and magic realism woven into a narrative that owed as much to the oral traditions of India as to the influence of writers such as Laurence Sterne, James Joyce, and Gabriel García Márquez—won a number of major awards, including the prestigious Booker Prize in 1981. A decade later, in 1993, to mark the twenty-fifth year of Booker awards, the novel was adjudged the Booker of Bookers.

Midnight's Children not only heralded the arrival of a major literary talent but it has also influenced critical discourse concerning postcolonial literature. It is no exaggeration to suggest that Salman Rushdie has made a singular contribution to the ongoing debate on postcolonial literature and its attendant theoretical formulations. Whereas an earlier generation of Indian anglophone writers whose works were read and appreciated in the West—including R. K. Narayan, Mulk Raj Anand, and R. Raja Rao—essentially adapted their Indian themes to Western form and language, Rushdie's reformulations in *Midnight's Children* (experimentation with language, melding of narrative traditions of East and West, cultural hybridity) signaled the arrival of a writer who resisted simple classification. His work thereby made it possible for Arundhati Roy, Jhumpa Lahiri, and others of Asian or Asian American origins to have their works received and read within a global context, freed from the constraints of labels such as "writers from the Commonwealth," a term that describes the federation of countries that were erstwhile colonies of the British Empire.

Midnight's Children was followed by *Shame*, an allegorical rendering of modern Pakistan and its political travails, in 1983. If *Midnight's Children* brought him fame, Rushdie found notoriety with his 1988 publication of *The Satanic Verses*. Centered around the misadventures of Gibreel Farishta and Saladin Chamcha, two Indian actors who fall to earth in Britain when their Air India plane explodes, the novel outraged devout Muslims all over the world because of its presumed disrespect for and blasphemy against Islam. The book was banned in India within a week of its British publication, both in response to the protest of British Muslims in Bradford, England, and out of concern for the sentiments of the large Muslim population in India, and similar bans followed in countries across continents. There were demonstrations and riots in India, Pakistan, and other Middle Eastern Muslim countries, resulting in injuries and deaths. Publishers and bookstores that sold the work were targeted for bombing, leading to the novel being pulled from bookshelves and public display. The fallout from the publication of *The Satanic Verses* was also ironic: It won the Whitbread Novel Award in 1988, but in February 1989, Ayatollah Khomeini, then the supreme leader of Iran, issued a *fatwā* (legal ruling) against Rushdie and the publishers and translators of his book, thus forcing Rushdie into hiding. With a price tag of millions of dollars on his head, Rushdie, with the protection of the British government, went into hiding for the next ten years. Eventually, the Iranian government distanced itself from the fatwā in the fall of 1998 (though the decision was far from universally accepted in the Muslim world), and Rushdie slowly began his reemergence into society.

The fatwā has had a profound effect on both Rushdie's worldview and his art. In 1990, in response to the fatwā and all that followed, Rushdie published an extended essay, "In Good Faith," in which he was both apologetic and defiant: "If *The Satanic Verses* is anything, it is a migrant's-eye view of the world. It is written from the very experience of uprooting, disjuncture and metamorphosis (slow or rapid, painful or pleasurable) that is the migrant condition, and from which, I believe, can be derived a metaphor for all humanity," though he also asserted that the novel is "in part, a secular man's reckoning with the religious spirit. It is by no means always hostile to faith" (*Imaginary Homelands* 394, 396). As to his own writing self, Rushdie had this to say: "I make no complaint. I am a writer. I do not accept my condition. I will strive to change it; but I inhabit it, I am trying to learn from it. Our lives teach us who we are" (414). It is worth noting that as a measure of his nonacceptance of the condition forced upon him by the fatwā,

Rushdie published *Haroun and the Sea of Stories* (1990), a children's book written for his son Zafar. An allegory about speech, silence, and the danger involved in storytelling, it won the Writers' Guild Award for Best Children's Book. Rushdie was greatly affected, not only by his own situation but by the collateral violence visited upon his Japanese and Italian translators of *The Satanic Verses*, the former stabbed to death in Tokyo and the latter barely surviving a knife attack in Milan.

If further evidence is needed of the effect of the fatwā on Rushdie's art and outlook, it is amply evident in his two collections of nonfiction, *Imaginary Homelands: Essays and Criticism, 1981–1991* (1991) and *Step Across This Line: Collected Nonfiction, 1992–2002* (2002). In the latter volume, Rushdie makes abundantly clear his views on censorship, fundamentalism of both the Right and the Left, and his renewed insistence upon the need for writers to speak unafraid. In the section titled "Message from the Plague Years," Rushdie recounts his almost decade-long life in hiding, his attempts to achieve a semblance of an orderly life, and his attempts to speak out against the fatwā. As he notes, "What has been done to *The Satanic Verses*, its author, publishers, translators, and booksellers, is a crime against freedom. The novel is not the crime; the author is not the criminal" (214). While it would be a stretch to suggest that Rushdie was radicalized by his experience, what is clear is that his vocal defense of art and the artist, and his support for those writers who, like him, were being targeted by fundamentalists and extremists, suggest the indelible effect his enforced exile from society had imposed on him. As he wrote in "A Declaration of Independence" in 1994:

> The art of literature requires, as an essential condition, that the writer be free to move between his many countries as he chooses, needing no passport or visa, making what he will of them and of himself. We are miners and jewelers, truth-tellers and liars, jesters and commanders, mongrels and bastards, parents and lovers, architects and demolition men. The creative spirit, of its very nature, resists frontiers and limiting points, denies the authority of censors and taboos.

As a confirmation, Rushdie expressed his solidarity with Taslima Nasrin, the Bangladeshi writer forced into exile by the same kind of intolerance suffered by Rushdie when she published her novel *Lajja* (*Shame*) in 1993, which was critical of both Islam and its treatment of women (*Step Across This Line* 250, 254).

Since 1990, Rushdie has published six additional novels, including *The Moor's Last Sigh* (1995), which tells the Zogoiby family story through the life of Moraes Zogoiby; *The Ground Beneath Her Feet* (1999), a reinscription of the Orpheus and Eurydice myth contextualized within contemporary popular music; and *Fury* (2001), a novel about exile and restlessness, set in New York City. *Shalimar the Clown* (2005), set in turbulent Kashmir (the lost "paradise") and California, recounts the life of Maximilian Ophuls, and Rushdie dedicated it "in loving memory" of his Kashmiri grandparents. Rushdie's *The Enchantress of Florence* (2008) is an encounter between East and West set in the time of the Mughal Empire. Most recently, he published *Luka and the Fire of Life* (2010), a sequel of sorts to his critically acclaimed *Haroun and the Sea of Stories*, recounting the adventures of Haroun's younger brother Luka, who is called upon to undertake a quest to once again save his father, the storyteller Rashid Khalifa, from doom. Rushdie also coauthored, with Tim Supple and Simon Reade, the stage adaptation of *Midnight's Children*, which the Royal Shakespeare Company premiered in 2002, and he coedited *Mirrorwork: 50 Years of Indian Writing, 1947–1997* (1997) with Elizabeth West and *The Best American Short Stories 2008* (2009) with Heidi Pitlor. *The Jaguar Smile*, a work of nonfiction published in 1987, recounts Rushdie's travels in Nicaragua the year before.

While Rushdie's novels, particularly *Midnight's Children* and *The Satanic Verses*, have been the focus of considerable critical attention, his collection of short fiction, *East, West: Stories* (1994), has only recently come under critical purview. The stories here point to Rushdie's preoccupation with cultural hybridity, identity, and the resultant conflicts they give rise to, themes he explores in his novels. *East, West* is demonstrable evidence of Rushdie's dexterity on a small canvas, inasmuch as he is viewed as a writer of "grand" narratives.

As a novelist and short-fiction writer, Salman Rushdie is not easily pinned down. While his works insistently point to issues of cultural hybridity, displacement, and the need to accommodate pluralism and secularism, he is equally a writer who draws upon the vast store of history, literature, mythology (of East and West), and contemporary cultural poetics in a language and form that delights and astounds. As he puts it, "The real risks of any artist are taken in the work, in pushing the work to the limits of what is possible, in the attempt to increase the sum of what it is possible to think. Books become good when they go to this edge and risk falling over it—when they endanger the artist by reason of what he has, or has not, artistically dared" (*Imaginary Homelands* 15).

If he has dared as an artist, Rushdie's personal life has also been tumultuous. He has been married and divorced four times: first to publishing executive Clarissa Luard, by whom he had a son, Zafar; then to American novelist Marianne Wiggins; next to freelance editor Elizabeth West, by whom he had a second son, Milan; and most recently to Padma Lakshmi, a model and television personality.

Meeting with greater success on the professional side, Rushdie sold his archive to Emory University in 2006 and began a five-year appointment there in 2007 as Distinguished Writer in Residence in the English Department. In recognition of his distinguished contributions to literature, Queen Elizabeth II of England awarded Rushdie a knighthood in 2007, which prompted renewed outrage among Muslims both in England and abroad.

Undoubtedly, Rushdie's works, as Rushdie himself, have influenced debates about postcolonial literature, as evidenced by the sheer number of articles and full-length critical studies published on Rushdie's novels to date. For Rushdie, the novel form remains his "first love," for "not only is it the art involving least compromises, but it is also the only one that takes the 'privileged arena' of conflicting discourses right inside our heads. The interior space of our imagination is a theatre that can never be closed down; the images created there make up a movie that can never be destroyed" (*Imaginary Homelands* 426). Another great writer and critic, John Updike, put it best: "Rushdie in his Manhattan retreat is no longer a third-world writer but a bard of the grim one world we all, in a state of some dread, inhabit" (386).

Works Cited

Haffenden, John, ed. "Salman Rushdie." *Novelists in Interview*. London: Methuen, 1985.

Rushdie, Salman. *Imaginary Homelands: Essays and Criticism, 1981–1991*. London: Granta, 1991.

_____. *Step Across This Line: Collected Nonfiction, 1992–2002*. New York: Random, 2002.

Updike, John. *Due Considerations: Essays and Criticism*. New York: Ballantine, 2008.

CRITICAL CONTEXTS

Critical Reception

Joel Kuortti

I. Introduction: Phases of Rushdie's Reception

Salman Rushdie's eleven novels and his other works have generated an exceptional amount of critical response throughout the world. This essay offers a survey of the reception of his major books and presents an outline of the major lines of response that have emerged among his critics. I have here divided the critical reactions into three distinct, approximately decade-long phases and several different directions. The first phase starts with *Grimus* and continues up to the publication of *The Satanic Verses*. During this time, Rushdie wrote *Midnight's Children*, *Shame*, and *The Jaguar Smile*. The second, most intensive phase of criticism begins with *The Satanic Verses* and lasts until *The Moor's Last Sigh*. The third, ongoing phase emerges with *The Ground Beneath Her Feet* and continues through *Fury*, *Shalimar the Clown*, and *The Enchantress of Florence*. The main directions that the reactions have taken are the literary, controversial, and political strands.

There is very little material prior to the publication of the epoch-setting *Midnight's Children* in 1981. After that, criticism began to proliferate, and Rushdie gained a distinctive position within the spheres of Indian, postcolonial, and Commonwealth literature. This intensive literary interest continued up until the publication of *The Satanic Verses* in 1988. The international furor created by the protests against the novel and its author, culminating in the *fatwā* (legal ruling) issued by Ayatollah Khomeini in February 1989, started a cornucopia of writings for and against Rushdie, rather than about his works. About a decade later, critical attention focused again on the novels but with a heightened sense of contextual problematics. Rushdie has now become a catchphrase for different, often contradictory, types of discourse—defense of freedom, Islamic apostasy, diasporic citizenship, cosmopolitan writing, Indian English literature—but many sources that refer to him still do not actually discuss his works. Such a unique history of criticism makes the assessment of Rushdie's reception both challenging and intriguing.

Apart from the studies of individual or selected novels, there are a number of general introductions to his works, titled simply *Salman Rushdie* (sometimes with a subtitle). The first was written by James Harrison in 1992; others include those by Catherine Cundy (1996), D. C. R. A. Goonetilleke (1998), Damian Grant (1999), Andrew Blake (2001), Andrew Teverson (2007), and Stephen Morton (2008). Since Uma Parameswaran's 1988 *The Perforated Sheet: Essays on Salman Rushdie's Art*,[1] the number of monographs (Brennan; Petersson, *Unending Metamorphoses*; Kuortti, *Fictions*; Dutheil; Sanga; Hassumani; Deszcz) and anthologies (Taneja and Dhawan; Fletcher; Booker; Bloom; Mittapalli and Kuortti; Ray and Kundu; Gurnah) focusing especially on Rushdie's works has been steadily growing. There is no proper biography of Rushdie yet, but Ian Hamilton published a noteworthy biographical article in 1995 and some of the introductory volumes contain useful biographical sketches and data. Many of Rushdie's interviews have been collected in two valuable volumes, by Michael Reder and by Pradyumna S. Chauhan, and these contain biographical material.

In the following, the critical reception of each of Rushdie's works is considered historically and thematically. As there is no end to the possible materials, the presentation is obviously selective. A fuller corpus of the materials up to 2001 can be found in the Rushdie bibliographies I have compiled as well as those by M. D. Fletcher in *Reading Rushdie: Perspectives on the Fiction of Salman Rushdie* (1994) and V. Indira Sambamurthy in *An Annotated Bibliography of Indian English Fiction* (2001). Presently, there is no up-to-date critical bibliography, but many recent books on Rushdie contain some bibliographical details on critical reception.

II. Early Criticism: From *Grimus* to *Midnight's Children* and *Shame*

Grimus

It was not until the 1981 publication of *Midnight's Children* that Rushdie's writing truly gained critical attention. His debut novel, *Grimus*, was published six years before, but there were very few reviews of it in the British newspapers, which usually discussed it together with other new publications and received it unsympathetically. Rushdie's agent at the time was Liz Calder, who has commented that "it got some terrible reviews, violently bad reviews, which is unusual for a first novel. I think, only one good one . . . Everyone else . . . all these sort of heavy weight reviewers, absolutely slaughtered it" (77). When the book was first translated into French in 1977, there were encouraging signals (Rushdie, "Interview" 24), and with the US publication in 1979, there were scant but more positive reviews. Reviewer Mel Gilden praised it as "science fiction in the best sense of the word" (8). This coincided with the inclusion of *Grimus* in *The Encyclopedia of Science Fiction* (1979), edited by Peter Nicholls. Even though Nicholls granted *Grimus* only a marginal status as science fiction, it is now usually categorized as belonging in that genre. Thus, Rushdie's intention of evading such a label finally failed. All of which has led to Rushdie himself belittling the book as "too clever for its own good" ("Interview" 25).

Grimus entered literary criticism in 1983 with Uma Parameswaran's article on *Midnight's Children*, where she regarded the novel as "remarkable" and already containing characteristics that *Midnight's Children* then made more prominent ("'Handcuffed'" 34). It took another two years for the next article to appear, when Ib Johansen published his "The Flight of the Enchanter: Reflections on Salman Rushdie's *Grimus*." Since then, there has been a steady—even if slight—flow of critical attention to *Grimus* (e.g., Parameswaran, "New Dimensions"; Rahimieh, "*Grimus*"; Rahimieh, *Oriental Responses* 84–89; Cundy, "Rehearsing Voices"; Syed; Massé; Petersson, *Unending*

Metamorphoses 61–90; Kuortti, "Allegories"; Petersson, *"Grimus"*; Souza Gomes Carreira; Johansen, "Tricksters"). The critical interest has been on such issues as Rushdie's themes and sources, elements of Menippean satire and postmodernism, and language and satire. In his intriguing study of Rushdie's first four novels, Roger Y. Clark gave one of the more compelling analyses of *Grimus* as an introduction to the "otherworlds" that would consistently appear in the subsequent novels (30–60).

Whatever may have been the merits or shortcomings of Rushdie's first novel, it has not remained simply a curiosity since it has been available through continuous printings. There are also at least eight translations, including the first translation into French by Maud Perrin in 1977.[2] While not among Rushdie's major works, *Grimus* is not going to disappear from the critical eye.

Midnight's Children

When *Midnight's Children* was published in February 1981, it was met with immediate applause and critical acclaim. It soon became a staple diet for literary critics, academics, *litterateurs*, and even journalists who were interested in finding out what contemporary India was "really" like. In a 1983 interview, Rushdie toyed with the idea of *Midnight's Children* being "the best introduction to India" ("Doing the Dangerous Thing" 220) and found this at the same time embarrassing, pleasing, and amusing. However, its allegorical elements were promptly identified, and the title phrase itself— "midnight's children"—was applied to both postindependence India as a whole and the many Indian writers who emerged in the literary tidal wave that followed the book's success as winner in 1981 of both the Booker and the James Tait Black Memorial Prizes.[3] Most critics have agreed with Meenakshi Mukherjee, who considered it "a landmark novel," "a catalyst" for the remarkable changes in India and Indian English literature in the 1980s, and "easily . . . one of the contenders for [the] position" of a seminal book of the late twentieth century (10–12).

Apart from reviews and shorter analyses, critical attention to the book did not begin immediately. The sheer extent of the novel—446 dense pages—gave critics something to mull over. Among the first critics were Ron Shepherd—who, in his 1982 essay "Growing Up," connected Rushdie with other emerging Asian writers' novels such as Lloyd Fernando's *Scorpion Orchid* (1976) from Malaysia and Russell Soaba's *Wampis* (1977) from Papua New Guinea—and Feroza Jussawalla, who studied Rushdie within Indian English writing in her 1983 doctoral dissertation (publicly published in 1985). Jussawalla did not like the emerging strand of literature the novel represented and considered it too parodic in comparison to such writers as Mulk Raj Anand and R. K. Narayan. She called for an interpretive community to provide a sustainable reading for intercultural texts (Jussawalla, *Family Quarrels* 119), an idea she returned to in relation to the problems of interpreting *The Satanic Verses* (Jussawalla, "Rushdie's 'Dastan-e-Dilruba'").

More articles analyzing *Midnight's Children* within the Indian English literary tradition followed from critics such as Shyamala Narayan (1983), Uma Parameswaran (1984), and Dieter Riemenschneider (1984). In the years to come, the history, development, and sociocultural status of Indian English writing was to become one of the core issues when discussing Rushdie's texts—as well as those of other Indian English writers. Rushdie's self-conscious usage and commentary on English further warranted that the language issue would receive critical attention (Rushdie, "Empire" 8; Srivastava; Gane, "Postcolonial Literature"). "Chutnification" became a buzzword—implying both a specific type of Indian English and cultural hybridity in more general sense (Sharma; Crane; Banerjee, *Chutneyfication of History*).

There were also critics who placed Rushdie within other literary histories: magic realism, postmodernism, metafiction, satire, fantasy, postcolonial literature, Commonwealth literature, and so on. Rushdie was compared to writers as diverse as Gabriel García Márquez, Günter Grass, Rudy Wiebe, Chinua Achebe, and Derek Walcott

(Parameswaran, "New Dimensions"; Bader; Howells; Sangari). This international literary legacy provided grounds for discussing issues such as cosmopolitanism, nationalism, and history—despite the fact that the book itself was very Indian and very Bombayite.

Even with its immense success, *Midnight's Children* really only attracted more extensive critical attention after the publication of *Shame*, when it was possible to consider Rushdie's works as an oeuvre, a totality with specific characteristics, themes, and techniques (Mahanta; Murti; Brigg). This has continued with the publication of each new book, and a wealth of comparative criticism is now available. There are specific volumes discussing it (Mukherjee; Schürer; Kortenaar and Louie; Mitra; Dey; Procter), and in David Smale's 2003 book there is a discussion of selected criticism of *Midnight's Children* and *The Satanic Verses* from a thematic point of view. All in all, *Midnight's Children* remains the most popular and the most studied of Rushdie's novels.

Shame

Since *Midnight's Children* received a lot of praise as well as some unsympathetic evaluations, it was going to be difficult for Rushdie to equal that with his next book. When *Shame* was published in September 1983, however, the critical consensus was that he had managed to produce a worthy successor. Even if the reviews were not as admiring, critical interest began immediately—usually in comparison with *Midnight's Children*—but there are no book-length studies of *Shame* exclusively yet.

With *Shame*, certain topics and features emerged and intensified in Rushdie's writing and the commentary on it. Gender issues had been marginal in the discussions of *Midnight's Children* but here, especially through the figure of Sufiya Zinobia, a critical interest in the representation of women appeared (Grewal; A. Ahmad; Moss; Parameswaran, "Impressive Women"), which has continued to be a focus of discussion of his other writing (Verma; Natarajan; Kamra; Kuortti, "Feminization"). Another strand in the criticism of *Shame* is political allegory. If

Midnight's Children was read as an allegory of the history of a nation, in *Shame*, the current political situation in Pakistan was turned into a fictional form more straightforwardly with Mohammed Zia ul-Haq as Raza Hyder, Zulkifar Ali Bhutto as Iskander Harappa, and Benazir Bhutto as Arjumand Harappa (Mahanta; Islam; Kortenaar, "Allegory"; Raza; Chakrabarti; Marwah).

III. *The Satanic Verses* and the Years of the Rushdie Affair

Prior to the publication of *The Satanic Verses* in 1988, Rushdie published his travel book *The Jaguar Smile: A Nicaraguan Journey* (1987). Apart from reviews, very little has been written on it, and it remains one of Rushdie's least successful books. Everything changed during the winter of 1988–89.

The Satanic Verses and the Rushdie Affair

When *The Satanic Verses* was launched in September 1988, the first reviews were positive, and reviewer Angela Carter called it a "populous, loquacious, sometimes hilarious, extraordinary contemporary novel" (30). However, soon there were protests against it in Britain, and in India, the book was banned in October. The conflict spread rapidly, with other countries banning it, and finally escalated in the scandalous *fatwā* (legal ruling) declared by the Iranian ayatollah Ruhollah Khomeini in February 1989. For a long time, this extraliterary context dominated the discussion of Rushdie. Thousands of articles and dozens of books were published that passionately sided with or against Rushdie and his book (Ruthven; Sardar and Wyn Davies), several books outlined the affair and collected writings on it (Appignanesi and Maitland; Ahsan and Kidwai), and a number of books tried to negotiate across the polarized debate (Cohn-Sherbok; Kuortti, *Place*).

Due to the overriding presence of the affair, for a decade, purely literary analyses of the novel were relatively few and far apart. Since then, analyses, especially comparative ones, have been published steadily, and among the thematic concerns—apart from the political, religious, intercultural, social, and other contentious issues—have been migrancy, violence, cinema, hybridity, postmodernism, language, and translation (e.g., Seminck; Gane, "Migrancy"; Cavanaugh). In 2004, the cultural and intertextual richness of the novel was captured in an extensively annotated web document by Paul Brians.

Clandestine Years

During his years of clandestine existence from 1989 to 1998, Rushdie managed to write and publish several works. These broadened the variety of genres of his production and—while not reaching the status of major works—met enthusiastic reception. The first publication was *Haroun and the Sea of Stories* (1990), a children's book like its sequel, *Luka and the Fire of Life* (2010). However, *Haroun* is mostly analyzed as a political allegory about freedom of speech and Rushdie's personal situation (e.g., König).

Rushdie also ventured into nonfiction with the book *Imaginary Homelands* (1991), a collection of his nonfiction writings over the previous decade. Much like Benedict Anderson's *Imagined Communities*, the title became a catch phrase among critics, and many of the articles in the collection are cited extensively. Later on, Rushdie published another, less influential collection of nonfiction, *Step Across This Line* (2002).

The other books from this period are a tribute book, *The Wizard of Oz* (1992); the short-story collection *East, West* (1994); and the anthology *The Vintage Book of Indian Writing, 1947–1997*, which Rushdie edited with Elizabeth West for the fiftieth anniversary of India's independence in 1997. These got relatively little attention, except for the introduction to the anthology, where Rushdie praises Indian English literature as "a stronger and more important body of work than most of what has been produced in the 16 'official languages' of India" and claims it "represents perhaps the most valuable contribution India has yet made to the world of books" (viii). This began a heated debate that has resurfaced frequently whenever Indian English literature is discussed (Bhaya Nair; Shankar 65).

The Moor's Last Sigh

In 1996, Rushdie published his first major novel since *The Satanic Verses*. *The Moor's Last Sigh* became another book that is often read as an allegory of Rushdie's own predicament and especially as a sign of life from his forced silence (Gray). Gradually, however, other themes have emerged and reemerged in criticism of the novel: postcolonialism and aesthetics, hybridity and diaspora, palimpsest, cinema (Schultheis; Gabriel; Salgado; Stadtler, "Nargis"). Reviewers were delighted with the book, which they described as "absolutely fabulous" and "a huge, sprawling, exuberant novel" (Kemp; Kakutani, "Rushdie on India").

In this novel, Rushdie's predisposition for controversy is manifest through the portrayal of the mechanisms of religious fundamentalism and especially the inclusion of a well-known contemporary Hindu nationalist, Bal Thackeray, in the character of Raman Fielding. This aroused protests and a ban on the book in Mumbai (Spaeth; Trousdale; D. Ahmad). Other aspects of Rushdie's rewriting history have also been the focus of several critical essays, including those by Paul Cantor and Mona Narain.

IV. New Critical Interest

The most recent phase in Rushdie criticism treats the novels he has written since he came out of hiding in 1998: *The Ground Beneath Her Feet* (1999), *Fury* (2001), *Shalimar the Clown* (2005), and *The Enchantress of Florence* (2008). It is in many ways a combination of the earlier phases, with both the literary interest and the controversial side. Often these are integrated in analyses, but sometimes they appear separately. Although a number of articles have already been published on each of the four books, it is yet premature to assess this last phase in any great detail as the material is still proliferating. In the following, however, a preliminary outline of the developments on Rushdie's latest four major novels is offered. Discussion of the last two books is predictably the most limited.

The Ground Beneath Her Feet

It was not until the 1999 publication of *The Ground Beneath Her Feet* that the balance in critical responses to Rushdie's books shifted. Sociopolitical issues did not vanish, but the focus on literary and aesthetic attention has been notable. A collection of critical articles—*The Great Work of Making Real: Salman Rushdie's* The Ground Beneath Her Feet (Linguanti and Tchernichova, 2003)—has already been published on this novel, indicating this shift in focus.

One of the new fields of thematic interest in discussions of this novel is popular music, and several articles analyze this feature (Rollason; Albertazzi), including a biographical connection. The title song from the novel was set to music and recorded by the band U2 (Glaister), and it later featured in the 2000 Wim Wenders movie *The Million Dollar Hotel*. Other avenues of analysis have concentrated on photography, travel, the urban space, trauma theory, myths, and globalization (Concilio; Upstone; Parashkevova; Keulks, "Preferring"; Glomb; Leonard).

Fury

With *Fury*'s publication in September 2001, Rushdie managed to precede and anticipate the September 11 terrorist attacks in the United States. This ominous foreboding brought yet another theme to the critical discussion of Rushdie: terrorism. This theme had been there already, especially in *The Moor's Last Sigh*, but now it became emphatic (Detmers). Rushdie had recently moved to New York, and *Fury* was seen as his "first American novel" (Sutherland).

Although the novel received some of the most negative reviews of Rushdie's career, critical interest in *Fury* has been extensive, and many comparisons have been drawn with his other novels as well as with other writers. Thematic concerns have ranged from cosmopolitanism to transnationalism, postmodernity to postethnicity, and authorship to technocapitalism (Zimring; Wiemann; Ng; Banerjee, "Postethnicity"; Brouillette; D'Cruz). While the autobiographic concerns are still strong in the analyses (Spencer 153), the sheer scope of other interests is remarkable.

Shalimar the Clown

The darker themes of terrorism that were present in *Fury* continue in *Shalimar the Clown* (Morton, "There"; Stadtler, "Terror"; Kung). The global reach of the novel invited many commentaries (Siddiqi), but the literary aspects were of interest to many (Murphy; Resta). Comparisons with *Fury* (Keulks, "New York"; Detmers) and *The Ground Beneath Her Feet* (Keulks, "Preferring") have been made. Rushdie's affection for Kashmir had appeared in *Midnight's Children* and *Haroun and the Sea of Stories*, but here it is given a full-fledged form in relation to contemporary terrorism (Updike). Other emerging themes in criticism have been psychology and history (Munjal and Sahni; Khasnabish).

The Enchantress of Florence

The Enchantress of Florence brought Rushdie back to one of the earliest interests in his art: that of storytelling (Deresiewicz), together with such themes as love and the problems of intercultural communication. Reviewers were divided about the book. To one, it was "a weary, predictable parody" (Kakutani, "Storytelling and Deception"), while to another, it was "brilliant, fascinating, generous" (Le Guin 6). The novel has already invited some critical studies, but the future will show which directions will draw sustained attention (Bharat; Rao; Dash; Thiara).

Conclusion

An evaluation of a contemporary writer's critical reception is in many ways a hopeless task. Emphases, categories, themes, and lines of development may change suddenly after the publication of yet another work. The way I have presented the reception of Rushdie's works here tries to do justice to the multiplicity of both the primary and secondary material in the popular and academic discussions. When I have referred to specific studies, usually only one aspect is mentioned, although there might be other, equally significant topics discussed. Due to the critical diversity, any possible canonization of Rushdie criticism is still pending. It is my hope that this outline offers some guidance in this and provides new avenues for analyses.

Notes

1. Parameswaran's book is actually a collection of her articles.
2. *Grimus* has also been translated into German by Gisela Stege (1998), Polish by Krzysztof Filip Rudolf (2000), Hungarian by Greskovits Endre (2002), Serbian by Lazar Macura (2004), Italian by Vincenzo Mantovani (2004), Romanian by Daniela Rogobete (2008), and Portuguese by Miguel Castro Caldas and Susana Baeta (2009).
3. In 1993, Rushdie was awarded the Booker of Bookers for *Midnight's Children* for the best novel in twenty-five years, which created another debate (Huggan).

Works Cited

Ahmad, Aijaz. "Rushdie's *Shame*: Postmodernism, Migrancy, and the Representation of Women." *Economic & Political Weekly* 26.24 (1991): 1461–71.

Ahmad, Dohra. "'This Fundo Stuff is Really Something New': Fundamentalism and Hybridity in *The Moor's Last Sigh*." *Yale Journal of Criticism* 18.1 (2005): 1–20.

Ahsan, M. Manazir, and A. R. Kidwai, eds. *Sacrilege Versus Civility: Muslim Perspectives on The Satanic Verses Affair*. Leicester: Islamic Foundation, 1991.

Albertazzi, Silvia. "Music in *The Ground Beneath Her Feet*." Ray and Kundu 124–32.

Appignanesi, Lisa, and Sara Maitland, eds. *The Rushdie File*. 1989. London: Fourth Estate, 1990.

Bader, Rudolf. "Indian Tin Drum." *International Fiction Review* 11.2 (1984): 75–83.

Banerjee, Mita. *The Chutneyfication of History: Salman Rushdie, Michael Ondaatje, Bharati Mukherjee and the Postcolonial Debate*. Heidelberg: Winter, 2002.

_____. "Postethnicity and Postcommunism in Hanif Kureishi's *Gabriel's Gift* and Salman Rushdie's *Fury*." *Reconstructing Hybridity: Post-Colonial Studies in Transition*. Ed. Joel Kuortti and Jopi Nyman. Amsterdam: Rodopi, 2007. 309–24.

Bharat, Meenakshi, ed. *Rushdie the Novelist: From* Grimus *to* The Enchantress of Florence. New Delhi: Pencraft International, 2009.

_____. "The Silvered Tongue: Storytelling in *The Enchantress of Florence*." Bharat 313–32.

Bhaya Nair, Rukmini. "What Did Rushdie Mean and Why?" *Hindu* 17 Aug. 1997: 33.
Blake, Andrew. *Salman Rushdie: A Beginner's Guide*. London: Hodder, 2001.
Bloom, Harold, ed. *Salman Rushdie*. New York: Chelsea, 2003.
Booker, M. Keith, ed. *Critical Essays on Salman Rushdie*. New York: Hall, 1999.
Boyagoda, Randy. "'Three Kings of Disorient': A Globalized Search for Home in *The Ground Beneath Her Feet*." *South Asian Review* 24.1 (2003): 130–43.
Brennan, Timothy. *Salman Rushdie and the Third World: Myths of the Nation*. London: Macmillan, 1989.
Brians, Paul. "Notes for Salman Rushdie: *The Satanic Verses*." Washington State University, 13 Feb. 2004. Web. 18 May 2012.
Brigg, Peter. "Salman Rushdie's Novels: The Disorder in Fantastic Order." *WLWE* 27.1 (1987): 119–30.
Brouillette, Sarah. "Authorship as Crisis in Salman Rushdie's *Fury*." *Journal of Commonwealth Literature* 40.1 (2005): 137–56.
Calder, Liz. "Interview med Liz Calder, fhv. redaktør ved Victor Gollancz, London, 25. maj 1999." By Rasmus Gissel. *Salman Rushdies* Grimus *og dens Receptionshistorie*. MA thesis. Aarhus University, 2000. Rpt. in Gisselnet.dk, 2009. 76–81. Web. 18 May 2012.
Cantor, Paul A. "Tales of the Alhambra: Rushdie's Use of Spanish History in *The Moor's Last Sigh*." Bloom 121–44.
Carter, Angela. "Angels in Dirty Places: *The Satanic Verses*." *Guardian* 23 Sept. 1988: 30.
Cavanaugh, Christine. "Auguries of Power: Prophecy and Violence in *The Satanic Verses*." *Studies in the Novel* 36.3 (2004): 393–404.
Chakrabarti, Santosh. "*Shame* as a Political Allegory." Ray and Kundu 152–62.
Chauhan, Pradyumna S., ed. *Salman Rushdie Interviews: A Sourcebook of His Ideas*. Westport: Greenwood, 2001.
Clark, Roger Y. "*Grimus*: Worlds upon Worlds." *Stranger Gods: Salman Rushdie's Other Worlds*. Montreal: McGill-Queen's UP, 2001. 30–60.
Cohn-Sherbok, Dan, ed. *Salman Rushdie Controversy in Interreligious Perspective*. Lewiston: Mellen, 1990.
Concilio, Carmen. "Worthy of the World: The Narrator/Photographer in Salman Rushdie's *The Ground Beneath Her Feet*." Ray and Kundu 133–44.
Crane, Ralph J. "The Chutnification of History." *Inventing India: A History of India in English-Language Fiction*. Basingstoke: Macmillan, 1992. 170–89, 200.
Cundy, Catherine. "'Rehearsing Voices': Salman Rushdie's *Grimus*." *Journal of Commonwealth Literature* 27.1 (1992): 128–38.
———. "Rushdie's Women." *Wasafiri* 18 (1993): 13–17.
———. *Salman Rushdie*. Manchester: Manchester UP, 1996.
Dash, Pratap Kumar. "Reader-centric and Text-centric Approaches to Novel: A Study of Intertextuality in Salman Rushdie's *The Enchantress of Florence*." *Language in India* 11 (Feb. 2011): n. pag. Web. 1 Aug. 2011.
D'Cruz, Adrene Freeda, and T. Ravichandran. "More Real than the Real: Technocapitalism in Salman Rushdie's *Fury*." *Meridian Critic B. Literature* 16.2 (2010): 41–55.

Deresiewicz, William. "Salman Rushdie's Imaginative New *The Enchantress of Florence.*" *The Nation.* The Nation, 15 Sept. 2008. Web. 8 Aug. 2011.

Deszcz, Justyna. *Rushdie in Wonderland: Fairytaleness in Salman Rushdie's Fiction.* Frankfurt: Lang, 2004.

Detmers, Ines. "Global Minds and Local Mentalities: 'Topographies of Terror' in Salman Rushdie's *Fury* and *Shalimar the Clown.*" *Local Natures, Global Responsibilities: Ecocritical Perspectives on the New English Literatures.* Ed. Laurenz Volkmann, et al. Amsterdam: Rodopi, 2010. 351–64.

Dey, Pradip Kumar. *Salman Rushdie's* Midnight's Children. New Delhi: Atlantic, 2008.

Dutheil de la Rochère, Martine Hennard. *Origin and Originality in Rushdie's Fiction.* Bern: Lang, 1999.

Fletcher, M. D., ed. *Reading Rushdie: Perspectives on the Fiction of Salman Rushdie.* Amsterdam: Rodopi, 1994.

Gabriel, Sharmani Patricia. "Hybridity, Nation, Diaspora and Representation: Masala Nationalism in Salman Rushdie's *The Moor's Last Sigh.*" *Migrating the Texts: Hybridity as a Postcolonial Literary Construct.* Ed. Alessandro Monti and John Douthwaite. Turin: Harmattan, 2003. 41–76.

Gane, Gillian. "Migrancy, the Cosmopolitan Intellectual, and the Global City in *The Satanic Verses.*" *MFS: Modern Fiction Studies* 48.1 (2002): 18–49.

_____. "Postcolonial Literature and the Magic Radio: The Language of Rushdie's *Midnight's Children.*" *Poetics Today* 27.3 (2006): 569–96.

Gilden, Mel. "*Grimus*: Turn Left at the Conscious Mind." *Los Angeles Times Book Review* 26 Aug. 1979: 8.

Glaister, Dan. "After the Satanic Verses, the Romantic Lyrics." *Guardian.* Guardian News and Media, 22 Jan. 1999. Web. 1 Aug. 2011.

Glomb, Stefan. "The Birth of Rock 'n' Roll out of the Spirit of Myth: Salman Rushdie's *The Ground Beneath Her Feet.*" *Zeitschrift für Anglistik und Amerikanistik* 54.1 (2006): 65–77.

Goonetilleke, D. C. R. A. *Salman Rushdie.* London: Macmillan, 1998.

Grant, Damian. *Salman Rushdie.* Plymouth: Northcote, 1999.

Gray, Paul. "Writing to Save His Life: *The Moor's Last Sigh.*" *Time* 15 Jan. 1996: 70–71.

Grewal, Inderpal. "Salman Rushdie: Marginality, Women, and *Shame.*" *Genders* 3 (1988): 24–42.

Gurnah, Abdulrazak, ed. *The Cambridge Companion to Salman Rushdie.* Cambridge: Cambridge UP, 2007.

Hamilton, Ian. "The First Life of Salman Rushdie." *New Yorker* 71.42 (1995): 90–113.

Harrison, James. *Salman Rushdie.* New York: Twayne, 1992.

Hassumani, Sabrina. *Salman Rushdie: A Postmodern Reading of His Major Works.* Madison: Fairleigh Dickinson UP, 2002.

Howells, Coral Ann. "Rudy Wiebe's *The Temptations of Big Bear* and Salman Rushdie's *Midnight's Children.*" *Literary Criterion* 20.1 (1985): 191–203.

Huggan, Graham. "The Postcolonial Exotic: Salman Rushdie and the Booker of Bookers." *Transition* 64 (1994): 22–29.

Islam, Shamsul. "Rushdie and Political Commitment: A Study of *Midnight's Children* and *Shame*." *Literature and Commitment: A Commonwealth Perspective*. Proc. of the Third Commonwealth-in-Canada Conf., Oct. 1985. Ed. Govind Narain Sharma. Toronto: TSAR, 1988. 125–31.

Johansen, Ib. "The Flight of the Enchanter: Reflections on Salman Rushdie's *Grimus*." *Kunapipi* 7.1 (1985): 20–32.

———. "Tricksters and the Common Herd in Salman Rushdie's *Grimus*." Gurnah 77–90.

Jussawalla, Feroza F. *Family Quarrels: Towards a Criticism of Indian Writing in English*. New York: Lang, 1985.

———. "Rushdie's 'Dastan-e-Dilruba': *The Satanic Verses* as Rushdie's Love Letter to Islam." *Diacritics* 26.1 (1996): 50–73.

Kakutani, Michiko. "Rushdie on India: Serious, Crammed Yet Light." *New York Times* 28 Dec. 1995: C13+.

———. "Storytelling and Deception in a Magic Kingdom." *New York Times*. New York Times, 3 June 2008. Web. 8 Aug. 2011.

Kamra, Sukeshi. "Replacing the Colonial Gaze: Gender as Strategy in Salman Rushdie's Fiction." *Between the Lines: South Asians and Post-Coloniality*. Ed. Deepika Bahri and Mary Vasudeva. Philadelphia: Temple UP, 1996. 237–49.

Kemp, Peter. "Absolutely Fabulous: *The Moor's Last Sigh* by Salman Rushdie." *Sunday Times Books* 3 Sept. 1995: 1–2.

Keulks, Gavin. "New York, Los Angeles, and Other Toxicities: Revisiting Postmodernism in Rushdie's *Fury* and *Shalimar the Clown*." *The Mourning After: Attending the Wake of Postmodernism*. Ed. Neil Brooks and Josh Toth. Amsterdam: Rodopi, 2007. 143–68.

———. "'Preferring the Composite Darkness': Trauma Theory and Narration in *The Ground Beneath Her Feet* and *Shalimar the Clown*." Bharat 247–63.

Khasnabish, Ashmita. "*Shalimar the Clown* and the Psychical Fantasy of Woman." *Humanitarian Identity and the Political Sublime: Intervention of a Postcolonial Feminist*. Lanham: Lexington, 2009. 71–92.

König, Eva. "Between Cultural Imperialism and the Fatwa: Colonial Echoes and Postcolonial Dialogue in Salman Rushdie's *Haroun and the Sea of Stories*." *IFR: International Fiction Review* 33.1–2 (2006): 52–63.

Kortenaar, Neil ten. "*Midnight's Children* and the Allegory of History." *ARIEL* 26.2 (1995): 41–62.

Kortenaar, Neil ten, and Kam Louie. *Self, Nation, Text in Salman Rushdie's Midnight's Children*. Montreal: McGill-Queen's UP, 2005.

Kung, Shao-ming. "Paradise Lost: Narratives of Violence and Terror(ism) in Salman Rushdie's *Shalimar the Clown*." *Tamkang Review* 40.2 (2010): 79–103.

Kuortti, Joel. "Allegories of Fiction: *Grimus* and *Haroun and the Sea of Stories*." Mittapalli and Kuortti 30–71.

———. "A Bibliography of the Rushdie Criticism." Mittapalli and Kuortti 177–217.

———. "Feminization of Narrative and *Shame*." *Zenith* 7 (2001): 45–49.

———. *Fictions to Live In: Narration as an Argument for Fiction in Salman Rushdie's Novels*. Frankfurt: Lang, 1998.

_____. *Place of the Sacred: The Rhetoric of the* Satanic Verses *Affair.* Frankfurt: Lang, 1997.

_____. *The Salman Rushdie Bibliography: A Bibliography of Salman Rushdie's Work and Rushdie Criticism.* Frankfurt: Lang, 1997.

Le Guin, Ursula K. "The Real Uses of Enchantment: *The Enchantress of Florence.*" *Guardian* 28 Mar. 2008: 6.

Leonard, Cecile. "Mapping Global Contexts in Salman Rushdie's *The Ground Beneath Her Feet* and *Fury.*" *Commonwealth Essays and Studies* 28.1 (2005): 100–08.

Mahanta, Aparna. "Allegories of the Indian Experience: The Novels of Salman Rushdie." *Economic & Political Weekly* 19.6 (1984): 244–47.

Marwah, Anuradha. "The Tattered Burqa and the Peeling Palimpsest of Rushdie's *Shame.*" Bharat 146–58.

Massé, Sophie. "Transfictional Identities in Salman Rushdie's *Grimus.*" *Études Britanniques Contemporaines* 8 (1995): 89–95.

Mittapalli, Rajeshwar, and Joel Kuortti, eds. *Salman Rushdie: New Critical Insights.* 2 vols. New Delhi: Atlantic, 2003.

Mitra, Reena, ed. *Salman Rushdie's* Midnight's Children. New Delhi: Atlantic, 2006.

Morton, Stephen. *Salman Rushdie: Fictions of Postcolonial Modernity.* Houndmills: Macmillan, 2008.

_____. "'There Were Collisions and Explosions. The World Was No Longer Calm': Terror and Precarious Life in Salman Rushdie's *Shalimar the Clown.*" *Textual Practice* 22.2 (2008): 337–55, 404.

Moss, Stephanie. "The Cream of the Crop: Female Characters in Salman Rushdie's *Shame.*" *International Fiction Review* 19.1 (1992): 28–30.

Mukherjee, Meenakshi, ed. *Rushdie's* Midnight's Children*: A Book of Readings.* Delhi: Pencraft International, 1998.

Munjal, Savi, and Rashmi Sahni. "'. . . The Collision Is Still Happening': Genealogies of the Present in *Shalimar the Clown.*" Bharat 293–312.

Murphy, Neil. "The Literalisation of Allegory in Salman Rushdie's *Shalimar the Clown.*" Murphy and Sim 351–64.

Murphy, Neil, and Wai-chew Sim, eds. *British Asian Fiction: Framing the Contemporary.* Amherst: Cambria, 2008.

Murti, K. V. S. "Secular Fantasy: Salman Rushdie's Fiction." *Journal of Indian Writing in English* 13.2 (1985): 41–47.

Narain, Mona. "Re-imagined Histories: Rewriting the Early Modern in Rushdie's *The Moor's Last Sigh.*" *Journal for Early Modern Cultural Studies* 6.2 (2006): 55–58.

Narayan, Shyamala A. "*Midnight's Children.*" *Literary Criterion* 18.3 (1983): 23–32.

Natarajan, Nalini. "Woman, Nation, and Narration in *Midnight's Children.*" *Scattered Hegemonies: Postmodernity and Transnational Feminist Practices.* Ed. Inderpal Grewal and Caren Kaplan. Minneapolis: U Minnesota P, 1994. 76–89.

Ng, Andrew. "Gothic Illuminations of the Post-modern and Post-colonial Conditions in Salman Rushdie's *Fury.*" Murphy and Sim 365–84.

Nicholls, Peter, ed. *The Encyclopedia of Science Fiction.* St. Albans: Granada, 1979.

Parameswaran, Uma. "'Handcuffed to History': Salman Rushdie's Art." *ARIEL* 14.2 (1983): 34–45. Rpt. in Parameswaran, *The Perforated Sheet: Essays on Salman Rushdie's Art* 1–11.

———. "'Impressive Women, but the Chains Are No Fictions': Women in Rushdie's *Shame*." *Women's Writing: Text and Context*. Ed. Jasbir Jain. Jaipur: Rawat, 1996. 141–57.

———. "New Dimensions Courtesy of the Whirling Demons: Word-Play in *Grimus*." Parameswaran, *The Perforated Sheet: Essays on Salman Rushdie's Art* 55–66.

———. *The Perforated Sheet: Essays on Salman Rushdie's Art*. New Delhi: Affiliated East-West, 1988.

———. "Salman Rushdie in Indo-English Literature." *Journal of Indian Writing in English* 12.2 (1984): 15–25. Rpt. in Parameswaran, *The Perforated Sheet: Essays on Salman Rushdie's Art* 12–20.

Parashkevova, Vassilena. "New Cities out of Old Ones: Catoptric Echoes and Reversals in Salman Rushdie's *The Ground Beneath Her Feet*." *Journal of Postcolonial Writing* 45.4 (2009): 414–25.

Petersson, Margareta. "*Grimus* and the Alchemical Tradition." Mittapalli and Kuortti 1–29.

———. *Unending Metamorphoses: Myth, Satire, and Religion in Salman Rushdie's Novels*. Lund: Lund UP, 1996.

Procter, James. *Salman Rushdie's* Midnight's Children: *A Routledge Guide*. London: Routledge, 2009.

Rahimieh, Nasrin. "*Grimus:* Salman Rushdie's First Experiment with Post-Modern Narrative." *Literature and Perspective*. Proc. of the Third Commonwealth-in-Canada Conf., Oct. 1985. Ed. Govind Narain Sharma. Toronto: TSAR, 1988. 116–24.

———. *Oriental Responses to the West: Comparative Essays in Select Writers from the Muslim World*. Leiden: Brill, 1990.

Rao, M. Madhusudhana. "Rushdie, the Enchanter of Tales." *IUP Journal of English Studies* 5.4 (2010): 21–25.

Ray, Mohit Kumar, and Rama Kundu, eds. *Salman Rushdie: Critical Essays*. 2 vols. New Delhi: Atlantic, 2006.

Raza, Hima. "Unravelling Sharam: Narrativisation as a Political Act in Salman Rushdie's *Shame*." *Wasafiri* 39 (2003): 55–61.

Reder, Michael, ed. *Conversations with Salman Rushdie*. Jackson: UP of Mississippi, 2000.

Resta, Donatella. "Cognitive Science and Literature: A Cognitive Analysis of the Metaphoric Processes in *Shalimar the Clown* by Salman Rushdie." *Cognitive Philology* 2 (2009). Web. 18 May 2012.

Riemenschneider, Dieter. "History and the Individual in Salman Rushdie's *Midnight's Children* and Anita Desai's *Clear Light of Day*." *Kunapipi* 6.2 (1984): 53–66.

Rollason, Christopher. "Rushdie's Un-Indian Music: *The Ground Beneath Her Feet*." *Studies in Indian Writing in English*. Ed. Rajeshwar Mittapalli and Pier Paolo Piciucco. Vol. 2. New Delhi: Atlantic, 2001. 122–57.

Rushdie, Salman. "'Doing the Dangerous Thing': An Interview with Salman Rushdie." By T. Vijay Kumar. Mukherjee 212–27.

_____. "The Empire Writes Back with a Vengeance." *London Times* 3 July 1982: 8.
_____. "Interview with Salman Rushdie." By Jean-Pierre Durix. *Kunapipi* 4.2 (1982): 17–26.
_____. Introduction. *Mirrorwork: 50 Years of Indian Writing, 1947–1997*. Ed. Salman Rushdie and Elizabeth West. New York: Holt, 1997. vii–xx.
Ruthven, Malise. *A Satanic Affair: Salman Rushdie and the Rage of Islam*. London: Chatto, 1990.
Salgado, Minoli. "The Politics of the Palimpsest in *The Moor's Last Sigh*." Gurnah 153–67.
Sambamurthy, V. Indira. "Salman Rushdie." *An Annotated Bibliography of Indian English Fiction*. 3 vols. New Delhi: Atlantic, 2001. 1225–310.
Sanga, Jaina C. *Salman Rushdie's Postcolonial Metaphors: Migration, Translation, Hybridity, Blasphemy, and Globalization*. Westport: Greenwood, 2001.
Sangari, Kumkum. "Marquez and the Politics of the Possible." *Journal of Arts and Ideas* 10–11 (1985): 37–58. Rev. ed. in *Cultural Critique* 7 (1987): 157–86.
Sardar, Ziauddin, and Merryl Wyn Davies. *Distorted Imagination: Lessons from the Rushdie Affair*. London: Grey Seal, 1990.
Schultheis, Alexandra W. "Postcolonial Lack and Aesthetic Promise in *The Moor's Last Sigh*." *Twentieth-Century Literature* 47.4 (2001): 569–95.
Schürer, Norbert. *Salman Rushdie's* Midnight's Children: *A Reader's Guide*. New York: Continuum, 2004.
Seminck, Hans. *A Novel Visible but Unseen: A Thematic Analysis of Salman Rushdie's* The Satanic Verses. Ghent: Studia Germanica Gandensia, 1993.
Shankar, Subramanian. "Midnight's Orphans, or, A Postcolonialism Worth Its Name." *Cultural Critique* 56 (2004): 64–95.
Sharma, D. R. "Chutnification of India." *New Quest* 33 (1982): 169–71.
Shepherd, Ron. "Growing Up: A Central Metaphor in Some Recent Novels." *The Writer's Sense of the Contemporary: Papers in Southeast Asian and Australian Literature*. Nedlands: U of Western Australia, 1982. 51–55.
Siddiqi, Yumna. "'Power Smashes into Private Lives': Violence, Globalization and Cosmopolitanism in Salman Rushdie's *Shalimar the Clown*." *South Asia Research* 27.3 (2007): 293–309.
Smale, David, ed. *Salman Rushdie:* Midnight's Children / The Satanic Verses: *A Reader's Guide to Essential Criticism*. Houndmills: Macmillan, 2003.
Souza Gomes Carreira, Shirley de. "Postcolonial Issues in Rushdie's *Grimus*." *Revista Eletrônica do Instituto de Humanidades* 2.8 (2004): 7–15.
Spaeth, Anthony. "Rushdie Offends Again." *Time* 11 Sept. 1995: 53.
Spencer, Alice. "The Puppet Master's Fury: Malik Solanka as Artist." Ray and Kundu 153–62.
Srivastava, Neelam. "Languages of the Nation in Salman Rushdie's *Midnight's Children* and Vikram Seth's *A Suitable Boy*." *ARIEL* 36.1–2 (2005): 207–32.
Stadtler, Florian. "Nargis and Aurora Zogoiby: Imaging Mother and Nation in Mehboob Khan's *Mother India* and Salman Rushdie's *The Moor's Last Sigh*." *Once Upon a Time in Bollywood: The Global Swing of Hindi Cinema*. Ed. Gubir Jolly, Zenia Wadhwani, and Deborah Barretto. Toronto: TSAR, 2007. 175–90.

———. "Terror, Globalisation and the Individual in Salman Rushdie's *Shalimar the Clown*." *Journal of Postcolonial Writing* 45.2 (2009): 191–99.

Sutherland, John. "The Sound and the Fury: Salman Rushdie's *Fury*." *Guardian*. Guardian News and Media, 24 Aug. 2001. Web. 1 Aug. 2011.

Syed, Mujeebuddin. "Warped Mythologies: Salman Rushdie's *Grimus*." *ARIEL* 25.4 (1994): 135–52.

Taneja, G. R., and R. K. Dhawan, eds. *The Novels of Salman Rushdie*. New Delhi: Indian Soc. for Commonwealth Studies, 1992.

Teverson, Andrew. *Salman Rushdie*. Manchester: Manchester UP, 2007.

Thiara, Nicole Weickgenannt. "Enabling Spaces and the Architecture of Hybridity in Salman Rushdie's *The Enchantress of Florence*." *Journal of Commonwealth Literature* 46.3 (2011): 415–31.

Trousdale, Rachel. "'City of Mongrel Joy': Bombay and the Shiv Sena in *Midnight's Children* and *The Moor's Last Sigh*." *Journal of Commonwealth Literature* 39.2 (2004): 95–110.

Updike, John. "Paradises Lost: *Shalimar the Clown*." *New Yorker*. Condé Nast, 5 Sept. 2005. Web. 1 Aug. 2011.

Upstone, Sara. "The Fulcrum of Instability: Salman Rushdie's *The Ground Beneath Her Feet* and the Postcolonial Traveller." *Wasafiri* 47 (2006): 34–38.

Verma, Charu. "Padma's Tragedy: A Feminist Deconstruction of Rushdie's *Midnight's Children*." *Feminism and Recent Fiction in English*. Ed. Sushila Singh. New Delhi: Prestige, 1991. 154–62.

Wiemann, Dirk. "Back to Back Stories: Salman Rushdie, Transnationalism, and *Fury*." *Mediating Indian Writing in English: German Responses*. Ed. Bernd-Peter Lange and Mala Pandurang. Berlin: Lit, 2006. 141–65.

Yaqin, Amina. "Family and Gender in Rushdie's Writing." Gurnah 61–74.

Zimring, Rishona. "The Passionate Cosmopolitan in Salman Rushdie's *Fury*." *Journal of Postcolonial Writing* 46.1 (2010): 5–16.

History and Myth: Rewinding the Past in "The Prophet's Hair" and *The Moor's Last Sigh*
Mona Narain

Explorations of the concepts of nation and nationality, the use of religion to define them, and national histories' complicity in the erasure of competing ideas that are perceived as threats are all central to Salman Rushdie's work. Though the canvas of his fiction is large, he is most interested in examining history and society through the lens of the experiences and stories of individuals. Indeed, history is the instrument through which people make meaning of their pasts, and Rushdie explores many histories, empirical and mythical, to give us a highly plural vision of the past. This essay examines his story "The Prophet's Hair" and the novel *The Moor's Last Sigh* (*MLS*) because they have similar themes that illustrate his hybrid constructions of the past. In each text, he simultaneously refers us to the complex stories of nations and cities as they are interwoven with the stories of families and individuals such as Hashim the moneylender and Moraes Zogoiby.

Scholars have read *The Moor's Last Sigh*, as well as several other Rushdie novels, as the writer's postmodern play on the breakdown of coherent historical narratives in the late twentieth century. Placing Rushdie's work in a global context and aligning it with his Latin American contemporaries, such as Gabriel García Márquez or Jorge Luis Borges, has produced important insights about its place within the genre of magic realism. Since "The Prophet's Hair" and *The Moor's Last Sigh* both incorporate magic and fantasy, reading them through the literary critical focus of magic realism or postmodernism offers interesting insights. For example, Fiona Richards has persuasively described the short story as "an exploration of the status of the iconic in Rushdie's writing" that exposes "the ineffable in material signs" (1, 3). She argues that though Rushdie is irreverent toward icons, his representation of the sacred icon in the story "reveals something dangerous about the icons themselves" and "open[s] it to radical doubt" (3, 15).

Moreover, Salman Rushdie grounds his work within the empirical realities of important historical events, though he uses imaginative means to explore them. This aspect of his work has not been discussed as often, so I am going to examine "The Prophet's Hair" and *The Moor's Last Sigh* within the less explored context of real events in recent Indian history and Indian notions of history and myth. Using Ashis Nandy's explanation of the cyclical nature of Indian history and myths, I analyze *The Moor's Last Sigh* within the context of the Babri Masjid religious conflict between Hindus and Muslims in modern-day India. Set in the city of Bombay (Mumbai) for the most part, the novel is deeply entwined with the city's history. I suggest that it is a text that is also Rushdie's direct political response to the right-wing political party Shiv Sena's recent rewriting of the city's past in militaristically Hindu terms. I trace Rushdie's interests in alternative notions of history to his early short story "The Prophet's Hair," set in Kashmir, which uses a cyclical form and myth to similarly comment on the practices of fundamentalist Muslims and Islam's place in Indian nationality. When added to considerations of postmodernity or magic realism in his writing, this different, non-Western context allows Rushdie's readers to understand the form and themes of his work in a richer, more complex way. Importantly, when we use this critical lens, Salman Rushdie's works also emerge as interventions in ongoing debates on Indian nationality, religious identity, and the future of the Indian people from within Indian historical and mythical traditions, rather than just an expatriate's comments from afar or a writer's aesthetic play.

Both "The Prophet's Hair" and *The Moor's Last Sigh* are based on actual events in Indian history. Indeed, the novel draws on a long expanse of time and historical events, which gave rise to violent conflicts between Hindus and Muslims, in part due to rigid fundamentalist beliefs. In an interview with Alastair Niven in 1994, Rushdie discussed the importance of India in his writing, stating, "I think there's been nothing more important in my life—as a writer—than that fact; both the fact of originating in India and then coming from there—both those things. I think I would not be this writer if I had never left, and I could not be this writer if I hadn't come from there" (Chauhan 231). Though the short story was first published in the *Atlantic* in June 1981, Rushdie put "The Prophet's Hair" together with other new short stories and republished it in 1994 as part of the collection *East, West* (*EW*). One of the other stories, "Christopher Columbus," imagines the events preceding Columbus's 1492 voyage and paints a cameo of Queen Isabella's ouster of Boabdil, the sultan of Alhambra. In *The Moor's Last Sigh*, which followed this collection in 1995, Rushdie develops this cameo further as he traces and locates the hybrid ancestry of the novel's protagonist, Moraes Zogoiby, to 1492, the ouster of Boabdil, and the exodus of the Jews. Thus, the collection and the novel are intimately linked together in thematic ways. Furthermore, aside from his children's tale *Haroun and the Sea of Stories* (1990), these two texts were Rushdie's first publications after *The Satanic Verses* in 1988, which incurred the wrath of many orthodox Muslims and led the ayatollah of Iran, Ruhollah Khomeini, to issue a *fatwā* (legal ruling) against Rushdie, a death sentence in effect. Rushdie wrote both these works while in hiding. Not surprisingly then, "The Prophet's Hair" and *The Moor's Last Sigh* are explorations of and an indictment of fanatical religious beliefs that give rise to violence and destruction.

In his article "History's Forgotten Doubles," Ashis Nandy argues that thinking of the past as the sole province of traditional or official history is problematic. This is an idea that Rushdie's work has also espoused through its articulation of alternative narratives for the same historical event. For example, in *Midnight's Children*, Saleem admits to getting the date of the death of Mahatma Gandhi, the "father" of the nation, wrong and posits other possible dates for it (189–90). Nandy's critique of the totalizing impulses of history particularly criticizes Enlightenment history's claim as the *only* story of the past and as a discipline that requires empirical facts, cause-and-effect explanations, in order to narrate a linearly progressive story about cultures and nations to explain this "one" past. He also asserts that this form of history is particularly problematic to understanding South Asian cultures and their past. He argues that in societies such as India, which Western observers sometimes considered "ahistorical" or without traditional, Western forms of written history by the Europeans, "millions of people still live outside 'history.' They *do* have theories of the past . . . but they also recognize, confront, and live with a past different from that constructed by historians and historical consciousness. They even have a different way of arriving at that past" (44; Nandy's emphasis). Instead, traditional Indian *itihāsas* (plural accounts or histories) are composed of a combination of legends, epics, myths, and real events that are often cyclical but "rarely linear or unidirectional" (63). Importantly, the past is not necessarily and always the precursor of the present. Instead, Nandy explains, "Time in much of South Asia is an open-ended enterprise," in which the present sometimes dictates an ethical construction of the past (63). "The conventional truth value of or empirical certitude about the past is not particularly relevant" in such formulations, according to Nandy (64).

This framework is more valuable to understanding Salman Rushdie's structural (in)coherence than Aristotelian demands for unities of time, place, and action. It also provides us with an understanding of Rushdie's works, such as "The Prophet's Hair" and *The Moor's Last Sigh*, as commentaries on important social and political problems, a perspective on the two texts' interventions in specifically Indian debates that more global, abstractly theoretical frameworks such as postmodernity, though viable and useful in their own way, do not necessarily reveal.

"The Prophet's Hair" is set in the capital of the beautiful valley of Kashmir, Srinagar, which is nestled among the Himalayas in the northernmost part of India. Indian legend has it that upon seeing the valley for the first time, the seventeenth-century Mughal emperor Shah Jahan exclaimed, "If there is a paradise on earth, this is it, this is it, this is it!" an idea that Rushdie uses explicitly and satirizes at the end of the story (*EW* 57, 58). Critics have remarked on how Kashmir, where Rushdie's ancestors lived, has recurred as an important mythic, psychological, and imaginative location in his fiction for over three decades—most fully and recently in *Shalimar the Clown* (2005)—and how the paradoxes of Kashmir, its beauty and its violent modern history, permeate "The Prophet's Hair." Kashmir is also the home of the Nehru-Gandhi family that produced three prime ministers of India. Divided between a larger portion in India and a smaller part in Pakistan, Kashmir is now familiar to the world as a disputed territory between India and Pakistan. Since the 1960s, the Indian province has been torn apart by the violence resulting from this dispute, with frequent terrorist attacks, ethnic and religious sectarianism between Muslims and Hindus, and government crackdowns. The Kashmiri territory on the Pakistan side of the border has been subjected to similar violence, though for somewhat different reasons. The short story and its location in Kashmir serve as a metaphoric and concrete space to depict the problems of the historical claims of hostile nation-states and the competing historical concerns of different ethnic communities, which give rise to separatist, religious violence and state repression. Given his interest in exploring the ramifications of large cultural and historical issues on the individual through smaller scale plural histories, or itihāsas, Rushdie masterfully distills these large concerns into the story of two families and one major historical incident—the 1963 theft of the Prophet's hair from the shrine—which had deep political and social repercussions still felt in Kashmir.

Set sometime in the second half of the twentieth century, "The Prophet's Hair" is the tale of Hashim the moneylender, his family, and the famous relic of Moi-e-Muqqadas, said to be the prophet Muhammad's own hair, housed in the sacred shrine of the Hazratbal mosque. It begins with incidents of individual violence. A wealthy young man named Atta is beaten almost to death by hoodlums as he searches for a thief in the darkest alleyways of the city. His sister Huma takes up the search, and she too bears the marks of violence on her face and body. The plot follows a cyclical trajectory as we go back in time to discover the reasons for the beatings and the search for a thief. The flashback reveals that the events began with Hashim's discovery of a glass vial containing the Prophet's Hair floating by the quay on the lake six days ago. This discovery leads to the family's present distress. Life had been good for Atta and Huma's family until then. Their father has a beautiful house on the shores of the Dal Lake in the middle of Srinagar and in the vicinity of the mosque. He lives in it with a beautiful wife and two grown children. Hashim is Muslim like the majority of Kashmiris, though he is not religious or even a believer, evidenced by the fact that he is a moneylender, a profession abhorrent to the Prophet and Islam, which forbids lending money for profit. He has a bizarre and ironic ethical code, which translates into charging his customers over 70 percent interest. He tells his wife that he charges high interest rates "to teach these people the value of money; let them only learn that, and they will be cured of this fever of borrowing borrowing all the time—so you see that if my plans succeed, I shall put myself out of business!" thus gulling himself and his family into a pretence of honorable living that is replicated in their formal, polite everyday family life (41).

Indeed, later in the story, we see Hashim express the violence of his contradictory ethical beliefs by seeking to dismember defaulting debtors with a knife to teach them a lesson. The cyclical nature of the plot allows readers to understand the extreme violence in the story, and when all the main characters die within hours of each other, we see violence and death as the inevitable result of such contradictory and false ethical beliefs.

Rushdie connects the story of the family and the broader implications of the theft of the relic within a set of thematic oppositions moving the plot inexorably toward its tragic and ironic end. The sacred vial finds its way into the hands of both the profane moneylender and the thief, Sheikh Sín, and the strange honor system and the religious beliefs of the thief's family are juxtaposed with the livelihood of the wealthy, secular moneylender's family, which is based on a different kind of thievery: extortion. We witness the most important, satiric contradiction in the effects of the holy vial, which works its powerful transformation on its viewers/possessors just as faithful believers would have it—for Kashmiri Muslims, the *deedar*, or viewing, of the Moi-e-Muqqadas is sufficient to transform a human being's life. Overnight, Hashim becomes truthful, revealing in "streams of awful truth" that he hates his wife and family and has a mistress (44). He also turns fanatically devout, ordering all books in the house other than the Qur'an to be burnt, starting to strictly observe an orthodox Islamic way of life by praying five times a day, and insisting that his daughter wear a veil and restrict herself to home. When his family refuses, he disinherits them and turns physically violent in order to force them into what he now believes is a more devout and righteous way of life. Yet Hashim's actual practices terrorize the people around him, having the opposite effect of what a religious "born again" conversion is promised to be. His son Atta decides that his family's slow destruction is the result of the illegitimate possession of the Prophet's Hair, so he steals it in order to return it to the mosque. But the vial inexplicably, magically, falls out of Atta's pocket.

Relieved that he no longer has the responsibility of returning the vial, Atta returns home. Unfortunately, he then finds out that Hashim has again found the "errant relic." When he learns that his father had beaten the truth out of Huma about Atta's theft of the vial, Atta "buried his face in his hands and sobbed out his opinion, which was that the hair was persecuting them, and had come back to finish the job" (50). Atta's despairing utterance to his sister highlights the boomerang effect of the magical powers of the Prophet's Hair, which destroys those who possess or use it illegitimately, and at the same time, it underscores the collateral damage, the destruction of relatively innocent people along the way. The sense that "all will not end well" gains inevitability as we realize that Atta was almost beaten to death when he went out to hire a thief and is found in a coma by a poor flower vendor and brought home. In the meantime, Hashim has physically beaten and verbally abused his daughter and wife. Huma, on seeing her dying brother, resolves to get the vial out of the house, bringing us to the opening scene of the short story when she sets out in search of an "employable thief" and engages Sheikh Sín to complete the theft. The short story rolls to its tragic end as Hashim is awakened from sleep the next night and alerted to the entrance of the thief, who is about to steal the vial again, when his son suddenly wakes up from his coma and shouts, "*Thief! Thief! Thief!*" before dying (54). More horrible events follow with breathless rapidity as Hashim murders Huma as she tries to prevent him from discovering the theft in progress and then subsequently commits suicide when he discovers that he has killed his own daughter rather than the thief. The destruction comes full circle as the police shoot Sheikh Sín in the stomach as he tries to escape—a fate the thief had sought to avoid all his life.

The story concludes with another seeming inevitability. Soon after the moneylender and his family are destroyed due to Hashim's illegitimate, profane possession of the sacred relic and the vial is returned to its rightful place in the shrine—"in the heart of the valley which was once closer than any other place on earth to Paradise"—the religious members of the thief's family are healed because they were in the presence of the vial for a short period of time. His crippled sons regain the use of their legs, and his blind wife regains her eyesight in a miraculous flurry of mythic poetic justice (57–58). The contradiction lies in the ironic twist: The sons are left even more destitute because they can no longer pursue their profession of begging. A close reading of the text leads us to see that Rushdie is using satire here to point out the continued destitution of the poor, which no miracle can easily cure, as well as the destructive results of fanatical religiosity that accepts no alternatives. The cyclical, mythical quality of the narrative is enhanced by the magical elements that structure the plot and draw their power from the legend of the Hazratbal mosque and Moi-e-Muqqadas.

Read within the context of the historical events of the theft of the holy relic containing the Prophet's Hair in 1963, Rushdie's satire becomes an important commentary on the violent sectarian politics of Kashmir and the dual claims of India and Pakistan on Kashmir. On

Friday night of December 27, 1963, thieves broke through three separate doors of the Hazratbal mosque and stole the vial containing the sacred relic from the special chamber housing it. Writer Ved Mehta describes the events following the theft in his documentary narrative: "The news swept through Srinagar. All offices and shops, schools and colleges were closed. The streets were cleared of all buses, taxis, tongas, rickshaws, and bicycles, and the waterways of boats" (129). Drawing on archives of contemporary newspaper and eyewitness accounts, Mehta reports that mourning crowds of about thirty thousand people dressed in black, wailing in bereavement at the desecration of a holy site and relic, one considered second only to Mecca by Kashmiri Muslims, started to converge on the Hazratbal mosque. Rumors started to fly about various conspiracies "to injure Muslim sensibilities," by the Hindus, the Sikhs, the Indian government, and the state's political leaders, or by the Pakistani government to fuel a religious war between Indian Muslims and Hindus (Mehta 129). For several tense days, there were clashes between different ethnic communities. The police imposed a curfew and arrested political activists. As the investigation into the theft continued, sympathy marches took place in Pakistan. "The General Secretary of the Kashmir Liberation Movement in Pakistan . . . hinted that India was behind the theft by calling it 'the latest attack on Muslim culture by the enemies of the people of Kashmir'" (Mehta 132). Sectarian violence broke out in locations far from Kashmir, causing retaliation riots in East Bengal (then in East Pakistan, now the modern nation of Bangladesh) in which thousands died. Hindu refugees fled to India, and many Muslims from India moved to East Pakistan in a grotesque, smaller scale reenactment of the Partition riots between India and Pakistan in 1947–48 (Mehta 132). Inexplicably, on January 4, 1964, newspapers and radio broadcasts reported that authorities had recovered the Moi-e-Muqqadas. It appeared that the thieves had returned the holy relic to the shrine, though no one had accepted blame or been arrested (Mehta 138). Violence continued with more deaths until February 3, 1964, when a group of fifteen Muslim holy men, in the presence of the Indian prime minister, Lal Bahadur Shastri, verified the authenticity of the holy hair (Mehta 147). The religious violence following the theft that gripped Kashmir and other parts of the subcontinent marked a defining moment in the ongoing fight over Kashmir between India and Pakistan and between the nation-state and separatists. India and Pakistan have since fought two limited wars, in part due to Kashmir, in 1965 and 1971. More recently, in 1993, Kashmiri separatist militants took over the Hazratbal mosque in the hope of gaining access to the holy relic and using the mosque as a political pulpit to air their demands. The resulting siege of the mosque by Indian government forces lasted several weeks before ending without bloodshed, but the standoff's result could have been much worse.

Republished in 1994, Salman Rushdie's short story thus neatly captures the mystery of the relic's original disappearance. In the story, we are never told who the actual thieves were, and the relic's appearance and disappearance thus aptly parallels the real Moi-e-Muqqadas's mysterious theft and miraculous return. Rushdie deliberately juxtaposes the mundane with the miraculous. He highlights the mythic quality of the sacred object and imaginatively narrates what happened to the vial by putting it in the possession of an ordinary individual, a mundane moneylender living only a few miles away from the mosque. This alternative, imaginative history of the theft seeks to deconstruct the belief in large conspiracy theories and historical narratives constructed at national levels that circulated through the subcontinent in late 1963–64, resulted in the deaths of thousands, and led, in part, to the continued wars and insurgencies that followed. Instead, the immense passion that the original theft has generated in South Asian (particularly Kashmiri) history is sublimated into the sudden and extreme violence Hashim subjects his family to and the subsequent destruction of his whole family, as well as the death of the thief who came to be their savior. The story shows how the sacred can become profane in the hands of illegitimate possessors if misinterpreted and misrepresented and if used as a means to repress and terrorize. This is Rushdie's profound commentary on the misuse of religious discourse and locations for political domination in the twentieth century in all parts of the world, but especially in South Asia. Though the violence in the story destroys a few individuals, the itihāsa of these individuals is a metaphor for the destruction possible in the hands of religious fanaticism. It gives a human face to the violence and its victims rather providing us a dehumanized statistical account of the death tolls in riots. Furthermore, the ostensible positive promise of the last line of the story—that the thief's wife can "spend her last days gazing once more upon the beauties of the valley of Kashmir"—becomes a false promise when contextualized within the reader's knowledge of the continued violence that has now destroyed the beautiful valley that was once a paradise on earth (*EW* 58).

Rushdie's next publication, the novel *The Moor's Last Sigh*, refers to the history of another famous holy location, the Babri Masjid in the city of Ayodhya, which was the scene of great violence from 1992 through 1994. Rushdie wrote *The Moor's Last Sigh* during this time, while he was under the shadow of the fatwā and his own life was under threat from Muslim fundamentalists. Moraes Zogoiby, the protagonist, refers to the demolition of the mosque explicitly: "The mosque in Ayodhya was destroyed. Alphabet-soupists, 'fanatics', or, alternatively, 'devout liberators of the sacred site' (delete according to taste) swarmed over the seventeenth-century Babri Masjid and tore it apart with their bare hands, with their teeth, with the elemental power of what Sir V. Naipaul has approvingly called their 'awakening to history'" (*MLS* 363).

This reference comes just before Moraes goes on to kill Raman Fielding, his one-time boss, by smashing his face with a frog phone to avenge Fielding's insult to his mother, Aurora Zogoiby, on national television. Retrospectively, Moraes's rumination about the Babri Masjid incident becomes important as he too is implicated in murder for the first time on the next page of the novel. Moraes's explanation for the murder, not his "excuse" as he insists, is that all of us are ultimately implicated in the violence that surrounds us and "who started it" is immaterial.

Rushdie's yoking together of the demolition of the mosque and the killing of Raman Fielding is not coincidental. Fielding rules the violent sectarian politics and the criminal underworld of Moraes's Bombay. In this, he is a challenger to the economic and criminal ascendency of Moraes's father, Abraham Zogoiby. He also stands for a special brand of thuggery disguised as a religiously motivated political mass movement. Fielding is, of course, a caricature of Bal Thackeray, the leader of the Hindu/Marathi fundamentalist party Shiv Sena, established in 1966, which came to political power in Maharashtra in the early 1990s. It was the Shiv Sena administration that renamed the island city Mumbai in 1995 to resurrect the premodern association it had with the local Indian deity, Mumbadevi, before it became an important eighteenth-century colonial outpost of the British, who called it Bombay. Shiv Sena can be broadly translated as the army of Shiv, or Shivaji, a seventeenth-century Hindu king whose realm included the territory of the modern state of Maharashtra with its capital at Mumbai. Shivaji fought several wars with the Mughal and Afghan Muslim rulers of the surrounding kingdoms, and his history has been used by the Shiv Sena to create a militaristic, anti-Muslim, Hindu past and lay claim to the economic center of India, Mumbai, as a city exclusively for Hindus and specifically for Maharashtrians. In the 1980s, the Shiv Sena joined a broader fundamentalist Hindu coalition known as Hindutva, which is the radical right wing of the Bharatiya Janata Party (BJP), the national party in power in India from 1998 to 2004. This Hindutva movement was largely responsible for the demolition of the Babri Masjid.

The demolition of the Babri Masjid on December 6, 1992, resulted from an amalgam of the passionate fury of religious fundamentalism, tangled historical and mythic accounts of the origins of this early modern mosque, and the contemporary desire of various political parties and ethnic communities in India to lay claim to a specific history as their authentic past. Indeed, it was a test case of the conflicts between itihāsas and empirical history in India that Ashis Nandy describes. Likely built under the Mughal Muslim emperor Babur in 1528, according to Indian myths the location of the mosque is also the birthplace of the important Hindu deity Rāma, whose birth is said to predate written history. Both these accounts have coexisted for a long time in Indian culture. In the 1980s, however, Hindutva leaders mobilized a large number of followers, whipping them to a high pitch of anti-Muslim sentiment by arguing that Babur had razed the Hindu temple that had stood on the spot and built the Babri Masjid to establish Muslim dominance over India's Hindu subjects. The retaliatory razing of the mosque was justified and necessary therefore to "take back" the space as well as, metaphorically, the nation, which a weak policy of secularism had gifted to minorities such as the Muslims. The demolition and the frenzy it created horrified Indian citizens across the country, including secularists, who sought to establish the history of the site and location through empirical historical and archaeological research. However, the empirically unverifiable nature of any of these historical "facts"—whether this location was indeed the birthplace of Rāma, the specifics of Babur's intentions as he built the mosque, or whether Babur even *built* the mosque—was completely irrelevant to the Hindu masses who stormed and tore down the mosque. It was also irrelevant to the thousands of Hindus and Muslims who rioted in Bombay and the adjoining state of Gujarat in waves of retaliation, killing thousands in turn, and to the five Muslim militants who attacked the site to "take it back" for Muslims and were killed by the Indian police in the summer of 2005.

It is this tangled web of history, mythology, and violence that the Moor, Moraes Zogoiby, is referring to when he observes, "So, bloodlust was in my history, and it was in my bones." He elaborates:

> Violence was violence, murder was murder, two wrongs did not make a right . . . In the days after the destruction of the Babri Masjid, "justly enraged Muslims" / fanatical killers (once again, use your blue pencil as your heart dictates) smashed up Hindu temples, and killed Hindus, across India and in Pakistan as well. There comes a point in the unfurling of communal violence in which it becomes irrelevant to ask, "Who started

it?" The lethal conjugations of death part company with any possibility of justification, let alone justice. They surge among us, left and right, Hindu and Muslim, knife and pistol, killing burning, looting, and raising into the smoky air their clenched and bloody fists. Both their houses are damned by their deeds . . . I do not exempt myself. I have been a man of violence for too long, and on the night after Raman Fielding insulted my mother on TV, I brutally put an end to his accursed life. And in so doing called a curse down upon my own. (365)

The specific incident that motivates Moraes to kill Raman is the theft of Aurora's paintings, literally Aurora's reimagined canvas of plural India. Raman links the fall of the mosque with the theft of the paintings and observes that it was good they had disappeared because "if the new nation is to be born, there is much invader-history that may have to be erased." Moraes recoils from these words and ruminates, "So we were invaders now, were we? After two thousand years, we still did not belong, and indeed, were soon to be 'erased'" (364).

It is not surprising that Aurora's paintings are stolen and "erased," very likely by Fielding's gangs, for they represent a different, pluralistic, secular vision of the nation that the one-dimensional view of national history espoused by Fielding in the novel, and by extension the religious fundamentalists across India, seek to challenge. Indeed, Aurora's project is to bring together twentieth-century India with early modern Moorish Spain—to layer them on top of each other and unify them through the figure of Boabdil, the last Moorish sultan of Spain, who is said to be the Zogoiby family's ancestor. Paul Cantor has observed that Rushdie seems to be "turning to Moorish Spain as a model of multicultural society . . . Moorish Spain appears to have solved the problem that has figuratively and literally torn India apart in the twentieth century" (324). Aurora's series of paintings about the Moor are as much about Boabdil's past—his defeat by Queen Isabella and King Ferdinand's armies and his sigh as he left the Alhambra—as it is about Moraes and a prophetic vision of her own death and her son's crumbling future. Moraes, the modern-day Boabdil and the last Moor, is a mixture of a Christian, Jewish, and Indian blood and upbringing, an ancestry that is significantly different from the common historical binaries of Hindu/Muslim used to describe India's past. Through him, Salman Rushdie seeks to rewrite India's historical past to reveal its extensive hybridity, which cannot be encapsulated in one history, one religion, and one community, or, for that matter, even two. Aurora's early murals depict multiple worlds that bring together public and personal narratives. They are peopled with real beings such as Queen Isabella of Spain, animals, and mythic creatures all drawn together "in a sweeping black line," so much so that Camoens, her father, exclaims, "But it is the great swarm of being itself" (59). I have discussed elsewhere how Aurora's murals and paintings are Rushdie's *ekphrasis*, his literary description through visual art, designed to paint a more romantic vision of a plural hybrid nation by drawing upon India's early modern histories. However, Moraes's flight to Benengeli and his dying, frantic effort to write the history of his life is an elegy to this plural, romantic vision of the nation and a hybrid individual national identity. With Moraes's death, we anticipate, another piece of the itihāsa will also die: that of the Da Gama-Zogoiby family, which brings together the early modern arrival of the Cochin Jews, the mythic ancestry traced to the Alhambra, and the Indian Christians. The failure the novel records is perhaps the failure of the writer's efforts to eventually create an achievable vision of a plural nation, so that Moraes and Aurora's, or the artist's, vision remains an allegory (Narain 63–64). Yet what does emerge is Salman Rushdie's studied intervention in Indian political and social discourses about important questions such as which past defines India, who is authentically Indian, and to whom the nation belongs. This intervention is not just postmodern play or a critique of modern master narratives or a literary commentary. Rushdie presents us with many cycles of histories, big and small, personal and public, that incorporate different mythologies and legends to consistently reimagine and rewind the past in order to describe and escape the impasse modern India faces.

Exploring the aesthetic dimensions of Salman Rushdie's work can provide a reader several pleasures, but reading its literary aesthetics without paying attention to its ethical and political dimensions at the same time erases, to an extent, its layered and multifaceted nature. If we attend to Rushdie's engagement with the specific Indian cultural and political debates evident in the actual historical events that inform his fiction, however—and if we do so using Indian knowledge frameworks, such as those described by Ashis Nandy—we can see different layers in the text rooted in a specific cultural, historical dynamic that may not be otherwise visible. Rushdie is often called a "cosmopolitan writer," which is accurate but incomplete. His incorporation of actual events from Indian history in his works is an attempt to step aside from the so-called rootlessness of modern cosmopolitanism and the recurring label of the "exiled" writer and to speak from within a culture. In doing so though, Rushdie also gives an imaginative twist to such "real" events that disrupts official historical accounts of certitude.

Through the alternative stories that Salman Rushdie narrates, whether they are stories that each Chinese tile conjures up in the Mattancherri synagogue described in the novel or the story of the moneylender who possessed the Prophet's Hair for several days, Rushdie insists on creating and incorporating mythologies or itihāsas that are deemed incorrect or ahistorical by traditional empirical viewpoints. This insistence can be understood through Ashis Nandy's explanation of the Indian mythological impulse, in which the art of telling many stories of the past is "on grounds of diversity, seen as a moral value in itself, especially when it is located in the worldview of the victims" (47). Indeed, Rushdie's efforts are similar to those of the character he creates, Moraes Zogoiby, who reveals his motivation to write when he says, "So, in writing this, I must peel off history, the prison of the past" (*MLS* 136). However, Rushdie takes his diverse stories further to prevent them from becoming just simple proliferations of alternative narratives that lead nowhere. The reader is unavoidably faced with the ethical intent of his narration—especially when it is read in the context of specific cultural and historical moments, as we confront the horrific results of religious fanaticism on two families in "The Prophet's Hair" and on both individuals and the nation in *The Moor's Last Sigh*.

Works Cited

Cantor, Paul A. "Tales of the Alhambra: Rushdie's Use of Spanish History in *The Moor's Last Sigh*." *Studies in the Novel* 29 (1997): 323–41.

Chauhan, Pradyumna S. "Salman Rushdie Talks to Alastair Niven." *Salman Rushdie Interviews: A Sourcebook of His Ideas*. Westport: Greenwood, 2001.

Mehta, Ved. *Portrait of India*. New York: Farrar, 1967.

Nandy, Ashis. "History's Forgotten Doubles." *History and Theory* 34.2 (1995): 44–66.

Narain, Mona. "Re-Imagined Histories: Rewriting the Early Modern in Rushdie's *The Moor's Last Sigh*." *Journal for Early Modern Culture Studies* 6.2 (2006): 55–68.

Richards, Fiona. "The Desecrated Shrine: Movable Icons and Literary Irreverence in Salman Rushdie's 'The Prophet's Hair.'" *SOAS Literary Review* 2 (Summer 2000): 1–17.

Rushdie, Salman. *Midnight's Children*. 1981. New York: Random, 2006.

_____. *The Moor's Last Sigh*. New York: Vintage, 1995.

_____. "The Prophet's Hair." *East, West*. New York: Vintage, 1994.

Hybridity and the Chutnification of History
Nicole Weickgenannt Thiara

The thread that runs through Rushdie's work is his interest in the working and significance of hybridity, the mixing and mingling of cultures, histories, ideas, and stories. Rushdie's concept of cultural hybridity is deeply influenced by the subcontinent's history, its colonial past, and the nationalist narrative of a hybrid India. Born in Bombay in 1947, the year of India's and Pakistan's independence, he grew up with the idea (and ideal) of India as exemplifying the motto Unity in Diversity, where various cultures, religions, languages, and people form a composite nation. The British colonizers considered the dizzying diversity in India uncivilized formlessness, but Indian nationalists such as Jawaharlal Nehru reinterpreted it as "evidence of the greatness of the indigenous tradition which was capable . . . of absorbing diverse social forms into a single unity without destroying the marks of difference" (Chatterjee 169). In his novels, Rushdie tries both to depict historical examples of cultural hybridity truthfully and to write hybridity into being imaginatively; drawing the line between those two approaches is often not easy and sometimes impossible. For example, when Rushdie conjures up images of hybridity in his novels—such as Bombay as the exemplary hybrid and cosmopolitan city or Kashmir before the partition of the subcontinent in 1947—he often does so by improving on historical phenomena and thereby creating a yearning for the realization of creative and mutually inspiring cultural encounters.

This essay will trace the representation of the history of hybridity in Rushdie's work in a roughly chronological fashion, from the depiction of cultural synthesis in sixteenth-century India in *The Enchantress of Florence* (*EF*) to his exploration of the turn of the twenty-first century cosmopolitanism in *Shalimar the Clown*. It will also discuss how Rushdie's novels engage with major strands of Indian historiography by comparing his fictional versions of history with the historical accounts and narrative strategies of nationalist, feminist, and subaltern historiography. When analyzing the relationship between historical accuracy and imagination in Rushdie's novels, this essay will draw on the method of "chutnification of history" he describes in his 1981 novel *Midnight's Children* (459). The novel's protagonist and first-person narrator, Saleem Sinai, reveals at the end of the story that his history of India in the twentieth century is preserved both in words and in pickles. He emphasizes that his record of history in pickled form aims at truthfulness but admits that he had to reconcile himself "to the inevitable distortions of the pickling process" in order to provide history with "shape and form—that is to say, meaning" (461). Arriving at an historically accurate representation of events is depicted as problematic in Rushdie's novels since narratives and histories change over time through retelling and by responding to an audience's and teller's needs and motives. His history as chutney constitutes another version of the formula Unity in Diversity by trying to preserve the integrity of such diverse individual elements as "memories, dreams, ideas" (460) and the more traditional ingredients of historical accounts like facts and interpretations and to blend them into a coherent and meaningful account of the past.

Rushdie's depiction of history is often remarkably accurate and well researched but also frequently invented. The eponymous heroine in *The Enchantress of Florence* (2008), the Mughal princess Qara Köz, for example, is entirely fictional, whereas Mughal India and Machiavelli's Florence are correctly represented and meticulously researched (as a six-page bibliography at the end of the novel attests). Rushdie's portrayal of the Mughal emperor Akbar, one of the most significant kings of the subcontinent who ruled from 1556 to 1605, includes all the elements that historians focus on: the consolidation and expansion of the Mughal empire until it became "the most powerful empire of the age" (Eraly 154), Akbar's policy of religious toleration, his far-reaching administrative reforms that sought to include diverse groups in the running of the empire, and his patronage of the arts. The chief characteristic of his reign, however, is represented as his fostering of cultural synthesis, which is most manifestly displayed by innovations in architecture and painting.

Akbar is one of the great heroes of nationalist history writing in India because his reign is perceived as a turning point that transformed the Mughals from foreign Muslim invaders into Indian rulers. A representative example of this nationalist historiography is Jawaharlal Nehru's *The Discovery of India* (1946), in which he portrays Akbar's nurturing of cultural synthesis as something that both tapped into and enhanced an originally Indian talent for hybridity:

> In him the old dream of a united India again took shape, united not only politically in one state but organically fused into one people. . . . It was in his reign that the cultural amalgamation of Hindu and Moslem in north India took a long step forward. Akbar himself was certainly as popular with the Hindus as with the Moslems. The Mughal dynasty became firmly established as India's own. (Nehru 259–60)

Rushdie's Akbar, though a rather more complex and modern figure than that depicted in nationalist historiography, by and large affirms the nationalist image of Akbar as creating a "culture of inclusion . . . in which all races, tribes, clans, faiths and nations would become part of the one grand Mughal synthesis" (*EF* 317).

In *The Enchantress of Florence*, the test of Akbar's experiment of inclusion depends on his decision on whether to adopt the far-traveled foreigner Mogor dell'Amore, who claims to be his uncle. Akbar feels unable to do so, and when Mogor is forced to flee at the end of the novel, Akbar's ambitious hybrid project is declared largely a failure. The drying up of the lake at Akbar's capital, Fatehpur Sikri, which leads to the abandonment of the city, is perceived by Akbar as Mogor's curse, which foreshadows hybridity's antithesis:

> It was the future that had been cursed, not the present. . . . But once he was gone, all he had thought, all he had worked to make, his philosophy and

way of being, all that would evaporate like water. The future would not be what he hoped for, but a dry hostile antagonistic place where people would survive as best as they could and hate their neighbours and smash their places of worship. . . . (*EF* 347)

In the novel, however, the figure conjured up by Mogor's tales remains with Akbar: Qara Köz, who traveled the globe and who, symbolically through her presence at Akbar's court, is testament to his inclusive cosmopolitan spirit. She is a headstrong character and powerful sorceress, who makes the cities of Florence and Fatehpur Sikri fall under her spell and, according to Mogor's account, can even bewitch the flow of time. This fairy-tale figure in the novel's chutnified history of the sixteenth century evokes the powerful transgressive potential of a woman who determines her own story; in the process, she becomes a symbol of the permeability of all kinds of frontiers, such as those between East and West, the foreign and the familiar, the forbidden and the sanctioned, and the past and the present (Thiara, "Enabling Spaces").

Midnight's Children (*MC*), the autobiography of Saleem Sinai and an allegorical history of India from 1919 to 1978, offers an often outrageously idiosyncratic and megalomaniacal account of the subcontinent's history, since Saleem, "mysteriously handcuffed to history," claims to be responsible for it (9). Even though the narrative often appears fragmented and incoherent, it gives the reader a sense of the most significant historical events in that period, such as independence in 1947, the wars with Pakistan and China, and Indira Gandhi's emergency regime in 1975–77, in a fairly straightforward chronological order. This history is combined with the novel's fictional premise that Saleem's birth coincides with the birth of the Indian nation on midnight, August 15, 1947, which endows him with the magical gift of telepathy and makes him part of the company of 1,001 magical children born in that fateful hour. These magical children incorporate the promises of the independent nation, but despite Saleem's efforts at organizing them, they fail to live up to their potential and are eventually deprived of their magical gifts by the Widow, Indira Gandhi, during the emergency rule.

The novel's history of India is conceived within the nationalist narrative of India with its central motto, Unity in Diversity. One of the chief proponents of this inclusive form of nationalism was India's first prime minister, Jawaharlal Nehru, and fragments of his speech at the moment of India's independence, in which he postulates his vision for the future of "free India, where all her children may dwell," are included in the novel (*MC* 118). Saleem and his fellow magical children are the literal embodiment of this vision, and none of them fares too well. The novel clearly shows that the country's history and the children's fate are riddled with inequality, poverty, corruption, and caste and religious prejudice. So Nehru's representation of India as a nation where from time immemorial "the widest tolerance of belief and custom was practised and every variety acknowledged and even encouraged" is portrayed as an ideal to work toward rather than a reality (Nehru 62). *Midnight's Children* nevertheless endorses this idea of a hybrid India, while emphasizing the glaring failures in the nation-state's attempt at realizing its promise of equality and justice for all citizens of the nation. Thus, when Nehru's daughter Indira Gandhi suspends democracy during her emergency regime, the novel condemns this development as a betrayal of her father's vision and ideals and demonizes her as the hope-excising, witch-like widow. This allegorical approach to the recording of India's postindependence history brings out in sharp relief the novel's representation of the emergency rule as the attempted annihilation of the idea of the hybrid democratic nation.

While Rushdie worked on *Midnight's Children*, the nationalist narrative of India was coming under attack from feminist historiography, which insisted on the need to rewrite history in order to represent accurately the role of women in the struggle for India's independence. *Midnight's Children* in many ways reflects this call to write women into history; for example, the fictional Rani of Cooch Naheen is represented as an important political figure in the freedom struggle. While feminist historiography studies the work of women's organizations, their demand for equal rights, and their strategies of negotiating between modernity and tradition, *Midnight's Children* focuses on Saleem's maternal grandmother, Naseem, and her fight against her husband on the domestic front. Naseem initially tries to become the "modern Indian woman" her husband would like her to be, but eventually she ends up resisting what she perceives as his "fancy foreign ideas" and holds on to her traditions and religion, thwarting him at every possible turn (*MC* 34, 61). Naseem's conflict reflects the nationalist attempt at selectively adopting the modernity imported by the colonial rulers while holding on to essential Indian traditions and virtues. Indian men were to expose themselves to the dangers of the hybridizing contact with the colonizers and learn from them, while Indian women were supposed to proceed more cautiously and absorb a much diluted form of modernity since they were responsible for embodying the authentic "national culture" (Chatterjee 120). Thus, to some extent, Naseem follows the nationalist script for women's guarded entry into modernity, even though her extreme resistance to her husband's demands is hardly condoned by patriarchal nationalism. The story of Naseem appears to bear little resemblance to the approaches of feminist historiography, but both offer a nuanced exploration of the almost unachievable nationalist demand for women to become modern while remaining traditional. On the whole, *Midnight's Children* represents women as resisting the way men envisage their subservient role in the Indian nation and as demanding to shape history through characters such as Mary Braganza, in whose pickle factory Saleem works, or Narlikar's "giant, noisy, omnicompetent women" (*MC* 178). The novel also records the deep anxiety the novel's strong women provoke in men, particularly in Saleem, whose hysterical account of his "too-many women" (*MC* 406) portrays them as rather monstrous (Thiara, *Rushdie and Indian Historiography* 56–87).

The nation that brings out the worst in women in Rushdie's novels, however, is clearly Pakistan. Saleem's indomitable and mischievous sister, the Monkey, is transformed into the demure, patriotic Jamila Singer, the Voice of the Nation, in Pakistan, and *Midnight's Children* represents Pakistan's version of an exclusive and god-fearing nationalism as responsible for the fanatical turn in her life (313). Pakistan is founded on M. A. Jinnah's two-nation theory; from the 1930s, he campaigned for an independent Muslim state of Pakistan, based on the theory that there existed two nations on the subcontinent, one Hindu and one Muslim. *Midnight's Children* rejects this theory and represents Pakistan's concept of the nation as intrinsically Muslim as problematic and built on the antagonism toward its neighbor India. Rushdie's Pakistan novel *Shame* (1983) resumes the negative portrayal of Pakistan and its dire effect on women. The novel is an eccentric critique of patriarchal practices, since it condemns the way in which the country "crushes its women beneath the intolerable burdens of honour and propriety" by creating a narrative in which men's worst fears are realized in its monstrous women (173). Sufiya Zinobia literally turns into a monster that unleashes a murderous violence, primarily directed at men, and her sister Naveed, who heeds her husband's demand to produce children, turns into a grotesque, self-destructive hyperbreeder. These monstrous women are obviously a narrative device, which is supposed to discredit Pakistan's patriarchal nationalism but nevertheless gives off the lingering odor of misogyny.

Shame's chutnified history of Pakistan has the predominant flavor of gossip. History as gossip is subversive of official historical accounts and focuses on women and women's alleged method of communication (even though men are portrayed as indulging in gossip, too). The gossipy history of Pakistan in *Shame* takes the form of a vicious satire of Pakistan's ruling elite, but it also refracts ingredients of official histories such as the role of political parties and the military with marginalized and suppressed stories. Women are largely excluded from the public sphere in Pakistan, so when women's stories in the novel "explain, and even subsume, the men's," they mainly relate to the domestic realm—private relationships, families, marriages, and affairs—in other words, to what is usually referred as gossip (173). An example of this focus on history as gossip in *Shame* is the way in which its account of the partition of the subcontinent into India and a West and East Pakistan, with the ensuing mass migration and horrific massacres, is brushed aside by the story of Raza Hyder and Bilquìs's first encounter and courting. Similarly, the war that West Pakistan waged on East Pakistan in 1971, which led to East Pakistan's secession and the creation of Bangladesh, is harshly condemned in *Midnight's Children* but only briefly mentioned in *Shame*. History as gossip self-consciously "gives only partial views" (Bhaya Nair 997) but views that complement and often contradict the official account of events. What we are ultimately left with in *Shame*, however, is pessimism with regard to the future of a country that is described as "*insufficiently imagined*" (87; Rushdie's emphasis).

The structure of *The Moor's Last Sigh* (1995), which covers the period from 1911 to 1993, is remarkably similar to that of *Midnight's Children*. Both begin with the national movement for independence and its success in establishing an independent nation-state. The main narrative emphasis is on the development of independent India up to a point where the idea of an inclusive hybrid nation is threatened with destruction—by Indira Gandhi's emergency regime in *Midnight's Children* or by Hindu nationalism, epitomized by the destruction of Babri Masjid in December 1992 and the ensuing communal violence, in *The Moor's Last Sigh* (*MLS*). The ideology of Hindu nationalism, which propagates the idea of India as an exclusively Hindu nation, gained great support in India in the 1980s and 1990s even though it had first been conceived by V. D. Savarkar and others in the 1920s. Rushdie warned of the dangers of Hindu nationalism in a 1987 essay, saying,

> The idea of nationalism in India had grown more and more chauvinistic, had become narrower and narrower. The ideas of Hindu nationalism had infected it. I was struck by a remarkable paradox: that, in a country created by the Congress's nationalist campaign, the well-being of the people

might now require that all nationalist rhetoric be abandoned. (*Imaginary Homelands* 32–33)

The idea that India could actually be transformed into a totalitarian, "fundamentalist" regime is a danger that Hindu nationalist ideology represents in *The Moor's Last Sigh*, but the novel suggests that this ideology cannot ultimately cope with India's irrepressible hybrid diversity. The novel nevertheless systematically demystifies the concept of the nation and its symbols such as the revered figure of Mother India (Thiara, *Rushdie and Indian Historiography* 149–57).

In the 1980s, a new strand of history writing became influential in India, namely that of the subaltern studies group, which questioned nationalist historiography's focus on the elite. Subaltern historiography and its chief proponent, Ranajit Guha, use the term "subaltern" to refer to those sections of the population who were not part of the British or indigenous elite and called for the study of the role of the people in the making of history (Guha 39–44). This differentiation between the people and the elite is explored and interrogated in Rushdie's India novels. Rushdie's protagonists are often part of the elite; Saleem Sinai's family in *Midnight's Children* belongs to the middle class and Moraes "Moor" Zogoiby's family in *The Moor's Last Sigh* is wealthy and politically influential. In both novels, however, subaltern figures play crucial roles in the shaping of history, as does Saleem's adversary Shiva (with whom he had been swapped at birth) or the Tin-Man Sammy Hazaré in *The Moor's Last Sigh*, who plays a significant part at the end of the novel when he goes on a bombing spree in Bombay. These unruly, anarchic subaltern figures gesture at a critique of the concept of the nation as an elite construct that takes the inclusion of the silent and silenced masses for granted. Simultaneous with the growing influence of subaltern studies in Indian academic historiography in the 1980s and 1990s, political participation deepened in India with people from lower-class and lower-caste backgrounds coming to the fore. Instead of welcoming this development as a success of the democratic process, however, the elite perceived this change as a "plebeianization" of politics, which undermined its belief in democracy (Hansen 8). The rise of the Shiv Sena, the Hindu nationalist party on which *The Moor's Last Sigh*'s Mumbai's Axis is modeled, is an example of this democratizing process, which provoked the Bombay elite's distaste and disenchantment with democracy. *The Moor's Last Sigh* does not hold back in its depiction of the brutal and criminal methods that a party such as the Shiv Sena employs, but it also unflinchingly represents the subaltern classes' support of and attraction to such parties. The Zogoiby family's gatekeeper Lambajan Chandiwala, or Borkar, is an example of a subaltern character who follows the Mumbai's Axis leader Raman Fielding, a fact Fielding gleefully points out to Moor: "Whose town do you think this is? . . . On Malabar Hill you drink whisky-soda and talk democracy. But our people guard your gates. You think you know them but they have also their own lives and tell you nothing" (*MLS* 293). The novel acknowledges the need for a deeper democratization but shares the elite's concern about its unpredictable consequences.

The Moor's Last Sigh depicts the lives of both subalterns and the elite and demonstrates how their visions of India often do not match. It scrupulously portrays the complacency of the elite and its blind spots in the conception of India, but it explicitly does not side with those critics of the Indian elite who see them as westernized, alienated hybrids, who are not part of the real India. Excessively westernized and anglophile characters who spout imperialist rhetoric—such as Moor's monocled uncle Aires da Gama or Saleem Sinai's father, who literally turns white in *Midnight's Children*, or *The Satanic Verses*' Saladin Chamcha—are often the butt of the joke in Rushdie's novels. However, his novels emphasize the fact that the subcontinent's colonial past cannot be obliterated by the excavation of an uncontaminated precolonial layer of authentic Indianness. After all, Saleem and *Shame* protagonist Omar Khayyam Shakil are specifically hybrid characters (with British biological fathers), and Moor defiantly objects to the portrayal of the elite as "English-medium misfits" (*MLS* 166) who "hate the best of India":

"We were not, had never been, that class. The best, and worst, were in us, and fought in us, as they fought in the land at large. In some of us, the worst triumphed; but still we could say—and say truthfully—that we had loved the best" (376).

The Moor's Last Sigh also presents us with images of cultural hybridity that the novel explicitly represents as idealized, such as the image of the inclusive nation in Aurora's paintings and the portrayal of Bombay as the cosmopolitan city par excellence. In Aurora's paintings, carnivalesque revelry, envisaged as "fancy-dress balls" to which the country's minority communities are invited, signifies the hybridity of the nation: "idealised? sentimental? probably—of the present, and the future, that she hoped would evolve" (227). Aurora's vision of the nation is deeply influenced by Nehru's, and when the Nehruvian concept of India comes under attack from Hindu nationalist and subaltern forces, she feels the need to revise her "myth of the plural, hybrid nation" and paint gloomy images of the future, which declare her belief in the creative potential of hybridity as flawed (227). Pictures of slum-dwellers in the form of collages of rubbish replace her carnivalesque paintings, since "Aurora had apparently decided that the ideas of impurity, cultural admixture and mélange which had been, for most of her creative life, the closest things she had found to a notion of the Good, were in fact capable of distortion" (303). The novel suggests that hybridity understood as the mixing and mingling of cultures does not guarantee that the result is inspiring and creative but can turn out to be ugly, precarious, or sterile instead.

The novel's representation of Bombay as the ideal hybrid Indian city with its "everyday live-and-let-live miracles" (351) is also qualified by doubts and misgivings. Bombay as "the most Indian of Indian cities . . . [where] all Indias met and merged" is depicted as open, cosmopolitan, and an example of India's vibrant democracy: "It was an ocean of stories; we were all its narrators, and everybody talked at once" (350). In the end, however, the city is represented as self-destructing, and Moor laments the annihilation of its hybridity: "We engineered our own fall.

And now can only weep . . . for what we were too enfeebled, too corrupt, too little, too contemptible to defend" (373). In *The Moor's Last Sigh*, the ideal of cultural hybridity is battered and demystified. Yet the novel also clearly depicts that there is no good alternative to embracing cultural hybridity. Hindu nationalism, which relegates all other religious groups to the status of tolerated minorities, and the predatory capitalism of "the new god-and-mammon India" are the ominous alternatives that the novel presents to an often muddled and contested but also innovative and effervescent hybridity (351).

The most idyllic example of inspiring cultural hybridity that Rushdie has so far conjured up in his novels is the "paradise" Kashmir of *Shalimar the Clown* (2005). This singling out of Kashmir "as a territory of desire" resembles that of nationalist historiography, which privileged Kashmir as the site where the modernity of the nation is complemented by both ancient and syncretistic cultural traditions and unspoiled nature (Kabir 98–101, 164). In contrast to this nationalist vision, however, the connection of Kashmir to the Indian nation-state is a more contested and ultimately unresolved problem in *Shalimar the Clown*. Yet the novel's representation of *Kashmiriyat* (Kashmiriness) as a local form of hybridity, whose main ingredients are the amalgamation of Hindu and Muslim culture with its specific cuisine and distinct folk-theater tradition, is an almost ideal-case scenario. As Rushdie portrays it in his imaginary Pachigam, the "words *Hindu* and *Muslim* . . . were merely descriptions, not divisions": "Here in Kashmir, our stories sit happily side by side on the same double bill, we eat from the same dishes, we laugh at the same jokes" (57, 71). *Shalimar the Clown* chronicles the destruction of this hybrid culture and the guilt of all participants, in particular of India and Pakistan, in this unfolding tragedy without offering a solution, glimmer of hope, or closure. The novel is an act of mourning and the preservation of the memory of a unique hybrid culture that is irretrievably lost.

Shalimar the Clown is also concerned with tracing the effects of global power structures—such as American foreign policy's repercussions in Kashmir and the way Kashmir's fate is influenced by the global networks of Islamist terrorism—on the local. The novel combines various histories with a globe-traversing fictional story of love, betrayal, and revenge in order to drive home the fact of the inescapable connectedness of humanity in the era of globalization. This shift away from writing the nation toward imagining the world in Rushdie's novels first occurred in *The Satanic Verses* (1988), a novel Berthold Schoene describes as "without doubt the single most important prototype of the contemporary cosmopolitan novel" (28). He argues that the novel's cosmopolitanism lies in its "arrangement as a multiplicity of differently located narratives telescoped one into the other" in a nonhierarchical fashion, so that "far-fetched and half-forgotten local narratives [are assigned] the same significance and pride of place as noisily attention-seeking metropolitan narratives" (28). For example, in a novel that irreverently interrogates the nature of revelation and religious experience, the story of Ayesha, the butterfly-clad seer who leads the villagers of Titlipur on a pilgrimage to Mecca, affirms the possibility of a genuinely miraculous encounter with the divine. This story's ending is allowed to stand in stark contrast and contradiction to the final book of the novel, in which the death of Saladin Chamcha's father is recounted in a way that leaves little room for the belief in the existence of god or an afterlife. *The Satanic Verses* comprises stories that reach almost every continent without offering a homogenized image of the world.

It is significant that there is a certain affinity between Rushdie's cosmopolitan narrative of the world in *The Satanic Verses* and his narration of the Indian nation, whose cosmopolitan openness is depicted as its chief feature to be cherished. It is, after all, in the globe-spanning *Satanic Verses* that we find Zeeny Vakil's formula of an idealized hybrid India. Her recipe for a productive hybridity, "the principle of borrowing whatever clothes seemed to fit, Aryan, Mughal, British, take-the-best-and-leave-the-rest" (52), is not just applicable to India. There is, of course, a crucial difference between narrating the hybrid nation and narrating the world, since a nation always defines itself through its boundaries, no matter how cosmopolitan its outlook may be. However, Rushdie's Nehruvian conceptualization of India's Unity in Diversity relies on the recognition of a common bond without the erasure of differences, and this concept can be translated onto a global level. The cosmopolitan novel can be a significant medium in which such a planetary bond can be envisaged.

The role of the migrant with her hybrid vision plays a crucial role in this cosmopolitan conceptualization of the world community. *The Satanic Verses* is predominantly about migration and the way it forces hybridity on the migrant. It does not represent the "migrant condition" with its experience of "disjuncture and metamorphosis" as easy or uncomplicated, despite the fact that Rushdie considers this novel a celebration of hybridity. "*Mélange*, hotchpotch, a bit of this and a bit of that is *how newness enters the world*. It is the great possibility that mass migration gives the world," he has said (*Imaginary Homelands* 394). In *The Satanic Verses*, the migrants' hybridity is restricted by racism and economic exploitation, as well as their longing to hold on to their roots and culture in as intact a form as possible, considering some cultural traditions too sacrosanct to be allowed to be bent out of shape by entering the gravitational field of another tradition or dissenting idea. Migration nevertheless fuels a cosmopolitan vision. London, the migrants' destination in *The Satanic Verses*, is represented as a microcosm in which the world is reimagined and often violently reconfigured as a cosmopolitan space by the novel's transplanted characters. Hybridity in the context of global migration can be a truly subversive force, desacralizing "the transparent assumptions of cultural supremacy" (Bhabha 228). So Uhuru Simba's defiant stance is embraced by many in the novel: "We are other than what we would have been if we had not crossed the oceans . . . We have been made again: but I say that we shall also be the ones to remake this society . . . It is our turn now" (414). At the end of the novel, cosmopolitan London is riven and devastated by the processes that bring newness into the world, but the text also makes clear that we must learn new ways of negotiating difference and diversity. *The Satanic Verses* creates a yearning for a better future where cosmopolitanism and hybridity are welcomed and enable a migrant to flourish rather than merely survive.

In Rushdie's work the sheer variety of examples of hybridity—the abstract hybridity of the nation, the premodern one of Kashmir, the chaotic, urban, and unruly one of Bombay and London—testifies to the untamable and almost unclassifiable nature of this phenomenon and the fuzzy boundaries between its different forms. In his novels, ideal hybridity implies the nurturing of a cultural distinctiveness born out of a curious and open encounter with the Other without the aim of diluting differences or effacing the local in favor of the universal. Rushdie's celebration of hybridity acknowledges the fact that genuine encounters with cultural difference can often be exhausting, difficult, and frustrating, as well as invigorating, stimulating, and creative. Whenever hybridity in its many guises is on the verge of being overly idealized in his work, the text deconstructs this optimistic portrayal of cultural mixing and mingling. In most cases, experiments with hybridity end in some form of failure, as in *The Enchantress of Florence*, or the forces of hybridity only barely survive the onslaught of the proponents of a purer, exclusive concept of culture, as in *The Moor's Last Sigh*.

What remains, however, is a yearning for the endless possibilities of hybridity. A representative image of the attraction and subversion of cultural and ideological encounters is *The Enchantress of Florence*'s Tent of the New Worship; an innovation of Emperor Akbar, it is "a place of disputation where everything could be said to everyone by anyone on any subject, including the nonexistence of God and the abolition of kings" (*EF* 36). In this space, philosophers and mystics, Muslims, Hindus, and Jesuits argue, debate, and utter the blasphemous and seditious. This portrayal of the Tent of the New Worship is another example of Rushdie's creative and prolific method of chutnifying history: A historical fact is amplified and fictionalized and thus turned into a metaphor for hybridity in process. This rowdy scene is furthermore an apt image for all of Rushdie's novels in which versions of history and concepts of the nation and the world are imagined, disputed, and recast amidst a "constant hubbub" (*EF* 79). Such hubbub "may be too strong for some palates," as Saleem Sinai remarks of his pickles of history: "Their smell may be overpowering, tears may rise to eyes; I hope nevertheless that it will be possible to say of them that they possess the authentic taste of truth . . . that they are, despite everything, acts of love" (*MC* 461; ellipses in orig.).

Works Cited

Bhabha, Homi K. *The Location of Culture*. London: Routledge, 1994.
Bhaya Nair, Rukmini. "Text and Pre-Text: History as Gossip in Rushdie's Novels." *Economic and Political Weekly* 6 May 1989: 994–1000.
Chatterjee, Partha. *The Nation and Its Fragments: Colonial and Postcolonial Histories*. Princeton: Princeton UP, 1993.
Eraly, Abraham. *Emperors of the Peacock Throne: The Saga of the Great Mughals*. Rev. ed. New Delhi: Penguin, 2000.
Guha, Ranajit."On Some Aspects of the Historiography of Colonial India." *Selected Subaltern Studies*. Ed. R. Guha and G. C. Spivak. New York: Oxford UP, 1988. 37–44.
Hansen, Thomas Blom. *The Saffron Wave: Democracy and Hindu Nationalism in Modern India*. Princeton: Princeton UP, 1999.
Kabir, Ananya Jahanara. *Territory of Desire: Representing the Valley of Kashmir*. Minneapolis: U of Minnesota P, 2009.
Nehru, Jawaharlal. *The Discovery of India*. 1946. New Delhi: Oxford UP, 1989.
Rushdie, Salman. *The Enchantress of Florence*. London: Cape, 2008.
_____. *Imaginary Homelands: Essays and Criticism, 1981–1991*. London: Penguin, 1992.
_____. *Midnight's Children*. 1981. London: Vintage, 1995.
_____. *The Moor's Last Sigh*. 1995. London: Vintage, 1996.
_____.*The Satanic Verses*. 1988. London: Vintage, 1998.
_____. *Shalimar the Clown*. London: Cape, 2005.
_____. *Shame*. 1983. London: Vintage, 1995.
Schoene, Berthold. *The Cosmopolitan Novel*. Edinburgh: Edinburgh UP, 2010.
Thiara, Nicole Weickgenannt. "Enabling Spaces and the Architecture of Hybridity in Salman Rushdie's *The Enchantress of Florence*." *Journal of Commonwealth Literature* 46.3 (2011): 415–31.
_____. *Salman Rushdie and Indian Historiography: Writing the Nation into Being*. Houndmills: Macmillan, 2009.

Salman Rushdie and Philip Roth: Parallels and Departures

David J. Zucker

In some important ways, Salman Rushdie and his older contemporary Philip Roth have led parallel lives. Both have achieved acclaim, admiration, and numerous awards for their works. For all their fame and fortune, however, each author has earned the wrath of his faith community. Philip Roth first offended some of his fellow Jews with his portrayal of Jewish life in *Goodbye, Columbus* (1959). He then caused an even greater scandal with his description of the life and the sexual conduct of his antihero in *Portnoy's Complaint* (1969). Salman Rushdie's *Satanic Verses* (1988), of course, caused an international furor that led to riots in Europe, Asia, and Africa, a sentence of death for its author, the murder of one of his translators and the stabbing of another, threats against his publishers, bombings of bookstores, and a decade during which he had to live underground. Rushdie's 2001 novel *Fury*, set in America, which seems in part both a parody of and homage to Roth's novel *Sabbath's Theater* (1995), suggests that Rushdie has thought about these Roth–Rushdie parallels himself. Rushdie has written that he was helped by knowing of Roth's "responses to being so vilified" by his faith community. Roth, he said, "seems to speak directly, profoundly, not only to, but *for*, me" ("Philip Roth" 347; Rushdie's emphasis).

Both Rushdie and Roth seem to take personal delight in treading on dangerous and provocative ground. In an interview prior to the publication of *The Satanic Verses*, Rushdie said, "One of my major themes is religion and fanaticism." He continued, "I have talked about the Islamic religion because that is what I know the most about" (Pipes 72). As Daniel Pipes observes:

> Rushdie's exquisite awareness of religion and censorship meant that he knew that writers dealing with religious subjects routinely got into trouble in the Middle East. . . . Further, as a well-informed student of history and

politics, he realized exactly what Muslim sensibilities he was offending, and what this would mean. He himself observed after the furor began, "the orthodox Islamic world is somewhat behind the attitudes of the other great world religions." (74)

In response to the reaction to *Portnoy's Complaint*, Roth freely admitted, "The rabbis have got their indignation to stoke, just as I do. And there are sentences in that book upon which a man could construct a pretty indignant sermon" ("On *Portnoy's Complaint*" 20). Yet, while Roth challenges a certain self-image of American Jews, he is proud to be part of the Jewish people, explaining:

> I have always been far more pleased by my good fortune in being born a Jew than my critics may begin to imagine. It's a complicated, interesting, morally demanding, and very singular experience, and I like that. I find myself in the historic predicament of being Jewish, with all its implications. Who could ask for more? (20)

Finally, there are interesting overlaps in the lives of these two authors. Each has been married multiple times, and each has a former wife with a very high profile. Rushdie's fourth wife was the actress and television host Padma Lakshmi, who is the basis for the character Neela Mahendra in *Fury*. Rushdie also dedicated the book to her. Roth's longtime companion and second wife was actress Claire Bloom. Following their divorce and her treatment of their relationship in her autobiography *Leaving the Doll's House* (1996), Roth responded through the character of Eve Frame in his 1998 novel *I Married a Communist*. He did not dedicate the book to her.

Salman Rushdie and *The Satanic Verses*

Rushdie's first literary success was *Midnight's Children*, which weaves together the narrative of a family and the history—sometimes purposely skewed—of modern India into one of the most famous examples of magic realism in contemporary fiction. It was *The Satanic Verses*, however, that catapulted Rushdie to international prominence.

Around the world, Muslims, Arabs, and some Christians and Jews immediately reacted to the book as an attack on both Muslims and Islam (Zucker 31). In their view, the religious history of Islam, as well as its rites and ethics, were of one piece. Moreover, as a people, Muslims were seen as inseparable from the religion, rites, and ethics of Islam.

The religious reaction to Rushdie's book, vociferous and eventually life threatening, was not immediate in Britain. The furor began in India, before the book even appeared, when prepublication interviews appeared in the papers. The critic Madhu Jain rightly predicted in *India Today* that *The Satanic Verses* was "bound to trigger an avalanche of protests from the ramparts" (Pipes 19). In October 1988, the book was banned in India; similar bans quickly followed in Bangladesh, Sudan, South Africa, Thailand, Singapore, Venezuela, Poland, and many other countries. The British umbrella organization the Union of Muslim Organizations decided to have the book "legally banned in Britain and Rushdie criminally prosecuted, both on the charge of blasphemy" (Pipes 21). By December 1988–January 1989, there were book burnings of *The Satanic Verses* in Bolton, near Manchester, and in Bradford, both cities with large Muslim populations.

In February 1989, the whole matter escalated exponentially. A *fatwā* (legal ruling) was issued by Iran's highest religious authority, Ayatollah Khomeini. This fatwā, which never has been rescinded, sought to

> inform all the zealous Muslims of the world that the blood of the author of the book entitled *The Satanic Verses*, which has been compiled, printed, and published in opposition to Islam, the Prophet, and the Qur'an, as also of those involved in its publication who were aware of its contents, is hereby declared forfeit. I call on all zealous Muslims to dispatch them quickly, wherever they may be found, so that no one will dare to insult Islamic sanctities again. Anyone who is himself killed in this path will be deemed a martyr. (qtd. in Lewis 185)

The accusation against Salman Rushdie that prompted this reaction and the fatwā was that he was guilty of both treason and blasphemy.[1] He was seen as having insulted and abused the Prophet, and "from the perspective of Islamic jurisprudence, presenting the Prophet as fiction, even in dreams, or presenting him as a devil, amounts to treason. . . . a blasphemy, [a matter] Rushdie himself acknowledges" (Sardar and Davies 164). Some leaders in the Christian and Jewish communities "showed considerable sympathy for the Muslim position—though not the murder threat, to be sure."[2]

Religious leaders were not the only ones who were offended and outraged, and criticism was not limited to the religious community. Secular Muslims and Arabs alike took offense at Rushdie's "insulting tone" and charged him with being a "provocateur in a highly gratuitous manner," "cynical," and "scornful" (Ali 296). In an essay titled "*The Satanic Verses*: A Secular Muslim's Response," Agha Shahid Ali writes that it is the sections that refer to Muhammad that give such offense to many Muslims:

> The tone is so irreverent that it seems everything, including some of Islam's most sacred narratives, has been turned into a joke . . . Muhammad comes across as a fake of sorts, not as the founder of a great religion. The Koran comes across as the work of a charlatan, a conniving, at times bumbling opportunist. (298)

Edward W. Said, a Christian Arab, wrote as both a noted literary critic and a self-proclaimed secularist. Said was shocked by what he read. The work was blasphemous. The novel had stepped over the line specifically because this was authored by "a Moslem who writes both in and for the West." The book itself is, he wrote, "in all sorts of ways, a deliberately transgressive work. It parallels and mimics the central Islamic narratives with bold, nose-thumbing, post-modern daring" (Appignanesi and Maitland 164–65).

A year following the publication of the book, Rushdie argued that "*The Satanic Verses* is not . . . an antireligious novel. It is, however, an attempt to write about migration, its *stresses and transformations*, from the point of view of migrants from the Indian subcontinent to Britain" ("A Clash of Faiths," emphasis mine). Rushdie in effect argued that he was addressing the question of overcoming social "disabilities." It was not a matter of self-hatred on his part.

One might take Rushdie's comment as unvarnished truth, as opposed to an attempt to mitigate the effect that the book had worldwide. Yet it seems clear to me that Rushdie was speaking tongue-in-cheek. If *The Satanic Verses* had only addressed the "stresses and transformations" of an immigrant group, in this case Indians moving to the United Kingdom, there would have been no brouhaha. At issue was not migration in the modern world, Indian or otherwise. Rather, the problem centered on the subplot that purported to narrate the stresses and transformations concerning the life of Muhammad fourteen centuries earlier and, more specifically, events that touched on the creation of, as well as the early historical migration of, Islam.

The Satanic Verses gave such offense, according to Shabbir Akhtar, because of its "allegations about the textual impurity of the Koran" and "the suspicion that Rushdie invents a mouthpiece to launch a bitter diatribe against Islam and all things Islamic" (10). Rushdie deliberately, consciously, and provocatively challenged the character, purity, and integrity of Muhammad, as well as his mission as a prophet—foundational tenets of Islam—for his artistic purposes. Surely, it was not a coincidence that the name of the person who reveals the "truth" about Muhammad—that the Prophet did not or could not discern between human speech and divine revelation— was *Salman* the Persian. Salman the Persian, Salman Rushdie, it took little imagination to make that connection. The novel explains that Salman, acting as scribe for Muhammad, "began, surreptitiously to change things. Little things at first." Salman then goes on to describe his actions:

If Mahound [the fictional name for Muhammad³] recited a verse in which God was described as *all-hearing, all-knowing*, I would write, *all-knowing, all-wise*. Here's the point: Mahound did not notice the alterations. So there I was, actually writing the Book, or rewriting, anyway, polluting the word of God with my own profane language. . . . Maybe he'd just missed out once, I thought, anybody can make a mistake. So the next time I changed a bigger thing. He said *Christian*, I wrote down *Jew*. He'd notice that, surely; how could he not? But when I read him the chapter he nodded and thanked me politely, and I went out of his tent with tears in my eyes. (367–68)

This contention that Muhammad did not know or care that Salman was making changes is an affront for Islamic readers, since "for Muslims the Qur'an *is* the word of God. . . . An essential article of belief for a Muslim is to accept the Qur'an as a direct, literal narration of God's word" (Sardar and Davies 144.)

The controversy over *The Satanic Verses* signaled a clash of civilizations, which still has not abated. The wrath aimed at Rushdie bled over to the West, to America, and to Israel. According to Daniel Pipes, "Anti-Westernism has a way of turning into anti-Americanism . . . American culture, with its global impact, symbolizes the entire West. . . . Where London and Washington forged ahead, Tel Aviv could not be far behind. No Middle East story is complete without Israel, even when that country has no role at all, as in the Rushdie case" (130–31).

How did this clash of cultures manifest itself? According to Ali Mazrui, the debate "was a classic case of the dialogue of the deaf, between the West and the world of Islam. The West was bewildered by the depth of Muslim anger. The Muslims were bewildered by Western insensitivity" (348).

That said, in the West, with its centuries-old history and respect for diversity (at least in principle), numerous well-known writers and dozens of politicians weighed in on the subject. One of those defenders was Philip Roth, who signed a World Writers Statement to that effect.[4]

At the same moment, these protesters supported free speech and denounced censorship.

Philip Roth and *Portnoy's Complaint*

As mentioned at the beginning of this essay, the brouhaha over *Portnoy's Complaint* had its precedent a decade earlier in 1959, when Roth raised the ire of some members of the Jewish community when he published the collection titled *Goodbye, Columbus*. The focus of the novella "Goodbye, Columbus" is the Patimkin family, which is nouveau riche, loud, brash, and brassy. The book's stories also include portraits of an adulterous Jewish husband, a Hebrew school student who humiliates his rabbi, a conniving and wheedling Jewish army recruit, and a Jewish community frantic to expel a Hasidic yeshiva that they feel undermines their efforts to assimilate into suburbia. Charges of anti-Semitism and self-hatred were quickly leveled against Roth. Jews were distraught with his work. They felt that Roth had gone out of his way to cause a serious blemish both on Jews as Jews and on Judaism. Further, he had done this with malice aforethought, deliberately, consciously, and provocatively.

"While Roth has insisted he does not speak for American Jews or expound Judaism, he has given America a gallery of semitic stereotypes. Sophie and Alexander Portnoy, Brenda Patimkin, Eli the Fanatic, and Nathan Zuckerman," alleges Professor Alan Cooper, "are household names" (1). While the description of these characters as household names is an exaggeration, Roth's characters certainly are familiar to many in the Jewish and wider community.

Yet, the firestorm over *Goodbye, Columbus*—among rabbis and communal leaders—paled into insignificance compared to the explosion of invective that greeted *Portnoy's Complaint*. Its reception was strong and mixed, inspiring both praise and censure. Critic James Idema praised Roth as "a skillful, witty craftsman," while deeming his work "a quantum leap over other novels that deal explicitly with sex. It is scatology and profanity so unrelenting as to mock those tests of obscenity the Supreme Court has been laboring over for decades," and "an elaborate dirty joke." Others characterized the book (and Roth) as dangerous, dishonest, and distorted.

Roth explained that *Portnoy's Complaint* was "at once such a hit and such a scandal . . . [because] a novel in the guise of a confession was received and judged by any number of readers as a confession in the guise of a novel ("Imagining Jews" 218). At the heart of the novel is a question: How can such a good Jewish boy (read: successful, intelligent, articulate) be such a bad boy (read: single, sexually obsessive, and focused on non-Jewish women)? The novel itself is a monologue, a verbal catharsis spoken to a psychiatrist.

Several weeks after the book's publication, newspaper columnist Richard Yaffe wrote, "One of the unexpected by-products of Philip Roth's sensational *Portnoy's Complaint* will be an increase in synagogue attendance in America, at least temporarily, as rabbis begin to deliver sermons about it and 'review' it." Indeed, many of America's rabbis rushed to respond to the *Portnoy* phenomenon. Reactions varied between "recoil" and "recall," although recoil won hands down.

In the view of most critics, the figure of Alexander Portnoy damaged the perception of Jews in the eyes of the general public; consequently, "he had to be annihilated. And so, from many pulpits and public forums, Philip Roth was murdered; or worse, diagnosed as having had a nervous breakdown from sexual excess" (Cutter 30). Well-respected theologian and Reform rabbi Eugene Borowitz put forth a less popular view: "Though its language is filthy, its focus on sex obsessive, and its Jews violate cherished public relations images, *Portnoy's Complaint* is one of the great moral documents and Jewish novels of our time" (48). Nearly a half dozen years later, Roth conceded that, with some time and distance to consider the matter, he now had a better understanding of what was behind the furor: A "key element" of his "wayward hero" was that "the man confessing to forbidden sexual acts and gross offenses against the family order and ordinary decency was a Jew." He continued,

Going wild in public is the last thing in the world that a Jew is expected to do—by himself, by his family, by his fellow Jews, and by the larger community of Christians whose tolerance for him is often tenuous to begin with, and whose code of respectability he flaunts or violates at his own psychological risk, and perhaps at the risk of his fellow Jews' physical and social well-being.... He is not expected to make a spectacle of himself, either by shooting off his mouth or by shooting off his semen, and certainly not by shooting off his mouth about shooting off his semen. That pretty much takes the cake. ("Imagining Jews" 222)

Philip Roth and *Sabbath's Theater*

In 1995, Philip Roth published *Sabbath's Theater*. Although the reception of this book was considerably more muted than that of *Portnoy's Complaint*, for many people in the Jewish community, the novel was an unwelcome return to the past. They thought, "Here we go again." Yet, in the twenty-five years between the books, society had changed, and there was a greater acceptance of works—in print, on the screen, and in music—that depicted or referred to sexual acts. *Sabbath's Theater* related the story of Mickey Sabbath, at sixty-four, an aging roué, his hands crippled with arthritis, penniless, and down on his luck. According to Alan Cooper, he can be described as "dangerous. More than that, the facts of the case prove him despicable: he seduces women, corrupts youth, betrays wives, encourages women to betray husbands (even when the husbands are his rescuers), steals money, tempts alcoholics to drink, even urinates on a grave" (281). Yet, at the same time, "*Sabbath's Theater* challenges the notion that at sixty-four the heyday in the blood must be tame ... It explores forbidden pleasures of the erotic life, a life almost everyone lives in fantasy but condemns when it threatens to lurch into reality" (Cooper 282).

Some critics saw *Sabbath's Theater* as too graphic, raunchy, and biting in its humor. *New York Times* critic Michiko Kakutani found the novel difficult to finish and characterized it as "distasteful and disingenuous." Yet it is compelling. As Al Alvarez wrote nearly a decade later in the London *Guardian*, *Sabbath's Theater* "reads like *Portnoy's Complaint* retold by a 60-year-old man raging not about sex, but against the injustice and ludicrousness of death."

Fury and *Sabbath's Theater*

Fury, set largely in New York City, chronicles a year or so in the life of fifty-five-year-old Malik Solanka, a temporarily expatriate British citizen and successful writer. Although *Fury* may draw upon many sources, at the very least, it is either a parody or an homage (or both parody and homage) to *Sabbath's Theater*. In both novels, the protagonists are strong, determined, larger-than-life personalities whose sexual exploits cross the line of generally accepted mores.

Before exploring the *Fury–Sabbath Theater* connections, it is worth noting that *Fury* also has connections to some of Rushdie's earlier books. Its subplot concerning the creation of a video-game fantasy series of an endless war between two cultures, for example, seems another statement about the wider culture wars between Islamic and Western values that Rushdie has engaged in such novels as *Midnight's Children*, *Shame*, *The Satanic Verses*, *The Moor's Last Sigh*, and *The Ground Beneath Her Feet*.

Like *The Ground Beneath Her Feet*, *Fury* both mocks and shares modern Western society's fascination with stars in the world of entertainment, be it in the world of sports, music, or acting. There are frequent references to the lives of real characters among the glitterati of the New York scene in the beginning of the twenty-first century. *Fury* is awash in references to such people, whose seemingly transient fame will surely require an annotated edition in a few decades. These names may or may not have a deeper significance and appear to have no direct connection to the plot but serve to create mood and color. For example, a list of at-the-moment celebrities included in one paragraph alone: Steve Martin, Al Pacino, Melissa Etheridge, Warren Beatty, Christina Ricci, Will Smith, Dennis Rodman, Marion Jones, Christina Aguilera, Jennifer Lopez, Todd Solondz, 'N Sync, Robert Wilson, and Robert

Lepage (119). Another ripped-from-the-headlines example is the reference to Elián González, the Cuban boy who briefly caused a diplomatic row in 2000. The connection between the son that *Fury*'s protagonist Malik Solanka left behind in England and the Cuban boy is tenuous, however. As usual, Rushdie has also woven references to other writers and other works into his novel—here, they include oblique references to the American novelist William Faulkner and the Indian writer R. K. Narayan (220).[5]

Some of the connections between *Fury* and *Sabbath's Theater* come in the form of mimicry, while others are deliberate dissimilarities. Like *Sabbath's Theater*, *Fury* is set in the contemporary world of late twentieth-century America, *Sabbath's Theater* in the 1990s and *Fury* in 2000. Moreover, a significant amount of the action in both books takes place in New York City, with a few pages set in London. In New York City, Solanka lives in a rented apartment located near West Seventieth Street and Central Park West. Much of the New York City part of *Sabbath's Theater* takes place at the apartment of Sabbath's friend, Norman Cowan, who also lives near West Seventieth Street and Central Park West. The protagonists share the same initials in their given names and surnames: Malik Solanka and Mickey Sabbath. They are of a similar age, less than a decade apart—Solanka is fifty-five and Sabbath is sixty-four. Both protagonists are puppet masters and, for a time, made their living through their puppetry; they have also taught at the university level but no longer do so. Each is in his second marriage and estranged from his current wife.

By turns, Rushdie contrasts and compares the lives of the protagonists. For example, at age fifty-two, Drenka Balich is much closer in age to her sixty-four-year-old lover Sabbath than Mila Milo, who is in her early twenties, is to fifty-five-year-old Solanka. But Sabbath also has sexual relations with several people who are younger than he is. Drenka grew up in Tito's Yugoslavia, and Mila Milo's father (originally named Milosevic) is Yugoslavian. While Solanka is on an upward trajectory (at least professionally), Sabbath is headed downward.

Solanka is a millionaire, active writer, and creative spirit, continuing to know commercial success. Sabbath is penniless, his hands crippled with arthritis, which prevents him from performing his art, and he is obsessed with what he thinks is his coming death. Solanka dresses with style; Sabbath wears old and shabby clothes.

At the close of *Fury*, Solanka's lover Neela has abandoned him, he remains estranged from his wife, and that marriage is headed toward divorce. In the last scene, he attempts to make contact with his young son who is playing in a nearby park. When we last see him, he is literally in the air, jumping on a kind of trampoline that is part of a children's jungle gym, calling out to his son. At the close of *Sabbath's Theater*, Sabbath is still in a very rocky relationship with his wife. When we last see him, he is standing in the darkness of the cold morning air in the woods near a cemetery, ankle deep in springtime mud, railing against the injustices of life. In a sense, both men are defeated at the close of their stories. Solanka is groundless, anguished and depressed. Sabbath is grounded, literally and figuratively, but already planning what he will do next.

If the reader needs an additional nudge to see these connections, Rushdie actually provides a direct Roth connection. Early on in the novel, Solanka describes a friend as similar to Alex Portnoy and, in case the reader misses that clue, a direct reference to author Philip Roth quickly follows (20).

Analyzing the Reactions to Rushdie and Roth

Decades apart and for different reasons, Rushdie, like Roth before him, grossly and knowingly offended members of his religious community. The reactions and responses to them, however, were strikingly different. Philip Roth's Alexander Portnoy and, to a lesser extent, Mickey Sabbath were regarded by many Jews as vile, revolting, and irredeemable characters. They were an embarrassment, a *shandeh* (disgrace, shame). People were ready to turn their backs on Philip Roth, accuse him of self-hatred, and castigate him in print and angry letters; no one called for him to be murdered. By contrast, the fatwā against Rushdie remains in effect. Although the Iranian government formally distanced itself from it at a meeting of the UN General Assembly, Iran's most senior spiritual leader, Ayatollah Ali Khamanei, reaffirmed the fatwā in September 1998 and again in January 2005. As Bernard Lewis noted, it seems likely that this threat will follow Rushdie for the rest of his life (196).

Although there are parallels between Roth and Rushdie and their writing, there are also significant departures. Roth's fiction is imaginative but rooted in reality. Rushdie is a master of magic realism. Each has provoked his faith community, but the responses were light-years apart.

Even those Jews who were most critical of Roth, who found his work offensive, deliberately transgressive, an example of self-hatred, and even anti-Semitic, never suggested that what he wrote was blasphemous. Undoubtedly, Roth parodied parts of Jewish life, but he did not challenge Judaism nor did he intend to. In contrast, Rushdie knew that his portrait of the Prophet, mockery of the truth of the Qur'an, and satirical treatment of the beginnings of Islam would cause offense and be viewed as an affront, considered blasphemous by many believers.[6] *The Satanic Verses* was a work of art but also of hubris and intellectual arrogance. In retrospect, Rushdie has not only acknowledged but embraced this. In his address to a graduating class at Bard College, he said that *"hubris,* according to the Greeks, was the sin of defying the gods" and that because he himself has been accused of this supposed sin, he has "come to believe that such defiance is an inevitable and essential aspect of what we call freedom." His advice to others who would be free is to continue the struggle. There are those "that will seek to limit and control your thoughts and lives," he says. "Defy them; that's my advice to you: Thumb your noses. For, as the myths tell us, it is by defying the gods that human beings have best expressed their humanity" ("A Commencement Address" 138–39).

Throughout his career, Salman Rushdie has addressed numerous times the kinds of stresses, strains, and transformation that migrants face when they move from the Indian subcontinent to Britain. He also has written often of the clash of cultures. That said, he should not have to live daily with the fear of reprisal. On the other hand, he surely had a sense of what kind of a reaction his work might provoke.

Many years now have passed since these novels first appeared. The Jewish community of the twenty-first century is considerably more secure than was the case fifty years ago. Then, there was some irrational fear that the Jewish community itself, not Roth, would be the recipient of a moral, or even a physical, backlash. There was no such reaction experienced by the Jewish community in terms of *Portnoy's Complaint*, and the reaction to *Sabbath's Theater* was even more muted. Philip Roth has become an honored and treasured part of the North American Jewish community. Regrettably, even today, this benign reaction still does not describe the response to Salman Rushdie within the world of Islam. As of the second decade in the twenty-first century, very few voices have had the courage to call for a change of attitude. One exception is the noted Muslim writer Ziauddin Sardar, who wrote:

> The magnitude of the terrorist attack on America has forced Muslims to take a critical look at themselves. Why have we repeatedly turned a blind eye to the evil within our societies? Why have we allowed the sacred terms of Islam, such as fatwā and jihad, to be hijacked by obscurantist, fanatic extremists? . . . Muslims are quick to note the double standards of America . . . But we seldom question our own double standards. For example, Muslims are proud that Islam is the fastest growing religion in the West. . . . But Christian missionaries in Muslim countries are another matter. They have to be banned or imprisoned. Those who burn effigies of [the American president] will be first in the queue for an American visa. . . . [As Muslims,] we have to go further. Muslims are in the best position to take the lead in the common cause against terrorism. The terrorists are among us, the Muslim communities of the world. They are part of our body politic. And it is our duty to stand up against them. . . . The silent Muslim majority must now become vocal. ("My *Fatwā* on the Fanatics")

In free societies, such as those in the West in general, freedom of expression and of the press, even when the subject matter is offensive to the majority, never mind a minority, is allowed within very wide boundaries. This concept is not embraced by Islam, at least as taught and interpreted by its religious leadership in the early twenty-first century. The years 2005–06 saw protests that led to lives being lost and property damage, simply because some Muslims were offended by cartoons depicting the founder of Islam, Muhammad, which appeared in a Danish publication, the *Jyllands-Posten*. The Arab Spring of 2011 may result in some form of more democratic life for a number of Middle Eastern countries. It will not, at least initially, bring about Western-style democracies, ones that recognize and honor religious, political, and ethnic differences, much less the freedom of expression granting authors the right to write whatever they may choose, even if it parodies religion or religious issues.

Salman Rushdie and Philip Roth throughout their careers have consistently and consciously challenged their readers to think about a variety of issues that often make people uncomfortable. These matters deal with censorship, personal freedom, and lifestyles, as well as what might be the limits of expression within what we term a civilized world. As these are salient and seminal questions, how they will be addressed by future generations will be part of Rushdie and Roth's lasting legacy.

Notes

1. See the chapter in Pipes, "How Is the Book Blasphemous?" (53–69).
2. Pipes noted that "*L'Osservatore Romano*, the Vatican's semi-official mouthpiece, criticized Rushdie . . . Cardinal John J. O'Connor of New York encouraged Catholics 'not to dignify the publication of this work'"; that the head of the Anglican Church "suggested that the British laws of blasphemy be extended to cover other religions as well"; and that the chief rabbi of the United Hebrew Congregations of the Commonwealth had "appealed for legislation to proscribe such 'excesses in the freedom of expression'" (163–64). See also Parekh and Weller.

3. The name Mahound itself is an exceptionally distasteful choice. Akhtar explains, "In the Middle Ages, Mahound was a devil believed to have composed the Arabic Koran. Muhammad was often referred to as Mahound because Christians took him to be a false prophet" (13). See Sardar and Davies's book for a detailed presentation of the offending sections in *The Satanic Verses*.
4. See Appignanesi and Maitland 109–12. "In the light of some Muslim leaders' charge that the publication of *The Satanic Verses* was part of a 'Zionist conspiracy,'" Bhikhu Parekh notes, "the Jewish participation in the debate makes fascinating reading. As one would expect from a sophisticated and politically diverse community, the Jewish commentators covered a wide spectrum, demonstrating how ill-founded the charge was" (81).
5. R. K. Narayan's short story "Fellow-Feeling" is anthologized in a work Rushdie coedited with his former wife, Elizabeth West, *Mirrorwork: 50 Years of Indian Writing, 1947–1997*. Its lead character is Rajam Iyer, a member of the Brahmin class (100). In *Fury*, the character Neela Mahendra is based on the real-life television celebrity and super chef Padma Lakshmi, who is from an Iyer family and was married to Rushdie for three years (2004–07).
6. Bhikhu Parekh credits the offending chapters in *The Satanic Verses* with being both "daring and highly imaginative" writing. He then goes on to suggest that nonetheless the work allows for criticism in several ways:

> First, some parts . . . reflect bad taste and handle a great theme in rather crude, abrasive and offensive language. Second, they show bad literary judgement. Rushdie could have easily handled the theme in a manner that did not bear such a close historical resemblance to Islam. It is disingenuous to say that he did not mean Islam and yet use names and events that are all drawn from its history. The Muslim suspicion that he was being deliberately provocative is not easy to dispel. Third, Rushdie showed a remarkable lack of political judgement. (93)

Works Cited

Akhtar, Shabbir. "Art or Literary Terrorism?" Cohn-Sherbok 1–23.

Ali, Agha Shahid. "*The Satanic Verses*: A Secular Muslim's Response." *Yale Journal of Criticism* 4.1 (1990): 295–300.

Alvarez, Al. "The Long Road Home." *Guardian* 10 Sept. 2004: 20.

Appignanesi, Lisa, and Sara Maitland, eds. *The Rushdie File*. Syracuse: Syracuse UP, 1990.

Borowitz, Eugene. "*Portnoy's Complaint*." *Dimensions* 3 (1969): 48–50.

Cohn-Sherbok, Dan, ed. *The Salman Rushdie Controversy in Interreligious Perspective*. Lewiston: Mellen, 1990.

Cooper, Alan. *Philip Roth and the Jews*. Albany: State U of New York P, 1996.

Cutter, William. "Philip Roth's Remarkable 'Patrimony.'" *Jewish Journal* [Los Angeles] 1–7 Mar. 1991: 30–31.

Idema, James. "Book's Pending Success May Be Dirty Trick." *Sunday Denver Post* 16 Feb. 1969 Roundup sec.: 13.

Jones, Judith Paterson, and Guinevera A. Nance. *Philip Roth.* New York: Ungar, 1981.

Kakutani, Michiko. "Mickey Sabbath, You're No Portnoy." *New York Times* 22 Aug. 1995: 17.

Lewis, Bernard. "Behind the Rushdie Affair." *American Scholar* 60.2 (1991): 185–96.

Mazrui, Ali A. "Is *The Satanic Verses* a Satanic Novel? Moral Dilemmas of the Rushdie Affair." *Michigan Quarterly Review* 28.3 (1989): 347–71.

Parekh, Bhikhu. "The Rushdie Affair and the British Press." Cohn-Sherbok 71–95.

Pipes, Daniel. *The Rushdie Affair: The Novel, the Ayatollah, and the West.* New York: Birch Lane, 1990.

Roth, Philip. "Imagining Jews." *Reading Myself and Others.* New York: Farrar. 1975. 215–46.

———. "On *Portnoy's Complaint*." *Reading Myself and Others.* New York: Farrar. 1975. 15–22.

———. *Portnoy's Complaint.* New York: Random, 1969.

———. *Sabbath's Theater.* Boston: Houghton, 1995.

Rushdie, Salman. "A Clash of Faiths." *Maclean's* 27 Feb. 1989: 24.

———. "A Commencement Address for Bard College, N.Y." *Step Across This Line.* New York: Random, 2002. 136–40.

———. *Fury.* New York: Random, 2001.

———. "Philip Roth." *Imaginary Homelands: Essays and Criticism, 1981–1991.* New York: Penguin, 1991. 346–48.

———. *The Satanic Verses.* New York: Viking, 1988.

Rushdie, Salman, and Elizabeth West. *Mirrorwork: 50 Years of Indian Writing, 1947–1997.* New York: Holt, 1997.

Sardar, Ziauddin. "My *Fatwā* on the Fanatics." *Observer.* Guardian News and Media, 23 Sept. 2001. Web. 12 Mar. 2012.

Sardar, Ziauddin, and Merryl Wyn Davies. *Distorted Imagination: Lessons from the Rushdie Affair.* London: Grey Seal, 1990.

Weatherby, W. J. *Salman Rushdie: Sentenced to Death.* New York: Carroll, 1990.

Weller, Paul. "The Rushdie Controversy and Inter-Faith Relations." Cohn-Sherbok 37–57.

Yaffe, Richard. "Philip Roth's Complaint." *Jewish Exponent* [Philadelphia] 4 Apr. 1969: 21.

Zucker, David J. "Roth, Rushdie, and Rage: Religious Reactions to *Portnoy* and the *Verses*." *Journal of Ecumenical Studies* 43.1 (2008): 31–44.

CRITICAL READINGS

Rushdie's Other Worlds
Roger Y. Clark

> If this world is not to our taste, well, at all events there is Heaven, Hell, Annihilation—one or other of those large things, that huge scenic background of stars, fires, blue or black air. All heroic endeavour, and all that is known as art, assumes that there is such a background, just as all practical endeavour, when the world is to our taste, assumes that the world is all. But in the twilight of the double vision, a spiritual muddledom is set up for which no high-sounding words can be found; we can neither act nor refrain from action, we can neither ignore nor respect Infinity. (E. M. Forster, *A Passage to India* 212)

Salman Rushdie's early fiction is replete with what Forster calls "huge scenic background." Rushdie's background, however, is less concerned with astronomy (the stars and black air) than with religious cosmologies (heaven and hell) and with the accompanying realms of mythology (the plots and figures who act on the cosmic stage) and mysticism, which provides a link between human experience and these settings and figures. Rushdie's first four novels are also full of a rich, angst-ridden "spiritual muddledom" that lies in the twilight between those other worlds and the one we usually inhabit. Not wanting to ignore the huge scenic background—particularly as it is central to the beliefs and politics of the Indian subcontinent—Rushdie builds it into the characters, structures, and meanings of his narratives. Unable to respect it fully, he pokes enormous holes in it, questioning the books that describe it, the figures that populate it, and the testimonies that claim to verify it. In his later fiction, he treats this background as a function of culture, psychology, and politics, whereas in his earlier fiction, he explores the joys and struggles of those who come face to face with it.

Rushdie's first four novels are challenging because their versions of the huge scenic background fuse or clash depending on the point he is making at the time. In *Grimus*, he conflates four cosmologies to promote iconoclasm and the free play of dimensions; in *Midnight's Children* and *Shame*, he sets other worlds on a collision course to dramatize the tension between open and restrictive forces in the subcontinent; and in *The Satanic Verses*, he constructs a maze of revelatory and diabolic scenarios to challenge the nature of fiction and the foundations of belief. An example of his unpredictable take on otherworldly paradigms can be seen in the way he uses the Hindu god Shiva in a very positive way in *Grimus* and then in a very negative way in *Midnight's Children*.

There is no easy formula to explain Rushdie's early fiction. There are, nevertheless, four overall points I would like to make.

First of all, his early fiction resembles his later fiction in one crucial point: It is relentlessly secular. Rushdie consistently attacks the idea that things such as angels, prophecies, or holy books should govern human affairs or put limits on intellect or imagination. In *Imaginary Homelands*, he argues the need for secularism in India:

> After the terrible communal killings of the Partition riots, it was plainer than ever that if India's remaining Muslims, Sikhs, Buddhists, Jains, Christians, Jews and Harijans (untouchables), as well as the Hindu majority, were to be able to live together in peace, the idea of a godless State must be elevated above all of the 330 million deities. (385)

Having received his master's degree in Islamic history from Cambridge in 1968, Rushdie knows that secularism does not sit easily in Islamic societies:

> We see in Christianity a willingness to separate Church and State, and admission that such a separation is possible and maybe even desirable. In the world of Islam, no such separation has ever occurred at the level of theory. Of all the great sacred texts the Qur'an is most concerned with the law, and Islam has always remained an overtly social, organizing, political

creed which, again theoretically, has something to say about every aspect of an individual life. (380)

Although Rushdie recognizes the difficulty of applying secularism in Islamic countries, he makes a special case for the subcontinent, arguing that secularism is indispensable to Muslims in India and that it is part of the inheritance of Muslims in Pakistan. The latter is not easy to argue, given that Pakistan started as a religious state. Yet Rushdie also applies his secular sensibilities, together with his belief in the absolute freedom of expression, to seventh-century Arabia and modern-day Iran. The more people resist his secular vision and his right to express himself on matters pertaining to belief, the more he insists on them. The consequences of this are well known: He eventually receives a *fatwā* (legal ruling) tantamount to a death threat and spends a decade under the protection of Scotland Yard.

My second point is that Rushdie's early novels take otherworldly concepts more seriously than his later ones. Before I explore this point, I should qualify it in regard to his fifth and eleventh novels: While *Haroun and the Sea of Stories* and *Luka and the Fire of Life* are constructed along otherworldly lines, the otherworldly does not take deep root in the real world as we know it because there is no real world as we know it. The two novels are fantasies in the manner of *The Arabian Nights* or *Alice in Wonderland*. *Grimus* is nearly uncategorizable here, in that it is largely fantastic, yet the realistic elements are unmistakable, and the otherworldly elements are more serious than fanciful. In the first four novels, otherworldly paradigms are taken seriously, even while the texts (with the partial exception of *Grimus*) are largely grounded in the real world. One might even use the phrase "otherworldly realism," rather than "magic realism," to describe *Midnight's Children*, *Shame*, and *The Satanic Verses*.

In his early fiction, Rushdie takes many jabs at the huge scenic background, yet it nevertheless plays a key role in the structures of his narratives and the mental frameworks of his characters. Several of these characters—Aadam Aziz, Omar, Chamcha, and Mirza—do not want to believe yet cannot help it. They have the otherworldly thrust upon them, so to speak. The list of characters in his early fiction who believe more willingly is even longer: Virgil Jones, Grimus, Deggle, Flapping Eagle, Saleem, Padma, Parvati, Raza, Dawood, the three mothers, the Imam, Ayesha, Allie, and Gibreel, among others. Chamcha and Gibreel are perhaps the most interesting pairing, as they represent disbelief and belief, yet neither is able to control the cosmic forces that he rejects or accepts. They both stake their prospective grounds—Chamcha tries to be a "secular man" and to "live without a god of any type" (43), while Gibreel sees himself as the "genie of the lamp" whose "master is the Roc" (461)—yet both are swept up in the cosmic vengeance of a figure who might be referred to as the satanic narrator.

In contrast to his later fiction, Rushdie's first four novels supply a large space in which his characters can assume, question, or otherwise be subject to Forster's huge scenic background. Rushdie writes what he calls, in an interview with Eleanor Wachtel, a type of fiction "which doesn't prejudge whether your characters are right or wrong . . . in which the idea of the miraculous can coexist with observable, everyday reality" (149). In his later fiction, on the other hand, the list of key characters who believe in a huge scenic background diminishes. Characters tend to be religious in cultural, rather than ontological, ways—like India in *Shalimar the Clown*, who is "contemptuous of religion, her contempt being one of the many proofs that she was not an India" (18), or like Boonyi, who cannot believe in the myth of Sita because if she "set fire to herself no god would protect her. . . . Once in despair she did ask the gates of hell to open in the earth below her feet, but no cavity yawned. She was already in hell" (264).

The otherworldly emphasis of Rushdie's earlier novels is important because the time-honored structures of cosmology, mythology, and mysticism carry unique weights of meaning. These weights sink deep into the psyche, reverberating to the beginnings of culture and art. Playing with these structures sets up vibrations that can challenge or disturb readers—particularly if they believe in these structures, but sometimes even if they do not. By lessening the role of these structures, Rushdie's later fiction does not delve into the same kinds of reverberative ontologies. This is not to say that his later fiction does not contain deep psychological, cultural, political, and historical interest—as in the torments of Malik in *Fury*, the comparison of Akbar's India and Renaissance Italy in *The Enchantress of Florence*, or the exploration of geopolitical terrorism in *Shalimar the Clown*. The latter helps us understand the mind of a religious terrorist, yet this terrorist is what John Duvall and Robert Marzec in "Narrating 9/11" call "a reluctant terrorist" who is "not in the least religious" (392). *Shalimar* helps us understand the political ramifications of religion but not the impulse to believe. It helps us to see "the mutation [that] spreads outward directly to the point of a full clash of civilizations: there are 'the enemies pretending to defend us . . . and behind them the enemies pretending to rescue us in the name of God . . . and behind them the enemies . . . bearing ungodly names . . . and behind them the enemies we never see, the ones who pull the strings of our lives'" (Duvall and Marzec 392; ellipses in orig.). Rushdie's later fiction takes us in interesting directions indeed. Yet because it does not take other worlds seriously in terms of entering this world of ours, it does not challenge the experience of believing, which, to believers, is the very basis of otherworldly concepts. On the other hand, veering away from this type of ontological exploration may allow Rushdie scope to explore religion as a function of history, culture, and politics rather than as a function of belief in things such as gods or prophets.

My third point is that Rushdie's later fiction becomes increasingly dark, increasingly immersed in realms of diabology and demonology. In *Grimus*, the trickster persona of Deggle is a blend of Loki and the devil, yet he is counterbalanced by Virgil, who helps to unify the multiple dimensions through which the hero journeys. Deggle even acts in concert with Virgil at times, since he is also opposed to the maniacal, Odin-like control of Grimus. In this sense, Deggle is as much a Promethean Satan as a conventional Satan. In *Midnight's Children*, the demonic elements are more threatening, especially when the prime minister (the Kālī-like Widow) and the most powerful general (Shiva) drain the hope from Saleem's body and from his vision of a democratic, unified India. The scenario in *Shame* is even more shrouded by dark forces, which can be seen by comparing early references to Farid ud-Din Attâr's Mountain of Qaf, a symbol of cosmic, mythic, and mystical significance. In *Midnight's Children*, Saleem's great-grandfather, old Aziz sahib, dreams of the birds who attend a conference and then fly to Qaf (as in Attâr's *The Conference of the Birds*). After the death of old Aziz sahib, the ideals linked to Qaf surface in various forms throughout the novel. In *Shame*, on the other hand, Omar's three witchlike mothers remove from their shuttered mansion a beautiful screen depicting Qaf. Almost no trace of the ideals linked to Qaf resurfaces in the novel. The demonic elements in *Shame* become more and more prominent, until finally a Kālī/devil figure executes the hero, rapes a mentally disabled girl, and dispatches the president. While *Midnight's Children* ends with uncertainty—Will General Shiva crush Saleem, or will Attâr's ideals of conference and unity prevail?—*Shame* ends with Kālī and the devil hovering triumphantly over a deeply troubled nation. In *The Satanic Verses*, Rushdie goes a step further into the murky realms of diabology: He creates a narrator who possesses Chamcha, incites Gibreel to murder the woman he loves, and gleefully superimposes a hellish topography on the streets of London. This narrator, as in the Rolling Stones' song "Sympathy for the Devil," is pleased to meet us and hopes that we guess his name. It is hard to decide whether *Shame* or *The Satanic Verses* delves more deeply into the dark side; *The Satanic Verses* is more disturbing narratologically and theologically, yet it also contains playful humor, cosmopolitan wit, and oblique allusions to Attâr's ideals of unity and love.

Finally, the secular and iconoclastic way that Rushdie plays with religion can be troubling to the orthodox and devout, notwithstanding his appeal to the mystical ideals of the twelfth-century poet Farid ud-Din Attâr. For instance, orthodox readers might be shocked when the hero in *Grimus* uses a phallic "bone," which his sister once challenged him to bury beneath her skirt, to destroy an altar and then rape the altar's iconic goddess. They may not be mollified by the idea that the rape is meant to correspond to an iconoclastic stage in Attâr's mystical progress, after which the seeker is free to continue his spiritual journey. They may not appreciate being reminded that iconoclasm is a fundamental concept in Islam and that it is integral to the vision of many Sufi poets. Nor would they agree with Rushdie's overall approach, which mixes mysticism and secular iconoclasm and which implies that there is no intrinsic conflict between an Infinity that cannot be defined and a social contract that insists upon absolute freedom of inquiry, belief, and expression. Yet even if they did have problems with *Grimus* and its altar scene, both are so removed from public notice and from the particularities of sacred doctrines that they could chalk the whole incident up to irrelevant irreverence. This is not so, however, when Rushdie turns his secular iconoclasm against Islamic tradition in a reworking of the Satanic Verses incident.

In what is perhaps the most controversial novel of the late twentieth century, *The Satanic Verses*, Rushdie takes this pairing of secularism and iconoclasm further. The novel includes a questioning of revelation and the Prophet, a demonized version of Ayatollah Khomeini, and a brothel featuring versions of Muhammad and his wives. While all of these take place in the mind of a fictional schizophrenic, it is hard for devout readers to countenance them under any circumstances. Indeed, many simply refuse to read the book or allow others to read it. It is unlikely that they would be mollified by the idea that Rushdie has built subtle evocations of mysticism into the text—as I will argue below. First, however, I would like to give a fuller account of the way Rushdie explores the huge scenic background in his first three novels. This account will establish a pattern, which, when applied to *The Satanic*

Verses, will show that the novel may possibly be Rushdie's most insulting text, yet it poignantly extends the secular form of mysticism that has haunted Rushdie from the start.

Rushdie's intertwining of otherworldly and worldly motifs begins in 1975 with the publication of his first novel, *Grimus*, which he entered in the Gollancz science-fiction contest. It did not win, perhaps because its dialogue is sometimes stilted (very unlike the dialogue in *Midnight's Children*!) or perhaps because it focuses more on other worlds of myth and religion than on the type of scientific world found in *Soylent Green*, *Planet of the Apes*, or *2001: A Space Odyssey*. While the novel contains intergalactic journeys and a race of extraterrestrial stone frogs, its setting is a unique conflation of four cosmographies, its characters have heavy mythological associations, and its structure derives mainly from the journeys of Dante and Attâr.

In *Grimus*, Rushdie fuses four otherworldly paradigms, the most prominent among them being the mystical journey found in Attâr's *Conference of the Birds*, a long poem written in twelfth-century Persia. Attâr's poem features the journey of thirty birds (*si murgh* in Persian) over numerous mountain ranges to Mount Qaf and the bird god called the Simurg. This journey toward mystical unity and annihilation is the main model for Flapping Eagle's journey up the Mountain of Calf (a false or golden version of Qaf), controlled by the egomaniacal Grimus, whose name is a negatively slanted anagram of Simurg. Rushdie conflates this journey, in a style reminiscent of T. S. Eliot's *Four Quartets*, with three other paradigms: Dante and Beatrice's trajectory from the mountain of Purgatory to the spheres of Heaven, Shiva and Parvati's cosmos-shaking intercourse on Mount Kailash, and the cataclysm of Ragnarök, after which the mountainous island of Gimlé rises from the sea. The fusion of these four paradigms highlights iconoclasm and infinite dimensionality, as well as the sense of adventure Walt Whitman celebrates in *Song of Myself*: "*When we become the enfolders of those orbs, / and the pleasure and knowledge of everything in them, shall we be fill'd and satisfied then? / And my Spirit said, No, we but level that lift to pass and continue beyond*" (1218–20).

Secularism and mysticism complement one another in *Grimus*: Rushdie suggests that if dimensions (or worlds) must have controlling objects (sacred truths or gods), then such objects must be used selflessly or remain hidden. In the novel, the Rose is such a divine object, which makes sense since the rose is a symbol of love and union in both Christian and Islamic tradition. The rose is a particularly powerful metaphor in Dante, bringing together the most devoted souls at the end of "Paradiso," and in Sufism, where it represents love, the loving soul, and God. As intimated in Virgil Jones's diary—and with a tip of the hat to Nietzsche—the Rose initially appears to be hidden, inactive, or dead. This status is suggested by the reference to the dead bird of paradise and by the Rose's location in the forest next to the cemetery. Virgil brings the Rose back into the world and then uses it to fly to the planet of the Spiral Dancers, an allusion to Rumi's order of the whirling dervishes. Virgil uses the esoteric knowledge he finds there to free Flapping Eagle from Khallit and Mallit, who represent dichotomous, dogmatic thinking. Virgil's use of the Rose is free from an agenda, except that of Dante's Virgil, who leads his charge out of hell and up the divine mountain.

Grimus, on the other hand, uses the Rose for his own purposes, reducing the lives of others to a "divine game" that increasingly constricts free will. Given that Grimus controls the town of K, one can read a Kafkaesque fate in the townspeople, who are ground down and dehumanized by a Greater Machine. In Attâr's narrative, the thirty birds (again, *si murgh*) find annihilation when they realize that together they are the Simurg. They do not then reconvene in the form of a grimacing, or *grimusing*, authority. Virgil concludes: "If there were no god, we should have to invent one . . . [and] since there is a Grimus, he must be destroyed" (101).

Grimus is a positive figure in some ways, yet in his coercion, he prefigures the villains in Rushdie's next four novels—the Widow,

Dawood, the Imam, and the Cultmaster. All these characters think that their belief in a higher truth means they have the right (or the duty) to make others believe as they do. Such characters are not limited to Rushdie's early fiction—as we see in *Shalimar the Clown*'s Talib the Afghan, who would fit in well in Khmer Rouge Cambodia, except of course that he would himself be killed for his beliefs. He tells Shalimar, "God spits on entertainment. I would also order the execution of dentists, professors, sportsmen and whores" (272). In *Enchantress*, we meet "the necromancer of Stamboul, the long-hatted long-bearded Sufi mystic of the Bektashi order, adept in the mesmerist arts and the building of [coercive] memory palaces, working at the behest of a certain newly minted Pasha" (187). We also meet Shah Ismail, who shouts out "I am very God, Very God, Very God!" and boasts "in the words of the Sufi saint Shaykh Zahid, 'I will break the polo sticks of my adversaries.'" The narrator comments, with barbed understatement, "Modesty, generosity, kindness: these were not his most renowned characteristics" (213). Rushdie's point here seems to be that if these are the types of men speaking in the name of Sufism, then it would be better not to speak of it at all.

The infinite dimensionality Rushdie champions in *Grimus* also crops up in his later fiction—obliquely in Lifafa Das's peepshow and Saleem's telepathic conference in *Midnight's Children* and directly in *Haroun and the Sea of Stories*. The latter is particularly relevant, as it, like *Grimus*, combines positive Hindu and Muslim paradigms. In *Haroun*, the ocean on the moon Kahani (Hindi for "story") is "the biggest library in the universe," containing "all the stories that had ever been told" as well as those "that were still in the process of being invented" (72). Rushdie combines this ocean, borrowed from the eleventh-century Hindu writer Somadeva, with Attâr's mountainous terrain, the union of Somadeva and Attâr suggesting a fruitful meshing of Hindu and Islamic paradigms. This meshing is less obvious in *Grimus*, yet it is crucial to the ending of the novel. Flapping Eagle's name underscores the link to Attâr's conference of birds, yet at the end of *Grimus*, he becomes linked to the Hindu god Shiva through the ideas of tantric sex and destruction. He has sex with Media, whose name suggests a variety of forms and styles and who takes on the roles of Shakti and Parvati, with whom Shiva has near-cataclysmic sex on Mount Kailash. The link to Shiva is doubly appropriate, as he at once is the god most closely linked to tantra—author Wendy Donniger O'Flaherty calls him "the erotic ascetic"—and embodies both destruction and creation in his famous *tandava* dance. In syncretic terms, Flapping Eagle flies across Attâr's mountainous terrain to arrive at Qaf, at which point he imitates Shiva by destroying the Rose, thus liberating the divine mountain from the control of Grimus. This destruction echoes the Norse apocalypse of Ragnarök, in which Grimus represents Odin, Deggle represents Loki, and Flapping Eagle and Media represent the human couple who survive in the trunk of the giant ash tree, Yggdrasil.

The mystical flight of Flapping Eagle is possible given the abstract topography of *Grimus*, yet such an ideal flight is not possible given the geographic and historical terrain of *Midnight's Children*. While *Grimus* is structured along the epic and mystic paths of Dante and Attâr, *Midnight's Children* is structured first and foremost along parallel lines of family and national history. This is not to say that *Midnight's Children* is a worldly text, for in it Rushdie refers repeatedly to mythic figures (Padma, Parvati, Shiva, Ravana) and to mystical ideals (characters assuming the role of Attâr's bird-guide and Saleem seeing himself as the *paramhamsa*, the Hindu swan who can live simultaneously in the worlds of matter and spirit). The novel is also structured—albeit obscurely at times—on a mythic cycle, starting with a fall from and ending with a return to Eden. Yet all of these otherworldly elements are used to enliven parallel histories and to ask one important historical and political question: Will India survive as an open society? Will it be ravaged by the religious forces it brags, or will it foster an Attâr-style democratic unity, a Scheherazade-style happy ending? Writing in the years immediately after Indira Gandhi suspended parliament, Rushdie realizes that India could have gone the other way, perhaps in the direction of Pakistan. A deep fear of disintegration and fragmentation lies behind Saleem's writing at breakneck speed: "I must work fast, faster than Scheherazade, if I am to end up meaning—yes, meaning—something. I admit it: above all things, I fear absurdity" (9). The metafiction here is not just a postmodern game. Rather, it derives from the hope that India will rise in tolerance and harmony and from the fear that it will collapse into communalism and chaos. The fact that democracy was reinstated after the emergency rule is a promising sign, yet the fact that there was an emergency at all cannot be forgotten.

Rushdie's use of other worlds in *Midnight's Children* is often more muted and more subtle than in *Grimus*. Whereas *Grimus* starts with Virgil, a character who has an obvious link to Dante's *Inferno*, *Midnight's Children* starts with Aadam Aziz, a more subtle reference to both Hebrew myth and English literature in its Forsterian passage to the East. Behind the mythic reference is a mystical one: Aadam's father, old Aziz sahib, converses with thirty species of birds and then dies in a state of blissful senility in Kashmir, which can be seen as a lost Eden. This oblique reference to Attâr's *Conference of the Birds* is taken in a variety of directions throughout the novel. Each highlights the notion of open, tolerant, democratic discussion or conference—from Aadam Aziz's involvement with the Hummingbird and his Free Islam Convocation, to Amina's valiant stand against the muhalla zealots, and to Saleem's attempt to chair the Midnight's Children's Conference, in which he assumes the role of Attâr's bird-guide. It is also alluded to in the ghazals of Jamila, which explicitly echo the birdsongs heard by old Aziz sahib, reaching up through the birds into the heavens, providing a melodious counterpoint to the authoritarianism of the Pakistani generals. Last but not least, it is alluded to in the lapis lazuli spittoon. This explicit symbol of the democratic ideals of the Free Islam Convocation (donated by the Rani of Cooch Naheen, the Queen of Nothing, whose name suggests that the glorious conference will eventually come to nothing) is used by the wise old men in Agra, while children dance around it, until it is run over by an army car. It also expresses the unconsummated love between Amina and Nadir, who hides from the assassins of the Hummingbird, and accompanies Saleem in his traumatic journey through life.

Old Aziz sahib's death signals the beginning of history, just as Aadam's fall from traditional religion signals a movement from a closed Edenic realm where everything once made sense to an open, modern, secular world in which everything goes wrong. Things get particularly dire for the generations that succeed Aadam: Ahmed is tortured by the demon Ravana and by corrosive guilt, and Saleem is possessed by his two-headed demon. While possessed, Saleem indirectly kills his favorite uncle, a man who tries to sell a film script that describes the later life of Saleem. The convoluted metafiction here suggests that Saleem kills his own future by listening to his two-headed demon and following "the wisdom of the snake." Saleem also temporarily becomes a mindless dog of war, sniffing out "traitors" for the Pakistani generals amid the slaughter of Bengalis in 1971. Unable to continue in this unconscionable role, Saleem tries to escape his guilt by losing himself in the vast spaces of the Sundarbans jungle. Yet the jungle becomes a purgatory, a heart of darkness where Saleem must face himself and where strange otherworldly forces drink his life-blood until there is almost nothing left of him. Yet Rushdie does not leave Ahmed and Saleem in despair. Ahmed is saved by the love of Amina (the faithful), and Saleem is saved by a magical wave that sweeps him out of the jungle. Saleem eventually reunites with Picture Singh (who reminds Saleem of the Hummingbird) and with Mary and Padma. Finally, the mythic cycle hints at completion when the Muslim Saleem and the Hindu Padma plan their honeymoon in Kashmir with their adopted son, whose name is—not surprisingly—Aadam.

Forces of unity and division, cohesion and disintegration, take the form of mythic figures toward the end of the novel. On the positive side, we have the life-sustaining figure of Padma/Sri Lakshmi, Mary as a figure of forgiveness and love, Durga as the great mother goddess, and the new Aadam with the powers of the god Abraxas. On the negative side, we have the legacy of the Widow—seen as Kālī in her bloodthirsty mood—who castrates Saleem and the magical children in the name of OM, the sacred, unifying syllable of Hinduism. We also have the ongoing threat of Shiva, who split from Saleem's conference to become a gang leader, a murderer of whores, and a general working for the Widow. Whether the forces of peaceful unity or violent division will prevail is not clear.

While there are pessimistic elements throughout the text, there are also subtle optimistic hints. The lucky number 1,001 from *The Arabian Nights* is linked in a tricky way to the ages of both Saleem and the post-Raj subcontinent (thirty), as well as to the number of chapters or pickle jars Saleem fills with his rambling, spicy stories (thirty). Just as Scheherazade uses her 1,001 tales to liberate herself and the other women who might have followed her into the clutches of a vindictive Shahriyar, so Saleem hopes that his stories will herald a type of freedom—symbolized by the stories that he hopes will come after his stories. One version of the future, referred to as "thirty jars and a jar" (461), combines the happy ending of Attâr's thirty birds and the more down-to-earth happy ending of the 1,001 tales of *The Arabian Nights*.

In *Shame*, Rushdie shifts his focus slightly to the west, from India to Pakistan, yet he again uses mythic figures in his attack on intolerance, militarism, and authoritarianism. His main point is that the secular authoritarianism of Iskander Harappa (Ali Bhutto) creates the conditions for the more invasive religious authoritarianism of Raza Hyder (Zia ul-Haq). Rushdie uses a cause-and-effect dynamic similar to the one in the later chapters of *Midnight's Children*. There, Saleem and his Pakistani comrades are part of the religiously inflamed attack on East Pakistan in 1971. They are punished for their part in the violence with a sort of poetic justice: The *houris* (heavenly virgins) promised them by the Muslim generals turn out to be life-draining *apsaras* (nymphs) from Hindu myth. *Shame* contains a similar dynamic, in which Raza promotes a militaristic religious state and is eventually punished and murdered by a strange mythic conflation of Kālī and the devil. This figure is also conflated with Madame Guillotine, her basket of heads becoming Kālī's necklace of skulls. In *Midnight's Children*, the positive elements are not snuffed out—the Muslim Saleem reunites with the Christian Mary and the Hindu Padma, and India survives the "sperectomy," or hope draining of the Kālī-like Widow. Yet in *Shame*, the positive elements are roundly defeated. Raza turns the beauty of Jamila's ghazals into military propaganda, and the complicit hero, Omar Khayyam Shakil, is devoured by the same beast that kills Raza and hovers over the nation. The comparative endings of *Midnight's Children* and *Shame* make a rough sort of political sense, given that Pakistan, unlike India, has been deeply torn apart by its cultural and religious differences and has been unable to sustain a working democracy. Rushdie builds a prophetic element into the end of each novel, and the three decades since their publication suggest that his assessment is not without merit.

Shame may be Rushdie's darkest novel, yet *The Satanic Verses* is his most infamous and his most complex. In it, Rushdie revisits the Satanic Verses incident, an episode in the life of Muhammad that, for Muslims, demonstrates the honesty of the Prophet but that Western scholars have often used to suggest the fallibility of both Muhammad and his holy book. Referred to by Muslims as the *gharaniq* (birds) incident, the "satanic verses" refers to the trick played on Muhammad by Iblis, the Muslim devil, who fools Muhammad into thinking that God has permitted goddesses (the "three high-flying birds") to act as intercessors between himself and humans. Muhammad initially accepts the goddesses, later rejecting them when he realizes that the idea came from Satan rather than Gabriel—that is, when he realizes that they are satanic rather than angelic verses. The power struggle between God and the devil that lies behind this incident works its way into the layers of Rushdie's narrative. It also lies behind his inclusion of an elusive satanic narrator, who slips in and out of the text like Shakespeare's Iago on a hot Mediterranean night, possessing Chamcha and manipulating him so that he steers Gibreel into a murderous rage.

Throughout the novel, Rushdie conflates the Satanic Verses incident and *Othello*, keeping the biblical story of Adam and Eve and the Sufi paradigm of Attâr's Qaf in the background all the while. In a reworking of Shakespeare's play, Gibreel plays the bright but falling star Othello; Chamcha, the deceptive Iago; Allie, the innocent and forgiving Desdemona. Rushdie inserts the Satanic Verses incident into his *Othello* scenario: The possessed Chamcha whispers doggerel satanic verses over the telephone, thus driving Gibreel into a monstrous green-eyed jealousy. Chamcha succeeds in turning Gibreel's Edenic garden of love with his Eve/Allie into a hellish labyrinth of jealousy. He thus brings to fruition the vengeance of the ancient serpent, whose mythic roles are to offer apples spiked with dangerous knowledge and to bite the heels of humans, particularly those who, like Allie/Alleluia, intend to climb up divine mountains. Like *Othello*, the novel ends bleakly, with only an echo of the spiritual freedom represented by the murdered Allie, whose unwavering love for Gibreel and intense desire to climb Everest give us yet one more version of Attâr's Impossible Mountain of Qaf.

The operations of the satanic narrator become a bit easier to see when one keeps in mind one of the texts Rushdie says influenced the novel—Bulgakov's *The Master and Margarita* (*Imaginary Homelands* 403). Rushdie uses the scenario in which the devil wreaks havoc on Moscow (replacing it with London), throwing the Satanic Verses episode and *Othello* into the mix. While critics do not agree about the satanic narrator, I see him in terms of strategic invasions. These are most obvious in the second chapter, which mirrors Bulgakov's second chapter with its clear instances of satanic narration, and most subtle in the parts where he manipulates events to get rid of Sufyan and Allie/Alleluia, who represent goodness, liberalism, cross-culturalism, and the ideals of a modernized, cosmopolitan form of Sufism. The conclusion underscores the triumph of cosmic evil: Chamcha/Satan/Iago drives Gibreel/Adam/Othello to murder Alleluia/Eve/Desdemona. The death of Alleluia or Hallelujah—meaning "God be praised!"—is of course what the traditional Satan wants most of all. I explain in detail my theory about the satanic narrator in "Dreamscapes of a Green-Eyed Monster" (Clark).

Allie may be annihilated and her love may be impossible, yet annihilation and impossible love are notions that Rushdie consistently associates with Attâr's *Conference of the Birds*. Allie thus joins *Midnight's Children*'s Hummingbird, whose murder puts an end to the Free Islam Convocation, which aims to unite Muslims and Hindus in an alternative to Partition. She also joins *Shame*'s Mahmoud Kemal, who dies when zealots blow up his cinema, after he insists on showing a provocative Hindu-Muslim double bill in protest against "all this partition foolishness." Rushdie refers to this humorously, yet sadly, as "the double bill of his destruction" (62). In *The Satanic Verses*, Sufyan also dies in an explosion, which is significant because his name and his philosophy suggest a contemporary, eclectic form of Sufism; Sufyan has a "pluralistic openness of mind" and is the "least doctrinaire of hajis" (245, 243). Finally, Allie joins *Midnight's Children*'s Jamila, who is not killed by an assassin, an explosion, or a jealous husband, yet whose fate is perhaps worse: Her heavenly voice, which once reached above the birds in the highest treetops, is used by generals to push their citizens into what they call holy war (420).

Works Cited

Attâr, Farid ud-Din. *The Conference of the Birds*. Trans. Afkham Darbandi and Dick Davis. Harmondsworth: Penguin, 1984.

Clark, Roger. *Stranger Gods: Rushdie's Other Worlds*. Montreal: McGill-Queen's UP, 2001.

Donniger O'Flaherty, Wendy. *Śiva, the Erotic Ascetic*. Oxford: Oxford UP, 1973.

Duvall, John, and Robert Marzec. "Narrating 9/11." *Modern Fiction Studies* 57.3 (2011): 381–400.

Forster, E. M. *A Passage to India*. Harmondsworth: Penguin, 1978.

Rushdie, Salman. *East, West: Stories*. Toronto: Knopf, 1994.

_____. *The Enchantress of Florence*. Toronto: Knopf, 2008.

_____. *Grimus*. London: Granta, 1975.

_____. *Haroun and the Sea of Stories*. London: Granta, 1990.

_____. *Imaginary Homelands: Essays and Criticism, 1981–1991.* London: Granta, 1991.
_____. *Midnight's Children.* London: Picador, 1981.
_____. "Salman Rushdie." Interview by Eleanor Wachtel. *Writers & Company: In Conversation with CBC Radio's Eleanor Wachtel.* Toronto: Knopf, 1993. 138–58.
_____. *The Satanic Verses.* London: Penguin, 1988.
_____. *Shalimar the Clown.* Toronto: Random, 2005.
_____. *Shame.* London: Picador, 1983.
Whitman, Walt. "Song of Myself." *Complete Poetry and Selected Prose.* Boston: Houghton, 1959.

History as Trope and Atrophying History in *Midnight's Children*

R. S. Krishnan

> I was born in the city of Bombay . . . once upon a time. No, that won't do, there's no getting away from the date: I was born in Doctor Narlikar's Nursing Home on August 15th, 1947. And the time? The time matters, too. Well then: at night. . . . On the stroke of midnight, as a matter of fact. Clock-hands joined palms in respectful greeting as I came. Oh, spell it out, spell it out: at the precise instant of India's arrival at independence, I tumbled forth into the world. . . . thanks to the occult tyrannies of those blandly saluting clocks I had been mysteriously handcuffed to history, my destinies indissolubly chained to those of my country. (Rushdie, *Midnight's Children* 11)

Thus begins Saleem Sinai's recounting of his tumultuous life as one of the 1,001 Midnight's Children. His birth, at the very instant of India's independence, is welcomed by none other than Jawaharlal Nehru, India's first prime minister, who identifies Saleem Sinai with an auspicious national destiny: "Dear Baby Saleem, My belated congratulations on the happy accident of your moment of birth! You are the newest bearer of that ancient face of India which is also eternally young. We shall be watching over your life with closest attention; it will be, in a sense, the mirror of our own" (122). At the novel's outset, Saleem Sinai defines himself in relation to India's history. At the age of thirty, emaciated and debilitated, despairing of his life, he notes, "I saw in the mirror of humility a human being to whom history could do no more, a grotesque creature who had been released from the pre-ordained destiny which had battered him until he was half-senseless" (431), his autobiography superimposing itself on and intertwining with the nation's history. However, what constitutes history is frequently obliterated in the process, and it is here, in the ambivalence of its margins, that Rushdie locates his novel.

Rushdie portrays the history of the putative postcolonial promise of the newly emergent independent India through the prism of its "mythical" past by historicizing his fiction and fictionalizing his history. In effect, history in *Midnight's Children* is history as a trope. Rushdie portrays India's history in terms of the metaphors, metonymy, and irony that constitute Saleem's recasting of it from the perspective of his own life—not as the traditionally mythologized version contained in Indian history books but as distortions, disjunctions, and venality that pervade the postindependence body politic to which Saleem bears witness and of which he is a victim. As Hayden White has argued, historical explanation

> need not be assigned unilaterally to the category of the literally truthful on the one hand or the purely imaginary on the other, but can be judged solely in terms of the richness of metaphors which govern its sequence of articulation. Thus envisaged, the governing metaphor of an historical account could be treated as a *heuristic rule which self-consciously eliminates certain kinds of data from consideration as evidence.* (46)

Saleem copes with the distortions in the body politic by parodying reality through a refracting prism wherein the ordinary and extraordinary occurrences and incidents, far from canceling each other out, in fact have simultaneous existence. By choosing to write history as autobiography and by extending the personal into history, Rushdie's text mixes forms, narratives, history, and culture, and the intersecting "intertexts" continuously trade places in a perpetual movement that constantly redefines them. Consequently, Rushdie's novel exemplifies both a structural and a symbolic atrophying of history: As much as Saleem searches for a "form," a coherent and unified way of telling his nation's history, his only recourse is to contain national history metonymically in his own, and as he does so, national history symbolically atrophies in the imminent dissolution of his own life.

In his essay "Nietzsche, Genealogy, History," Michel Foucault notes that "history is the concrete body of a development, with its moments of intensity, its lapses, its extended periods of feverish agitations, its fainting spells; and only a metaphysician would seek its soul in the distant ideality of the origin" (145). In eschewing "traditional" history, Foucault suggests that "history becomes 'effective' to the degree that it introduces discontinuity into our very being," in that it enables us to recognize the events of history, not as a linear progression, but rather as "fragments" (154, 147). In delineating the political travails of postindependent India, Rushdie collocates historical consciousness with the personal, the one seeping into and inseparable from the other, the "vicissitudes" of the nation's "history" reflecting, refracting, and indeed, paralleling, the genealogy of textual voices, most especially that of Saleem. This has led critics such as Michael Reder to suggest that "*Midnight's Children* challenges the notion that any type of historical discourse can make claims of accurately representing past events" (226).

Thus, in *Midnight's Children*, the fantastic becomes real—Tai the boatman's claim that he has seen "emperors die" (16); the real, fantastic—Parvati-the-witch's thirteen-day labor corresponding to the thirteen-day political chaos ensuing from Indira Gandhi's refusal to resign after being convicted of electoral corruption (419). In such instances (and the novel is replete with them), Rushdie blurs the distinction between history and autobiography, and parody and irony prevail, which is the only way Saleem can hope to cope with the absurdities both in his life and in the postindependence politics of India. Mikhail Bakhtin notes, "Literary parody serves to distance the author . . . further from language, to complicate still further his relationship to the literary language of his time, especially in the novel's own territory. The novelistic discourse . . . is itself turned into an object and itself becomes a means of refracting new authorial intentions" (309). In *Midnight's Children* Rushdie deals with the absurdities of politics and culture by engaging in a parody of literary form that subverts itself, so that its "overall theme of fragmentation makes Saleem Sinai more a postmodern parody of a national allegory than national allegory proper" (Booker 139).

By adopting a nonlinear narrative and writing in hybrid English, Rushdie embodies a dialogic relationship that reflects what Bakhtin identifies as the discourse's "stratification of literary language, its speech diversity [which] is an indispensable prerequisite for comic style, whose elements are projected onto different linguistic planes while at the same time the intention of the author . . . does not wholly give itself up to any of them" (311). This stratification is evident throughout the novel, as it draws both explicit and implicit parallels between autobiography and history through its language. It is also made clear through the interspersions of reality and parody of Saleem's life history and India's social and political history, both of which are tied to the larger themes of institutionalized power versus individual powerlessness and of individual and political freedom. In particular, the long Indian cultural tradition of presenting mythologized history through the figure of the *sutradaar* (storyteller)——in this case, Saleem Sinai, the Midnight Child—attests to the undeniable presence of India's cultural and political history in this novel. At the same time, Rushdie's narrative technique keeps this presence perpetually hovering on the verge of absence by means of intrusions, chronological contradictions, and self-conscious asides of the narrator in a way that can be simultaneously unsettling and fascinating.

Working in a pickle factory—prematurely aged and "unlovely, buffeted by too much history" (38), a personal history paralleling that of his country—Saleem tells the story of the first thirty years of his life to Padma, his illiterate working-class companion, a woman who cares for and looks after him. She also provides the "more immediate atmosphere . . . with her interjections, her comments on the narrative, her misguided efforts to get Saleem's 'other pencil' to work, all of which add up to giving that realistic and tangible foil so necessary to keep the narrative to the ground" (Parameswaran 10).

Each of the 1,001 children, born on the auspicious night of independence, is endowed with a distinct magical power, and "the closer to midnight [their] birth-times were, the greater were [their] gifts" (195). The most powerful among the Midnight's Children then are Saleem and his rival Shiva, who were both born at the first moment of the hour. Saleem's very large nose gives him "the ability to look into the hearts and minds of men," whereas Shiva's huge knees give him "the gifts of war" (196). By the time Saleem is ten years old, 420 of the original 1,001 children are dead: "It is possible to hypothesize that these deaths . . . had their purpose, since 420 has been, since time immemorial, the number associated with fraud, deception, and trickery" (193). Rushdie is slyly alluding to the infamous Indian Penal Code number codified in law and mythologized in Indian cultural practice, whereby anyone booked under that section of the penal code is assumed a cheat and a liar, therefore a less-than-exemplary citizen. Thus, the 420 Midnight's Children, though dying of "malnutrition, disease, and the misfortunes of everyday life" (193), are delegitimized by the nation-state, ironically belying the augur of their birth.

In Saleem's case, he loses his telepathic powers when he undergoes an ear operation in November 1962 but emerges with an even more acute sense of smell. Thereafter, he goes through a number of misadventures: becoming a Pakistani citizen; fighting in East Pakistan (soon to be Bangladesh) in 1971; and "sniffing" out Sheik Mujibur Rehman, the leader of the revolt against Pakistan and later the first prime minister of Bangladesh (345). Saleem fortuitously meets Parvati-the-witch, pregnant with Shiva's child, who aids in his escape to India and marries him on February 23, 1975. Parvati delivers her baby on June 25, 1975, the very day that Indira Gandhi, the Indian prime minister, in a bid to hold on to power, declares emergency rule. In the roundup in the aftermath of this declaration, Saleem is arrested, tortured into giving the names and identities of all of Midnight's Children, and then sterilized (418, 421). Now, three years later, in 1978, he is writing his autobiography and reading it aloud to Padma.

In terms of plot, *Midnight's Children* looks like a mere recounting of Saleem's life: his welcomed birth at the moment of Indian independence, his early life filled with difficulties and disappointments, all of which parallel and reflect the first thirty years of postindependence Indian history and politics. However, Rushdie's account constantly and deliberately works at undermining any linear narrative or sense of order or meaning in such a representation of history: "Family history," Saleem says, "has its proper dietary laws. One is supposed to swallow and digest only the permitted parts of it, the halal portions of the past, drained of their redness, their blood. Unfortunately, this makes the stories less juicy; so I am about to become the first and only member of my family to flout the laws of halal. Letting no blood escape from the body of the tale" (59). As David Price has noted, "Saleem presents his history as a performance of narration, as opposed to a representation of events that took place in the past" (93). More specifically, his method underscores the subjectivity involved in the telling of history. As Saleem notes,

> I told you the truth . . . Memory's truth, because memory has its own special kind. It selects, eliminates, alters, exaggerates, minimizes, glorifies, and vilifies also; but in the end it creates its own reality, its heterogeneous but usually coherent version of events; and no sane human being ever trusts someone else's version more than his own (207).

Rushdie deconstructs history by deliberately avoiding a monoreferential narrative requiring adherence to fact or fiction. His narrative constantly undermines and indeed highlights the irreconcilable forces at work here—in Saleem's life story on the one hand and Indian history on the other—as the founding ideals of the independence movement are confronted and overwhelmed by the new forces of sectarianism and control of political power. Such forces are represented by Saleem's classmate Cyrus Dubash, who founds a religious cult and calls himself Lord Khusro Khusrovand, the "most successful holy child in history" (260–61); by Saleem's uncle Zulfikar, who aids in General Ayub

Khan's 1957 military coup (281–82); or in the surreal, terrifying portrait of the Widow (Indira Gandhi):

> No colours except green and black the walls are green the sky is black (there is no roof) the stars are green the Widow is green but her hair is black as black . . . the Widow's hair has a centre-parting it is green on the left and on the right black. High as the sky the chair is green the seat is black the Widow's arm is long as death its skin is green the fingernails are long and sharp and black. Between the walls the children green the walls are green the Widow's arm comes snaking down the snake is green the children scream the fingernails are black they scratch the Widow's arm is hunting see the children run and scream the Widow's hand curls round them green and black. (204)

By weaving the threads of personal genealogy into national history and metonymically containing national history in the personal, Rushdie subverts the traditional historical narrative and unsettles the readers' presuppositions about history through a collocation of voices that impinge on and ultimately destabilize the formal structures of fiction and history. *Midnight's Children* not only opens up a textual world that allows for a free play of heteroglossia, a multiplicity of voices and perspectives, but also reconstitutes Saleem's misadventures into statements about the subjectivity of history and the historicizing of the subject. This constant movement and displacement in the interaction between Saleem and India's history is what helps the novel avoid a singular fictional or historical frame, thus making its heteroglossia serve a multivalent representational purpose. To cite Bakhtin again:

> Authorial speech, the speech of narrators, inserted genres, the speech of characters . . . are merely those fundamental compositional unities with whose help heteroglossia . . . can enter the novel; each of them permits a multiplicity of social voices and a wide variety of their links and inter-relationships (always more or less dialogized). (263)

Indeed, this diffusion is captured in Saleem's increasing difficulty in providing some cohesion and form to his tale.

Saleem plays fast and loose with dates and undermines chronology, characteristic of traditional historical writing, by frequently shifting from past to present, rearranging events, digressing into anecdotes, and prominently proclaiming his causal role in shaping historical events. Indeed, he resists the urge to linearize, to adhere to a chronological narrative, even as he subscribes to his nation's "longing for form" (300). For example, Saleem changes the date of Gandhi's death but does not retract this even when he realizes his error. "Rereading my work, I have discovered an error in chronology," he admits. "The assassination of Mahatma Gandhi occurs, in these pages, on the wrong date. But I cannot say, now, what the actual sequence of events might have been; in my India, Gandhi will continue to die at the wrong time" (164). Again, Saleem writes that the election of 1957 took place "some time in the spring" of that year, but he has his mother campaigning in the summer of 1957. The discrepancy is not an oversight because Saleem realizes it: "And then it occurs to me that I have made another error—that the election of 1957 took place before, and not after, my tenth birthday; but although I have racked my brains, my memory refuses, stubbornly, to alter the sequence of events" (217). Saleem also realistically describes the language riots of 1956 but then claims responsibility for them and for the partitioning of Maharashtra state into Maharashtra and Gujarat. In his version, it was his bicycle accident in the midst of a demonstration—in which, goaded to speak Gujarati by the Marathi demonstrators, he repeats a nonsensical rhyme taught him by Keith Colaco, his Goanese schoolmate, *"How are you?—I am well!—I'll take a stick and thrash you to hell!"* (188)—that provoked the riots that led to the partition. Although the reality, as Saleem indicates, is that "the boundaries of these states were not formed by rivers, or mountains, or any natural features of the terrain; there were, instead, walls of words. Language divided us" (186).

Thus, as the recorder of history—his own and the nation's, which is to say, history according to Saleem—he tends to blur the realities of time and place. Such oversights and subsequent retractions leave the readers with a collage of suspended moments and freeze-frames in the narrative. As Linda Hutcheon has noted, "In [Rushdie's] postmodern storytelling there is no mediation that can act as a dialectical term for establishing relationships between narrative form and social ground" (460). Or, as Timothy Brennan points out, "History is 'altered' by rhetorical devices—either after-the-fact revision (the rewriting of history) or persuasion of those who can in fact change it" (109).

Paradoxically then, the collocation of history and autobiography and Saleem's digressions and interjections undermine each other precisely because of their indeterminacy; historical characters such as Indira Gandhi keep intruding into fiction, even as the fictional characters (for example, Zulfikar and Parvati-the-witch) encroach into history. Additionally, this crossing of texts and voices—Saleem's certainly, but also those of Shiva, Parvati, Padma, and, to a lesser extent, other characters, both historical and fictional (Sheikh Abdullah, Homi Carnack)—hovers in the indefinable space between text and reader, thus subverting both history and fiction. As Saleem the historian notes, "Reality is a question of perspective; the further we get from the past, the more concrete and plausible it seems—but as you approach the present, it inevitably seems more and more incredible" (164). Or, as Rushdie as writer points out, "In all literature, what actually happened is less important than what the author can manage to persuade his audience to believe" (263). "Saleem Sinai," Rushdie observes in one of his essays, "is an unreliable narrator, and . . . *Midnight's Children* is far from being an authoritative guide to the history of post-independence India" (*Imaginary Homelands* 22–23).

If Saleem is self-conscious as a narrator, he is also self-referential with his narrative: "I must interrupt myself," Saleem says; "I wasn't going to today, because Padma has started getting irritated whenever my narration becomes self-conscious, whenever, like an incompetent puppeteer, I reveal the hands holding the strings" (65). He frequently interrupts his narrative to provide glimpses of real events, such as the Jallianwallah Bagh massacre and the emergency declaration by Indira Gandhi. Yet in each of these instances, the events are so intertwined with Saleem's life and vision that they function less as history than as trope. Saleem seems to offer a matter-of-fact record of the Jallianwala massacre: "Brigadier Dyer's fifty men put down their machine-guns and go away. They have fired a total of one thousand six hundred and fifty rounds into the unarmed crowd. Of these, one thousand five hundred and sixteen have found their mark, killing or wounding some person. 'Good shooting,' Dyer tells his men, 'We have done a jolly good thing'" (36). Saleem carries over Dyer's nonchalant attitude toward the massacre he had ordered to the rumored killing of Tai by the opposing Indian and Pakistani forces over his stand on Kashmir: "R. E. Dyer might have commended his murderers' rifle skills" (37). Such documentary insertions call attention to the narrative itself, which is by turns ironic, parodic, terrifying, and above all, self-reflective. He also neatly metaphorizes Indira Gandhi's emergency proclamation in his description of Parvati giving birth, which Uma Parameswaran has aptly described as a "precise and nightmarish" tableau (6):

> Come on Parvati, push push push, and while Parvati pushed in the ghetto, J. P. Narayan and Morarji Desai . . . were forcing Mrs. Gandhi to push . . . the Prime Minister was giving birth to a child of her own . . . suspension-of-civil rights, and censorship-of-the-press, and armoured-units-on-special-alerts, and arrest-of-subversive elements. (*MC* 404)

In West Pakistan, Saleem witnesses human suffering due to the two Indo-Pakistan Wars of 1965 and 1971. As a result, he develops amnesia, metaphorized in his forgetting of historical reality: "History, it turns out, depends a great deal on who remembers it, how it is retold, and upon the teller's political/personal stake in it. Saleem has a vested interest in the events he narrates and he uses the past for his own, personal ends: he cuts up and retells history in a manner that allows him to be its central protagonist" (Hassumani 36).

If history involves interpreting the past in order to understand the present, then Rushdie sidesteps proscribing history into *Midnight's Children*. Specifically, he prefers an inversion of history, the novel beginning and ending in the present, subverting historical narration by its fictional representation. As White suggests, "The beginning state of affairs and the ending one are invariably poetic construction, and as such dependent upon the modality of figurative language used to give them the aspect of coherence" (98).

Rushdie's depiction of the struggle of Midnight's Children suggests what he perceives as the denigration of the ideals that signified the independence movement and its success. As Brennan observes, "Although much of *Midnight's Children* unfolds within a modern and political mode, repeatedly recalling the sectarian violence of contemporary Indian political life and the class tensions against which any national unity is artificially constructed, it is nevertheless designed to suggest the living presence of India's mythical past, not as 'vital tradition' but as false consciousness" (101).

Thus, history is "other" to Rushdie because the author's personal vision of India is displayed in an admixture of satire and realism, comedy and nightmare, which is the only means of coping with the absurdity of representing the subcontinent's history and politics. "[Saleem's] story is not history," Rushdie notes elsewhere, "but it plays with historical shapes" (*Imaginary Homelands* 25). On the other hand, Rushdie reminds his readers of the implicit difficulty of maintaining any objective view of history: As Saleem says, "The first lesson of my life: nobody can face the world with his eyes open all the time" (125). History is bearable only to the degree that it is reconstituted through memory and fantasy. As Neil ten Kortenaar suggests, "Saleem's self-conscious thematization has the effect of heightening the events of national history and rendering them fantastic" (32). In this sense, history in *Midnight's Children* is determined contextually in that as it is depicted, it becomes part of the matrix of autobiography. Precisely this dilemma is articulated by David Carroll when he suggests the difficulty of representing history in fiction, "if its representations of the past were not determined by either a historical or aesthetic ideal, if its representations were indications of the contradictions of history, of history as the conflict of opposing forces, rather than their resolution (suppression)" (110). As Aruna Srivastava notes, "By using the romantic literary/historical genre of the historical novel, then, Saleem is, at the beginning of the novel, apparently supporting the conventional or traditional view of history; however, he subverts this view more and more, not only in terms of a change in his thought, but by his trouble with his story's form and structure" (64). Or, as Saleem says, "Things—even people—have a way of leaking into each other . . . like flavors when you cook . . . the past has dripped into me," concluding, "So we can't ignore it" (39).

The past may have dripped into Saleem's present to confound his life, but he views both the past and the present, his own and the nation's, at an angle to reality: "On the day the World War ended, Naseem developed the longed-for headache. Such historical coincidences have littered, and perhaps befouled, my family's existence in the world" (28). It is worth noting that in a post–*Midnight's Children* essay entitled "'Errata': or, Unreliable Narration in *Midnight's Children*," Rushdie observes that "history is always ambiguous. Facts are hard to establish, and capable of being given many meanings. Reality is built on our prejudices, misconceptions and ignorance as well as on our perceptiveness and knowledge. The reading of Saleem's unreliable narration might be, I believed, a useful analogy for the way in which we all, every day, attempt to 'read' the world" (*Imaginary Homelands* 25).

In narrating his life, in interweaving his autobiography with India's history, however, Saleem knows precisely what he is doing—"destroying the unities and conventions of fine writing" (230). As he says, "There are so many stories to tell, too many, such an excess of intertwined lives events miracles places rumours so dense a commingling of the improbable and the mundane! I have been a swallower of lives; and to know me, just the one of me, you'll have to swallow the lot as well" (11). In short, Saleem says, "To understand me, you have to swallow a world" (370). The heteroglossic implication of swallowing the world rests in the uncertainty and instability of what is said, by whom, and about what, since neither the subject in question nor the narrative nor the context can be taken at face value. Indeed, in what must be an affectionate nod to the traditional Hindi movie plots based on substitutions at birth, Saleem's own origins are called into question. Saleem, it turns out, is the product of an affair between a street-singer's wife, Vanita, and Methwold, rather than the son of Aadam Aziz and Amina Sinai, as he originally claims.

Saleem's genealogy proves as suspect as the myth-laden history of Indian independence he purports to write. As he says, he has come to feel that he has "entered into the illusion of the artist, and thought of the multitudinous realities of the land as the raw unshaped material of [his] gift" (172). As Michael Gorra observes:

> Within himself he encompasses the whole of that India to which history has handcuffed him, not an individual so much as the choral voice of national consciousness. [. . .] Yet in describing that vision . . . the adult Saleem, at work in the pickle factory where he preserves his past in vinegar and spice, sees himself as suffering from a peculiarly "Indian disease . . . [an] urge to encapsulate the whole of reality." (112–13)

Striving to provide a semblance of form to his tale, Saleem discovers that his attempts provide no cohesion, except perhaps as an ordeal, a witness bearing to events located in and leading back to his present condition. As he says, "He was the child of a father who was not his father; but also the child of a time which damaged reality so badly that nobody ever managed to put it together again" (405).

The connection between history and autobiography is thus both dissonant and resonant. In recognizing the impossibility of shaping such disparate materials—not just those of his own autobiography but those of a partitioned and even more fragmented India—into a coherent narrative, Saleem's personal disintegration "becomes a metonymy for that of the national collage as a whole" (Gorra 114). In one of his interviews, Rushdie observes that "if *Midnight's Children* had any purpose . . . it was an attempt to say that the thirty-two years between independence and the end of the book didn't add up to very much, that a kind of betrayal had taken place, and that the book was dealing with the nature of that betrayal" (Haffenden 249).

At the end of *Midnight's Children*, Saleem finds that he is "no longer connected to history" (426). Facing disintegration, he hopes that "one day, perhaps, the world may taste the pickles of history. They may be too strong for some palates, their smell may be overpowering, tears may rise to the eyes; I hope nevertheless that it will be possible to say of them that they possess the authentic taste of truth . . . that they are, despite everything, acts of love" (444; ellipses in orig.).

Despite this sliver of optimism—that thirty years of his life, represented by "thirty jars [of pickles] stand[ing] upon a shelf," are "waiting to be unleashed upon the amnesiac nation" (443)—Saleem nevertheless recognizes that in the end "they will trample me underfoot . . . reducing me to specks of voiceless dust" (446). He then acknowledges that "it is the privilege and the curse of midnight's children to be both masters and victims of their times, to forsake privacy and be sucked into the annihilating whirlpool of the multitudes, and to be unable to live or die in peace" (446).

Concerning his own future, Saleem is ambivalent. As he says, "I shall reach my birthday, thirty-one today, and no doubt a marriage will take place, and Padma will have henna-tracery on her palms and soles," but he also recognizes the "rip tear crunch, and a stench issuing through the fissures, which must be the smell of death" (444). At the outset, Saleem says, "Above all things, I fear absurdity" (11), but he ends resigned to the collocation of the absurd and the horrifying in his personal and national history: "In words and pickles, I have immortalized my memories, although distortions are inevitable in both methods" (442). As with his own imminent dissolution, so with the "chutnification" of national history he had tried so hard to encapsulate for "a nation of forgetters" (38).

Rushdie reconstitutes the traditional monologism of historical narrative in favor of establishing multivalent fields of reference through multiple perspectives. Thus, the epistemological and ontological force that enters into the novel's very conception of history suggests both the impossibility of finding the "form" to represent history as well as the atrophy of that history.

Works Cited

Bakhtin, M. M. *The Dialogic Imagination: Four Essays*. Trans. Caryl Emerson and Michael Holquist. Ed. Michael Holquist. Austin: U of Texas P, 1981.

Booker, M. Keith. *Colonial Power, Colonial Texts*. Ann Arbor: U of Michigan P, 1997.

Brennan, Timothy. *Salman Rushdie and the Third World: Myths of the Nation*. New York: St. Martin's, 1989.

Carroll, David. *The Subject in Question: The Languages of Theory and the Strategies of Fiction*. Chicago: U of Chicago P, 1982.

Foucault, Michel. *Language, Counter-Memory, Practice: Selected Essays and Interviews*. Ed. Donald F. Bouchard. Ithaca: Cornell UP, 1977.

Gorra, Michael. *After the Empire: Scott, Naipaul, Rushdie*. Chicago: U of Chicago P, 1997.

Haffenden, John, ed. *Novelists in Interview*. London: Methuen, 1985.

Hassumani, Sabrina. *Salman Rushdie: A Postmodern Reading of His Major Works*. Cranbury: Associated UP, 2002.

Hutcheon, Linda. *The Politics of Postmodernism*. London: Routledge, 1989.

Kortenaar, Neil ten. *Self, Nation, Text in Salman Rushdie's* Midnight's Children. Montreal: McGill-Queen's UP, 2004.

Parameswaran, Uma. *The Perforated Sheet: Essays on Salman Rushdie's Art*. New Delhi: Affiliated East-West, 1988.

Price, David W. "Salman Rushdie's 'Use and Abuse of History' in *Midnight's Children*." *ARIEL* 25.2 (1994): 91–107.

Reder, Michael. "Rewriting History and Identity: The Reinvention of Myth, Epic, and Allegory in Salman Rushdie's *Midnight's Children*." *Critical Essays on Salman Rushdie*. Ed. M. Keith Booker. New York: Hall, 1999. 225–49.

Rushdie, Salman. *Imaginary Homelands: Essays and Criticism, 1981–1991*. London: Granta, 1991.

_____. *Midnight's Children*. New York: Knopf, 1981.

Srivastava, Aruna. "'The Empire Writes Back': Language and History in *Shame* and *Midnight's Children*." *ARIEL* 20.4 (1989): 62–78.

White, Hayden. *Tropics of Discourse*. Baltimore: Johns Hopkins UP, 1978.

On Reading *Midnight's Children* Politically
Asma Abbas

> Like all novels, *Midnight's Children* is a product of its moment in history, touched and shaped by its time in ways that the author cannot wholly know. I am very glad it still seems a book worth reading in this very different time. If it can pass the test of another generation or two, it may endure. (Salman Rushdie, *Midnight's Children*, xv–xvi)

Midnight's Children have turned sixty-four, and *Midnight's Children* is a little over thirty—give or take a few years. These are about the same ages as my mother and I. The multiple reverberations of *Midnight's Children* in our lives and beings suggest an extension of Ray Bradbury's metaphor at the end of *Fahrenheit 451*: In dark times, redemption might lie in books themselves becoming living beings, our not taking on their lives but giving them whatever we can of ours, allowing them and other works of art and thought that make life possible to continue becoming. This act of giving and affirming life, while not necessarily or only maternal, is contrary to the spirit of today's time when distance, objectification, stultifying repetitions, and the disregard of life come so easily.

The gifts and curses of the spawns of that midnight in 1947 are many, and there is something inescapable and profound about the realization that they continue to shape and be shaped by the midnights that have accosted the people of the South Asian subcontinent since then—as thresholds into nights of possibility or doom, as moments of decision, as new etchings on the palm. The 1980s, when I grew up in Karachi, were a proverbial "dark night" for the people of Pakistan, and today is too—proof that we ran into the wrong midnight at some point, but also evidence of other unrealized possibilities. As has been proven with my mother in Karachi and me in the United States for many years, no spatial boundary can dare to contain a destiny. While in different places and at different distances from the originating midnight that is Salman

Rushdie's topic, my mother and I experience oddly similar afflictions of history and time, as no new space is free from the gifts and curses we carry on our bodies and psyches. This is not just true for her and me, however: All of us remain haunted by those midnights, are enclosed in the same times, should be aware how important it is to recognize the possibility of renewing or undoing the curse of many past midnights, and even wish that, in some sense, it were still *only* midnight.

The independent nation-states of India and Pakistan plod along, appearing sometimes like amnesiac tigers, sometimes like beloved homelands, sometimes like killing fields, sometimes like infantile bullies resentful of and reliant on those who will suffer and survive anything. In the present moment, their people are besieged with wars and terrors of a considerably different stripe and a much more total nature than those set in motion by the dictatorships and states of emergencies in times past. Moreover, they are accompanied by a much graver retreat of politics, memory, and possibility than what drives me mad about those earlier times. I understand why Rushdie speaks of a "very different time," because like everywhere else in the world, what South Asia suffered through in the 1980s informs its current afflictions. In the twenty-first century, terror, the war against terror, neoliberalism, and finance capitalism structure a more heartless, militant, and abstract antipolitics than even the most undemocratic times of the 1980s in which my generation learned about democracy and politics. Although none of this would be possible without what happened in and before the 1980s, it is tempting to feel nostalgic for those modes of unfreedom. Even if they were a precedent for present reactionary politics, the relative simplicity and immediacy of resistance and travail, the evil politicians of yesteryear and their imperialist bedfellows, and the existence of a political discourse that was neither pure reaction nor one-dimensional almost seem quaint, especially when one encounters the easy credulities of those born too late to have experienced, let alone remember, them—those born after Indira Gandhi's assassination, after the onset of the Kashmiri freedom movement, after all the Afghan refugees came, the

VCR and the Kalashnikov came, and the democratic "reawakening" in Pakistan and "the return of democracy."[1]

Consequently, so much of how *Midnight's Children* lives, endures, and becomes has to contend with the erasure of the contexts that, if responsibly revived, could make this moment's defeats look and feel different. For many born either too late or born again—as the aggressively passive bourgeois living-in-the-moment types or as feudal-capitalist-nationalist-yet-global elite or as fundamentalist fanatics—such contexts might even enable a recognition that what they think are triumphs are actually defeats.

A writer's knowledge, Rushdie suggests, is necessarily incomplete, even at the time of a work's inception. To extend that, I believe that a reader has not only the power but also the responsibility to make and remake the novel in times and spaces beyond those in which it first became possible. The reader and the writer are both effects of history, and as much as their actions and interactions with a work of literature shape and contrive what becomes of history within and without them, they themselves are subjects shaped within this process. If this force field of interactions between histories and subjects is taken to constitute the realm we call politics, then the relation between politics and literature is not only a symptom of, but a site for negotiating, human social existence and possibility. Thus, history irrupts into the scene of reading not only through the embodied writer, but also through the embodied reader and all the characters and figurations in between.

This essay explores how a novel such as *Midnight's Children* endures and what kind of reading it invites at this later, very different time. The book especially lends itself to this exploration, not only because as a novel (functioning at a metaphysical or infrastructural level), it is congenital to the triangulation of politics, history, and subjectivity, but also because these elements are characters in motion on the narrative surface—desublimated, sanguine, messy, physical, incarnate, abject, and grotesque. Thus, the question of enduring history and enduring *through* history—the real crux of human political activity—is this novel's special burden to carry, at many levels. Concerning himself with the embodied inheritances of memory and history, Rushdie tackles the issue of our dynamic and dialogic interactions with history as its subjects and objects. These interactions are the proper constituents of politics as defined above; they transpire in the work of the senses in the novel, operate by way of multifarious sentiments such as desire, love, hope, and guilt, and infuse the very act of writing and reading such a novel.

The true test of endurance for a contemporary political novel is the extent to which it can raise and engage the question of our current crisis as a crisis of politics itself—of what politics is, of what it can be instead of the state apparatus complicit in violence, war, greed, conspiracy, manipulation, injustice, and betrayal to which most people reduce it, and of where it lives above and beneath the visible divisions of ideology. Political subjects are interesting then not as consumers of ideology or heads counted in an opinion poll, but as those who love and suffer in particular ways, relate to history and ideology in their embodied acts, and shape the realm of sensibility, subjectivity, and politics itself as they go. Moreover, given the dynamism of history in politics defined as a life activity rather than a modern manipulative institution, reading politically requires expanding and pluralizing the notion of history itself to include the unfolding forms of life that we inherit, contend with, and seek to go beyond. I want to bring this kind of reading to *Midnight's Children*.

To Read Politically

> In a stratified society all literature is engaged politically and morally, whether it's so perceived by the author or not. It will be so perceived by the readers it validates and by the readers it affronts.... Art is only partly rational. It acts on all the levels of our brain and influences us through sounds and silences, through identification and imagery, through rhythms and chemistry. (Piercy 119)

One can only imagine how intense this engagement is when the stratification Piercy speaks of is most essentially material, manifest at the very level of sensuous, embodied life across a society. One can further try to imagine the imperative or necessity of this orientation when that society is not merely stratified but traumatized: riven by partitions, inequalities, xenophobia, ghettoization, the drought of political discourse, the inability to learn from history, and the overwriting of political debate by neocolonial and imperialist politics of war and capital. Karel Kosík's interpretation of the 1968 crises as not political or national crises but the crisis of politics itself is instructive here. It is a crisis because "politics as mass manipulation in some sense transforms and undermines the understanding of political activity that we have traditionally held": the sense of politics as human life activity, expressing and cultivating humanity in creating a common space for us to be available and sensible to each other in our speech and deeds (Kosík 9). Kosík enabled a rethinking of the role of political literature in Czechoslovakia in terms that moved from predictable ideological battles of persuasion and propaganda toward addressing this crisis by not settling but raising the question of the meaning of politics in the modern world, literature not as edifier but as creative praxis.

Even when classic, historically sensitive, and progressive treatments of the political novel acknowledge the relations between politics and literature, politics is treated as a setting, ingredient, or concern, as something outside the text. For instance, in *Politics and the Novel*, Irving Howe riffs on Stendhal by comparing politics' intrusion into literature to a "rude disharmony" that interrupts an ongoing concert: "something loud and vulgar, yet a thing to which it is not possible to refuse one's attention" (17). Howe commits himself to examining the life and nature of this concert before and after the "violent intrusions" of politics, where politics appears as an external and perhaps extraneous pressure equated with ideology and often etched against epic historical circumstances that provide the staging ground for human action (17). For Howe, the political novel is not a separate genre or a consistent category but a convenient way of corralling works in which "*we take to be dominant*" the role of political ideas or the political milieu that serves as the setting (19; Howe's emphasis). The stakes are a little higher when Lionel Trilling invokes the "dark and bloody crossroads where politics and literature meet" (11), where "matters of life and death are taken up and the fate of 'society' hangs always in the balance" (Boyers 1). In line with Kosík's turn, regarding literature as creative praxis entails moving away from thinking of politics as external to the text. For literature to be creative praxis, I would suggest, it must be not merely a response to but a site for politics, giving life to the texts and producing politics anew. For the reader, this involves not merely putting texts to political use or reading political novels but reading politically.

In this moment of abiding crisis, reading texts politically presumes at least this much: that texts narrate something fundamental to our existence, craft current mythologies, encapsulate fantasies, and contrive fairy tales that allow us to live and that the outcome of this reading yields insights into our history and into possibilities of the present and the future. Reading politically is different from a hermeneutics of the novel's true politics and original intent, for both politics and literature bear different burdens depending on where and when the reader and writer meet. It is imperative that we carry this burden and not assume that it merely amounts to a subjective idiosyncratic interaction. Rather, this kind of reading acknowledges the novel as a space for interaction, a space that structures an experience as much as being structured by a politics that is a force outside the novel.

Instructive here is Hannah Arendt's claim that politics is inseparable from the creation and conservation of a space where individuals encounter each other as members of a community, engage in speech and deeds, and thus realize their humanity.[2] Putting these thoughts next to Jacques Rancière's notion of political subjectivity as "an enunciative and demonstrative capacity to reconfigure the relation between the visible and the sayable, the relation between words and bodies . . . 'the partition of the sensible'" (115), I find that reading politically does not require decoding the writers' declarations but judging how they, as political subjects, parse the sensible and render our current shared conundrums of political subjectivity. Reading politically further involves approaching the text with the capacities Rancière mentions. Bringing Arendt and Rancière together, reading and writing are acts of political subjects when citizens interact with other subjects and objects of creative praxis in society, judging them politically and accounting for the manner in which they configure and reconfigure one's imagination, sensibility, and availability to another. This effort at navigating the "sayable" and the "sensible," in the construction of common spaces where we can be heard or sensed, amounts to negotiating the meaning of politics itself and our relation to it.

With this spirit, I turn back to *Midnight's Children*, to understand its abundances, lacks, and chosen sensibilities, rummaging for a possibility that resonates today. Hope, I will argue, is in short supply in Rushdie's work for an area of the world that struggles politically and existentially, one whose current sorrows cannot be separated from the ones inherited by Midnight's Children or from the Hegelian curse or blessing that beginnings contain ends. Maybe that is what living through a time of great fear, mistrust, abuse, terror, and betrayal—one that has already rivaled the twentieth century's claim as the bloodiest—looks like.

In This Very Different Time

> The truest, deepest motive behind the declaration of a State of Emergency was the smashing, the pulverizing, the irreversible discombobulation of the children of midnight. (Salman Rushdie, *Midnight's Children* 492)

Midnight's Children endures not merely as a chronicle of a time past. So much of what Rushdie has lamented, maligned, and feared in his writing—specters of nationalisms and sectarianism, sanguinity of identity, murderous malleability of history, militant hypocrisies of power, bloodthirsty moralism, corrupt plutocracies, and feudal oligarchies nestled atop the abandoned and unrequited South Asian subcontinent—has continued in ugly ways in the years since the novel first appeared. These very issues have plagued or necessitated postcolonial literature and theory and are the ones that continue to pound and pulse through our veins.

However, I find myself being sensitive to very different aspects of Rushdie's work from the technical and metaphorical flourishes that once made me alternatively gasp, exhale, nod, reverberate, cringe, and roll my eyes. Seeing literature as at once a weapon and a symptom, I am now drawn to cast a second glance and critically reapproach *Midnight's Children* as one among many cultural products that meant to save us by turning the immediate into the grotesque, the fantastical, or the "magic realist." Today—when the grotesque is immediate and banal, cannibalizing both the magical and the real, and when the ruins of everyday life are much more pervasive—there is nothing fantastic about the body or the body politic that combusts much more easily at its own or another's hands than in the scenes of *Midnight's Children*. So it is important to keep asking what the redemptive political imperative of literature might be. While Rushdie's disgust with ideology is palpable and understandable, it is also needful to go a bit further and see how his narrative of the nation can help us key into whose romance and whose nostalgia is embedded in that bloody myth. None of this is the writer's burden to carry alone; I am interested in the cocreation and re-creation of meaning and life that happens between reader and writer in different times and spaces.

The biggest casualty of the tryst with destiny set in motion one night in August 1947 is hope itself—as Saleem calls it, "Sperectomy: the draining-out of hope" (503). Throughout the novel, the narrative of hope has to do with how these special children, these embodied possibilities of a free India, would turn out and how this beginning ultimately must confront the ugliness of its disappointment. This hope for freedom is really a hope for politics—its imagination and its possibilities. The loss of hope begins with the god-shaped hole that makes Aadam Aziz "vulnerable to women and history" (6, 4); how the novel formulates hope (in order to reject it) is directly reactive to the god-shaped hole bored inside Aziz when he stops believing, a lack that haunts the entire book. The encounter with the ground "knocked [him] forever into that middle place, unable to worship a god in whose existence he could not wholly disbelieve" (6). This serves as the template for the pathology that runs amok in *Midnight's Children*, taunting both the reader and Aziz's progeny of addicts throughout history with the curse that nothing can ever be enough while engulfing the possibilities of other beliefs, attachments, and devotions that are not fetishistic semblances of god (such as the nation, the nation-state, and so on). As I read the novel, I find the eruptions of sensuous powers, ultimately of sentiment and attachment—often in service of the sensual economy of the market and the state—to be in awe of a faith and a devotion that has already been denied to God at the outset. This is why I find Rushdie's severity toward the source and shape of the hole, but not toward the "hole" itself, to be very telling; I feel that he has missed an opportunity that we, as readers, can resuscitate.

In the face of our current challenges, Rushdie's emphasis on identity, exile, hybridity, postcolonial nationhood, and the superiority of liberal secularism, his tragic reconciliation with notions of privacy, and his refusal to rethink the possibility of politics beyond corrupt institutions and evil leaders seem ineffective. Neither his work nor the politics of the last century have convinced me that liberal ideology or metaphysics—with its private individual and proprietary liberties, instrumentalist orientation, distancing and rationalization of notions of the public, view of citizenship as a mere role, and holy grail of secularism—has the key to addressing the scourge of xenophobia, fundamentalist idealism, and fascism. I feel that Rushdie found his way to sit atop the riffraff of "believers" with ironic misogyny, hoarded metaphors, and emphasis on history's abundant promiscuities, but never really with any true love or intimacy. The exclusion of hope in this time when things are actually worse bites differently, since a satirization of devotion, belief, and faith is no protection when all that was insistently repressed and rejected continues to haunt the present and any possibility for the future.

The novel's declaration of the end of hope *could* potentially partake in an ontological critique of time, history, and the politics of modernity—along with pessimist philosophy and critiques of futurism—but it does not. While Rushdie masterfully deploys the ironic and the fragmentary, he comes across as overly detached from the metaphysical (and hence political) content of his aesthetic techniques. For instance, despite the implicit pathos of the loss of hope, the manner in which Rushdie's partiality to the multivocal postmodern genre manifests—in disavowing any principle of unification, celebrating irreducible singularity, and overdoing numbing self-referentiality—is all too loveless and casuistic. The novel's illocutionary exhaustion of hope is the luxury of a moment that could afford to treat the abject only as a principle of art rather than as a principle of existence. No such luxury, if it ever was available, is ours today.

Rushdie's confessed failure to "write about strong feeling, cathartic emotion, obsession" (qtd. in Marzorati), which is a key symptom of our times, makes me wonder if this failure, his emphases as outlined above, and his commentary on the end of hope are related. I cannot seem to respond to writing that is not, in some manner, dealing with what Rushdie has, by his own admission, failed to address. "Post-Rushdie" writing emerging from South Asia in recent years that has given the issues of the East-West encounter a needed break (as in Muhammad Hanif's *A Case of Exploding Mangoes* and *Our Lady of Alice Bhatti*) or a severe politicizing twist (as in Nadeem Aslam's *Maps for Lost Lovers* and *Leila in the Wilderness*) in order to address graver inheritances just resonates more with my urgencies. It steps away from symbolisms that address swooping questions of fate and hope for the rest of us in order to find and be with all the life between the poles of birth and death: loving, suffering, obsessing, failing, fearing, desiring, destroying. While these writers tread the path carved by Rushdie's attention to detail, the inconsequential, the filmic, and the artistry of speech across translation, they seem to provide a much more ontologically rich engagement with time and space in the face of lost hope. Theirs is a closer phenomenology of very precarious life that has seen Rushdie's prophecies come true with much less hilarity than he imagined, of the compulsive regard for beauty amid a very proximate ugliness, with no room to fake artistic detachment. All this confirms that art is always already partaking in the real; that different times bring different political aesthetic imperatives for both writer *and* reader; and that conversations across different midnights often amount to a changing of the guard. This new crop of writers is writing about and responding to other midnights, closer and later, without the benefit of hindsight. How their works will look to readers in another thirty years remains to be seen.

Body Politics: The Tale of Two Tais

> Perhaps, if one wishes to remain an individual in the midst of the teeming multitudes, one must make oneself grotesque. (Salman Rushdie, *Midnight's Children* 121)

In *Midnight's Children*, history "irrupts" into the body (59). In thematizing these irruptions—their physical and sensuous content, their forms, where and when they happen, and how they are economized and managed—Rushdie reveals his thoughts on history, memory, subjectivity, and hope, and thus on ethics, aesthetics, and politics.

Rushdie manifests his own concerns about the subcontinent in the bodies and beings of his characters. The body in this book becomes the threshold and the site for the encounter and interpenetration of history and memory, the personal and the political, the bounded and the unbounded, the conscious and the unconscious. The novel shows a society composed of different bodies absorbing history in different ways, being shaped by and bearing its marks. This irruption is navigated in many ways, since body and history never simply merge with or submit to each other. This allows the relation to continue, evading closure, though one could say that, over the course of the novel, bodies keep reconciling themselves to their reduced possibilities in order to keep going on. We also are shown what happens when body and history expel each other, as in Saleem's murderous escapades as a misogynist vigilante or patriotic militant or when the only possibility of survival is the body becoming a decaying repository of history, like midnight curses enclosed in deformed bodies and pickled umbilical cords reminiscent of Charles Bovary's collection of aborted fetuses. At a time, as I said earlier, when the fundamental orientation to the body and the conflicts it imbibes have changed so much, the way in which embodiment is parsed is important in assessing and moving on from the time to which *Midnight's Children* responds. How are we to judge the sensuous activity in which the novel's characters experience and manifest their politics—in the form of relations to memory, hope, truth, belief, desire, possibility, and the humanity of self and other—when, today, the body appears not only as grotesque but as infinitely destructible and disposable?

In such a time, how could one not turn to the incarnate margins, to the bodies of those who are usually written out of history, or challenge its writing altogether? Let us imagine the novel *politically* as a space in which individuals encounter each other as members of a community, by engaging in speech and deeds, and in doing so, realize their humanity. The novel, then, is thus necessarily a space where the sensible is parsed in negotiating the limits and meaning of politics and political subjectivity—the margins that hem, *and* hem in, the subjectivities, sensibilities, and politics, posited and normalized in the creation of this work of art. Encountering Rushdie this way is exciting and tricky. After all, how is one to locate those who signify a challenge to experience and politics as usual within a novel that promiscuously normalizes the extraordinary and sends the "real" into a tailspin?

Two rather unlikely characters in *Midnight's Children* convey what is involved in this sensual politics by providing frames within which questions of embodiment, experience, and alternative visions of politics and history are invoked: Tai the Boatman, who is attached to the nascence of Saleem Sinai's story and its arbitrary origins, and Tai Bibi, the 512-year-old prostitute who can mimic every smell in the world. They exceed, mirror, and haunt the usual political protagonists. They bring into relief the novel's body politics: its understanding of senses as political powers and its normative take on the nature and possibility of politics in different times and spaces. With their own special relations to smell, Tai and Tai Bibi bracket Saleem's signature nasal adventures, as the fate of his gifts undulates through the novel, pegged to various containments and releases from spaces. Now he is tied to ancestors where blood plays only a farcical role (he inherits his nose from Aadam Aziz, without actually being related to him), then caught in a washing machine in the bathroom; here banished to Karachi, there exiled from other places, even liberated from congested snot. In the last instance, he exchanges the gift of telepathy with the ability to smell every smell, a weapon that undercuts its usefulness repeatedly after he can no longer listen in to the minds of others, including his fellow Midnight's Children.

Tai inhabits the vast land of Kashmir and its vaster history, and Tai Bibi is found in a brothel in Karachi somewhere close to Jinnah's tomb. The ruler of the lake, of its whirlpools that swallow and expel dead white women, and of the mountains that spew and resound with the secrets and judgments of Kashmir, Tai the Boatman is the guardian of time and history—judge, executioner, martyr, and hero in more ways than Saleem can ever be. As a punishment for his trysts with Western medicine and pigskin briefcases, Tai also holds Aadam Aziz hostage with his three-year stench insurgency and drives his treasonous Westernness out of the valley. His actions can be seen as a metaphor for a form of nationalism that has often proved expedient in resisting colonization and occupation. His relation to memory and space lacks a dynamism that might allow a culture to breathe and find its way without resorting to a myth of cultural purity prior to colonization, a myth that demonizes and romanticizes earlier invaders and rulers fairly instrumentally and whimsically. This lack, this myth, and their consequences for our present lives expose the dark and potentially fascistic underbelly of any kind of idealist politics. These consequences are not limited to a heavy-handed Indian nationalism harkening back to the glory of nobles prior to British colonialism, effectively compromising class politics as well. They also extend to the nostalgia for bourgeois metropolitan life of colonial and postcolonial Bombay that one finds in Rushdie's own work. Further, they are a curse the colonized cannot break when the colony continues to symbolize a place of loss as well as a locus of enchantment.

Tai reappears, at least nominally, as Tai Bibi. Hers is a 512-year-old body, whose mimicry of smell brings to mind the strange space of action enclosed in the imitations to which the colonized are subject, a metaphor for domination producing its own unsettling resistances. Jacques Lacan writes,

> Mimicry reveals something in so far as it is distinct from what might be called an itself that is behind. The effect of mimicry is camouflage.... It is not a question of harmonizing with the background, but against a mottled background, of becoming mottled—exactly like the technique of camouflage practised in human warfare. (qtd. in Bhabha 125; ellipses in orig.)

Homi Bhabha places this mimicry next to the colonial act of producing an Other who is alike but different enough for the colonizer to remain distinct and in power. As an act that produces the colonized as subject, mimicry is a practice through which the colonized (who is made to be sensible in only a certain way) negotiates political subjectivity and thereby upsets the prescribed and predictable structures of relations with the colonizer.

The two Tais are the only mirrors available to those in the novel who have accepted the limits of desire, hope, thought, and sensuousness. Both signify a counterpoint to any claim of Saleem to his gifts, his story, and his ability to sniff out the truth. In Tai Bibi's ability to mimic all smells in order to test Saleem's "truth," the sensuous is invoked as the way to a memory of the present, to the truth of history in our beings rather than technical facticity. This illuminates modes of sensing, remembering, knowing, and expressing that are intersubjective and dialogic. To recall the space Arendt and Rancière envision, the possibility of sensing and making sensible in concert and collaboration with other individuals and entities is the very essence and the promise of politics itself. Not only are such capacities reminiscent of Rancière, they are not among those valorized by the technical-rational discourse of conventional politics. In Tai and Tai Bibi I find abundant and multidirectional links between mimicry, remembering, the production of smell, the reception of smell, the knowledge of the secrets of Kashmir, the knowledge of past lives and loves, and an inescapable sense of a different mode of power wielded by abject bodies and beings in the world into which Rushdie takes us. Their respective abjections might be seen as not always in service of, or mere props for, our protagonist's odyssey but as forces that anticipate, induce, and provoke the forms taken by the protagonist-subject. This way, we may discover more relations and interdependencies beyond the hijinks of accident and, in doing so, illuminate a range of marginal political subjects that are together constructing political realms, even in acts that seem incomprehensible or irrational to us, rather than just passively or reactively existing among static or hierarchical logics.

That scenario is a possibility that inheres in the capacities and locations of these characters, but there are no guarantees. As the story unfolds, the Tais also offer another angle on acts of remembering and sensing: that, in and of themselves, these capacities save no one, not to mention that the modes of remembering, sensing, and knowing available to us at a given moment also reek of a history of their own, of what produced them and what they produce. For instance, we see the brutality of these characters erupt as they guard history's secrets or discover those in another's heart: when they cling to their confident truths, freezing history and knowledge, make us fight, kill, and die for it, and limit individual "politics" to a place of pure and prescribed reaction. I am thinking here of how the encounter with Tai Bibi sends Saleem on a "truth" terror binge of his own that claims the Sabarmatis as casualties before he joins the military, not only buying into the truth of the state but also reinforcing it with his detective senses.

At the same time as Saleem is freed from having to carry the burden of others' deepest truths, he is relegated to being captive to all smells, and instead of expanding and making his subjectivity more abundant, this enlarged sensual scope only depletes and cheapens his subjectivity. The road from a young bourgeois lad, sold to cheap delights, running from truth, not quite knowing what to do with all the information his nose catches, to his and his nose's conscription into the Pakistani army is a slippery one. He learns politics through guilt, betrayal, and masculinist vigilantism. Petty mercantile desires, patriarchy, nationalism, and militarism never let his powers mean anything without their sanction. The cycle of loss and recovery that keeps Saleem (and us) reconciling to a new, less remarkable equilibrium for his sensibility and action also tells the story of a downward adjustment in the scope of politics and political subjectivity. The novel depicts how history and politics become external to and disconnected from us: technical, rational, objectified, utilitarian, manipulating, and manipulated.

The encounters with Tai and Tai Bibi fail to provoke a burst of Rancièrian political subjectivity in Saleem since he ultimately succumbs to antipolitical sensual economies of the market and the state rather than challenging them. At the same time, the two Tais fail to politicize their potent abjections in a way that counters the terms of nation, state, ideology, and misogyny. They could provide an effective counterpoint to existing politics or an impetus to an enhanced political subjectivity for Saleem, but they do not. In Saleem's trip to Karachi and his romance of Bombay or in prostitutes who will emote for us what they can never be, we see sad, impossible desire inherited from colonial and postcolonial ideological constructs of nationhood and identity—desire that *could* be dispensed with or reworked anew. Instead, Rushdie takes the god-shaped hole as immutable or indispensable, admitting the end of hope despite its bipolar attachments to the nostalgic and the new. In my judgment, then, the novel's overarching verdict on and tragic submission to the abiding power of the god-shaped hole obscures the fact that other sensuous, embodied practices might yet effect new forms rather than filling old ones.

This is where the idealist philosophy of Rushdie's magic realism departs from the materialist core of Rancière's philosophy and breaks loose to conjure fictive exceptions to hegemonic senses. These authors offer two ways of coping with the trauma of the present moment: Rancière's emphasis invests more faith in the abject and the miscounted than does Rushdie's, whose radical newness is available only in magic reality, tainting the Tais and dooming them (and Saleem and the *Midnight's Children* project) to failure. In this case, a begrudging courtship of the impossibly new or the magical necessitates many compromises on subjectivity and politics. Even with all the magic at the author's disposal, the novel performs a fateful normalization of perceptions and judgments already given at the start—prejudices that populate bourgeois politics to this day.[3] Maybe it is a sign of my time that Rushdie's fictive license feels more jarring than liberating, perhaps because its flight remains tethered to a structure of bourgeois individual life, operating with categorical understandings of politics as inimical to life's possibilities, an external imposition rather than an immanent logic. The denouement of the body in *Midnight's Children* is finally not a reconciliation with, but a purging of, the history that continues to irrupt into Saleem's body, at the cost of life and hope itself. Is the culprit politics per se? Or is it our (and the novel's) unfortunate reconciliation with, or ironic distance from, what politics has come to be?

> I betrayed the children of midnight. (499)
> Children, children, I am sorry. (502)

Notes

1. Also, of course, after Reagan and Thatcher and the Soviet Union and the Berlin Wall, and all those who may seem distant from Pakistan's fate but really are not; the fiction of independence and newness is always overstated to obscure the fact of entwined fates as far as the eye can see in any direction.
2. Arendt's notion of politics invokes a realm of political life that entails "the joy and gratification that arise out of being in company with our peers, out of acting together and appearing in public, out of inserting ourselves into the world by word and deed, thus acquiring and sustaining our personal identity and beginning something entirely new" (263). This sustenance of personal identity and the possibility of the new beginning are staked on the presence of a political community rightly understood as a realm of human plurality and freedom. Whenever the premises that might lead to a community of meaning in common with other free actors capable of producing such life have been razed, politics itself is in crisis; Arendt urges political judgment. She builds on Kant's notion of reflective judgment, which relies on the faculties of cognition and imagination, the ability to look at the particular, as in a work of art, and to see it from a perspective beyond the private—a gift that Saleem Sinai loses over the course of the novel. For Arendt, political judgment is necessary to counter politics as a condition wherein everything become an object, alien and external to us, and a realm to which we are attached only as consumers or spectators or manipulators, but not essentially as cohabitants or producers or authors or citizens.
3. It is interesting that this is usually the inverse of how philosophy and literature are *supposed* to behave, with their confessed partialities; here Rancière promises a little more figurality, intimacy, and possibility, and Rushdie's magic yields very confident declarations of the end of hope and an oddly reconciled paring down of the scope of subjectivity.

Works Cited

Adams, David. *Colonial Odysseys: Empire and Epic in the Modernist Novel*. Ithaca: Cornell UP, 2003.

Arendt, Hannah, and Jerome Kohn. *Between Past and Future: Eight Exercises in Political Thought*. New York: Penguin, 2006.

Bhabha, Homi. "Of Mimicry and Man: The Ambivalence of Colonial Discourse." *October* 28 (1984): 125–33.

Boyers, Robert. *The Dictator's Dictation: The Politics of Novels and Novelists*. New York: Columbia UP, 2005.

Howe, Irving. *Politics and the Novel*. New York: Columbia UP, 1992.

Kosík, Karel, and James H. Satterwhite. *The Crisis of Modernity: Essays and Observations from the 1968 Era*. Lanham: Rowman, 1995.

Marzorati, Gerald. "Rushdie in Hiding." *New York Times* 4 Nov. 1990: 30.

Piercy, Marge. "Active in Time and History." *Paths of Resistance: The Art and Craft of the Political Novel*. Ed. Isabel Allende, Charles McCarry, and Marge Piercy. Boston: Houghton, 1989. 91–123.

Rancière, Jacques, and Davide Panagia. "Dissenting Words: A Conversation with Jacques Rancière." *Diacritics* 30.2 (2000): 113–26.

Rushdie, Salman. *Midnight's Children: A Novel*. New York: Random, 2006.

Trilling, Lionel. *The Liberal Imagination*. New York: New York Review of Books, 2008.

Shame: "A Sort of Modern Fairytale"
Harold Branam

It is curious that *Shame*, Salman Rushdie's third novel, coming between his blockbusters *Midnight's Children* and *The Satanic Verses*, has not been as widely read or received as much critical attention as these other two novels. It could be argued that the three novels together form a kind of postcolonial epic or trilogy focusing on India (*Midnight's Children*), Pakistan (*Shame*), and the relationship of the subcontinent's diaspora to the former imperial power (*The Satanic Verses*). All three novels were written at the height of Rushdie's powers, are in a magic realist style, and use many of the same narrative techniques. In an interview with Anita Phillips at the time of *Shame*'s publication, Rushdie called it "the most intense writing I've ever done" (37). Like the other two novels, *Shame* won a major literary prize, France's Prix du Meilleur Livre Étranger.

Also like the other two novels, *Shame* is a complex, multilayered work, interweaving at least three strands: an allegorical bildungsroman of the fictional but politically peripheral main characters, Omar Khayyam Shakil and Sufiya Zinobia Hyder; a roman à clef political history of Pakistan from 1947 to 1982; and the author's commentary about Pakistan and this novel. In one of the commentaries, Rushdie describes *Shame* as not a "realistic novel" but "a sort of modern fairy tale" (65, 68). *Shame* also contains intertextual references to actual fairy tales (especially "Beauty and the Beast"[1]), proverbs, the Qur'an, and works by other authors including Saul Bellow, Milan Kundera, and Niccolò Machiavelli (307).

Besides the literary experience that it provides, *Shame* offers an assessment of Pakistan's history, politics, and culture. Although it is a work of fiction written by an author who admittedly never "lived there for longer than six months at a stretch" (66), *Shame* depicts the history of Pakistan from its founding in 1947 up to 1982 with a disturbing authority and prescience, significant not only for the people of Pakistan and India but also for people in the West and elsewhere. *Shame* pictures Pakistan during this period as a corrupt, violent, self-defeating country practicing repression and censorship, paranoid and aggressive toward India, dominated by the military, and uncertain of its own identity. This grim, unattractive picture might help explain why *Shame* is less read, but at the same time, it is another reason to read the novel since, unhappily, things seem not to have changed much in Pakistan since the period *Shame* covers. Among other newsworthy items, Pakistan has acquired nuclear weapons, political assassinations and terrorist attacks are still common, and in 2011, the planner of the September 11, 2001, terrorist attacks on New York and Washington, Osama bin Laden, was found hiding there. What is one to make of such a murky, unhappy, dangerous country?[2] The insights offered by *Shame* could be useful, beginning with the major one that Pakistan should not be made to feel so much shame that it explodes.

The novel itself begins during the waning years of the British Empire in "the remote border town of Q. [Quetta?]," whose "dumb-bell shape" consists of "old town and Cantt [Cantonment district], the former inhabited by the indigenous, colonized population and the latter by the alien colonizers, the Angrez, or British, sahibs" (3–4). The old town is dominated by the bazaar; Cantt by the "mirage" of the Hotel Flashman,

> whose great golden dome was cracked even then but shone nevertheless with the tedious pride of its brief doomed glory . . . under which the suited-and-booted Angrez officers and white-tied civilians and ringleted ladies with hungry eyes would congregate nightly, assembling here from their bungalows to dance and to share the illusion of being colourful. (4)

This nightly colonial ritual in a hot, sweaty place far from British shores, parodying similar scenes from writers such as Joseph Conrad and E. M. Forster, immediately shows the roots of Pakistan's future troubles: a segregated, privileged colonial elite that maintains its illusion of civilized splendor with the help of a military garrison. The British are not depicted as good role models.

Neither are the local indigenous elites, the Shakil family. The patriarch, Old Mr. Shakil, hating both the natives and the British, had "for many years remained immured in his high, fortress-like, gigantic residence . . . equidistant from the bazaar and the Cantt" (4). Here he, a widower, had in seclusion raised three daughters, nicknamed Chhunni, Munnee, and Bunny. He had also become deeply indebted to creditors and moneylenders. As the novel opens, he dies, raining down on everyone "passages of obscenity, oaths and curses of a ferocity that made the air boil violently around his bed" (3). The three closely intimate but ignorant daughters, with their "vast estates around Q . . . lost in their entirety," are "left with nothing but the unmanageably infinite mansion stuffed from floor to ceiling with possessions" (7). Upon learning this, they, "as is perhaps the universal custom of aristocratically bred persons . . . reacted to the news of their ruin by resolving to throw a party" (7).

The three sisters confirm their uppity, foolish ways by inviting mostly British guests to their extravagant party, serving alcohol, and dancing the night away to Western music. To the bazaar's delight, the party results in one of the sisters becoming pregnant, and all three again lock themselves away in their mansion. A mule-driver delivering the enormous padlock quizzes their old servant: "'For what your begums want this lock-shock now? Invasion has already occurred.' Hashmat replied, crossing her eyes for emphasis: 'May your grandsons urinate upon your pauper's grave'" (9). Thereafter, the household communicates with the world only via a dumbwaiter rigged both for the bottom to fall out and for intruders to be impaled with "eighteen-inch stiletto blades" (10). Then, in a performance deserving an Oscar, the three sisters simultaneously exhibit the same signs, symptoms, appetites, and swollen bellies of pregnancy and, together in a private room on old Mr. Shakil's deathbed, deliver the hero of the story, Omar Khayyam Shakil. (Like Omar, who is named after the Persian poet who died in

1123 CE, a number of characters are named after important historical figures, with largely comic effect.)

Western readers will understand that the sisters' performance is an effort to avoid shame, but, as the narrator emphasizes, the English word "shame" is not adequate for translating everything at stake here in their society. Instead, the narrator introduces the concept of *sharam*, "containing encyclopaedias of nuance" (33). The Urdu word *sharam* means "not only shame . . . but also embarrassment, discomfiture, decency, modesty, shyness, the sense of having an ordained place in the world, and other dialects of emotion for which English has no counterparts" (33). Sharam involves not only individual but family honor (hence the performance of all three sisters), so families will do anything to avoid it or its appearance, even to the extent of embracing shamelessness (for which the elite have better means, as shown in the way sharam operates throughout the novel). The narrator concludes, "What's left when *sharam* is subtracted? That's obvious: shamelessness" (33). The three sisters forbid Omar from feeling sharam, even as they suckle him from six breasts for six years, refuse to identify his father (who is probably British), and keep him locked in the old mansion, whose contents they pawn bit by bit to support their lifestyle. Meanwhile, Omar grows fat, roams the decaying rooms, discovers a library, accumulates knowledge (including learning several languages and hypnotism), and comes to embody shamelessness.

Society, with its pent-up passions, its simmering tensions and resentments, does not so easily forgive and forget, however. Twelve years after he is born, Omar finally ventures outside the mansion to attend school. Before he does, word gets around town that the sisters are purchasing school supplies, and a street vigil begins outside the mansion. On his first day, as Omar exits the dumbwaiter, he is greeted by a mob of the idle, the curious, the aggrieved, the vengeful, and the religious. Among the religious are the postman Muhammad Ibadalla, who has a "*gatta* or permanent bruise" on his forehead from praying, and "the beardy serpent" through whose "malign influence" Ibadalla got his job, "the local divine, the notorious Maulana Dawood" (36). As epithets and execrations fly through the air, Dawood prostates himself repeatedly at Omar's feet to call down hellfire and brimstones on the youngster's head—only to end up with a necklace of smelly old shoes thrown at the young offender, the ultimate insult, around his own head. Luckily, the schoolmaster, Mr. Eduardo Rodrigues, appears in time to rescue Omar from the mob.

These and other scenes from *Shame*'s opening chapters contain some of Rushdie's funniest writing and set a comic or satiric tone for the whole novel, even if at times the content can become grim and the comedy dark. The tone is established in large part by the novel's main narrator, who adopts a flowery, finicky style of magic realism that blends realism and fantasy, echoes authors ranging from William Faulkner ("its brief doomed glory") to Jane Austen ("perhaps the universal custom"), and mixes diction from the learned to the obscene. The narrator also takes on a fussy, digressive, evasive, and teasing personality of his own. The evasions about whether something is fact, rumor, gossip, or sheer speculation function as a blanket disclaimer and, at the same time, capture the ethos of the bazaar or "street." The teasing references to future events and even to the novel's ending whet a reader's appetite and help connect the novel's disparate parts. Altogether, the narrator could be considered the most interesting character in *Shame*—which has both good and bad implications.

The narrator could simply be described as the famously rich storytelling voice of Rushdie himself, a put-on "oral voice" that the Russian formalists call *skaz* (Teverson 49)—which entertains page by page, whatever else is going on—but, in *Shame*, it is useful to distinguish the main storytelling voice from inserted passages of authorial commentary. In these passages, Rushdie speaks more seriously, directly, and openly in his "real" voice, balancing the storyteller's playfulness with straightforward, behind-the-scenes observations. For instance, Rushdie reveals that the idea for *Shame* originated from a case of sharam in London's East End: a Pakistani father's honor killing of his teenage daughter, an only child, on suspicion of sleeping with a "white boy," an accusation later proved untrue. Rushdie was "appalled" by the gruesome story, by the friends and relatives who defended the father, and most of all, by his own "understanding." He saw "how colossal a force" sharam could be, to make a father kill his only child and, one might add, reach halfway around the world (117). He also saw powerful psychological extremes at work in "shamelessness, shame: the roots of violence" (118). Despite this, writing the dead girl's story "eluded" him until he realized that "to write about her, about shame, I would have to go back East, to let the idea breathe its favourite air" (118). In *Shame*, the character embodying shame, Sufiya Zinobia, is based on the "murdered girl" (118) and draws on other London stories about the rage and shame of street rioters, a girl attacked in the subway, and a mysterious boy who self-combusted in a parking lot.

This explanation that *Shame* was inspired by London incidents tends to exonerate Rushdie from any charges that he deliberately set out to make a direct attack on Pakistan in the novel. Instead, Rushdie seems more focused on the local racial and cultural tensions behind the incidents—a subject he expands on in his next novel, *The Satanic Verses*, and in his later collection of essays and criticism, *Imaginary Homelands* (1991). Rushdie himself resents the way the British lump all "Asians" together (117, 119), but a novel about sharam could take place almost anywhere "back East," especially India and some Arab or Islamic countries. Thus, in this sense, Pakistan seems only an incidental setting, a kind of testing site for an Eastern psychological concept that explains such things as honor killings, days of rage, and perhaps even irrational (as distinct from rational) hatred of the West.

On the other hand, by setting *Shame* in Pakistan, Rushdie could be seen to be mining sharam's mother lode. This interpretation is suggested by Rushdie's explicit set of disclaimers about where the novel takes place, which are shifting and problematic, beginning to sound like the evasive, teasing narrator: "The country in this story is not Pakistan, or not quite" (*Shame* 22); later Rushdie says, "Let it be [called]

Peccavistan" (87; Rushdie's italics). In yet another commentary, the terms change again: "If this were a realistic novel about Pakistan . . . I would be talking about my youngest sister [Sameen, to whom the novel is dedicated]. Who is twenty-two, and studying engineering in Karachi; who can't sit on her hair any more, and who (unlike me) is a Pakistani citizen" (65–66). Rushdie frankly admits he has come to know Pakistan, like his sister, only through brief visits, though he has "felt closer to each successive incarnation" (66). Despite this growing fondness, he concludes, "I think what I'm confessing is that, however I choose to write about over-there, I am forced to reflect that world in fragments of broken mirrors" (66). Therefore, he has chosen to write "a sort of modern fairytale," an innocuous story that does not "need" to "upset" anyone or be taken "too seriously." So, he notes hopefully, "no drastic action need be taken, either," such as a lawsuit or fatwā (68).

Yet everybody knows that fairy tales often have teeth. In Rushdie's case, the mouth that disclaims volubly also protests too much by itemizing what he would have to include if he were writing a "realistic novel." Among these, he lists the greenness of lawns as a measure of water thieves in a rich Karachi suburb; the Sind Club of Karachi sign warning "Woman and Dogs Not Allowed Beyond This Point"; the television executive "who once told me solemnly that pork was a four-letter word"; "genocide in Baluchistan"; knee-jerk anti-Semitism; "smuggling, the boom in heroin exports, military dictators, venal civilians, corrupt civil servants, bought judges, newspapers of whose stories the only thing that can confidently be said is that they are lies," and budgets "for defence (huge) and for education (not huge)" (66–67). In short, the authorial comments are double-edged: While seeming to issue explicit disclaimers, they actually supply anecdotal evidence that supports the narrator's "modern fairytale," as if—to do it justice—the reality of Pakistan can be described only in terms of fantasy and magic realism.

In his interview with Anita Phillips, Rushdie dropped all pretenses about where *Shame* takes place: "One of the problems with Pakistan, particularly, is that of its 30 odd years of independent history, it's almost never had a free society" (37). Because censorship had stifled Pakistani fiction, he felt that in writing *Shame*, he was "operating in completely virgin territory" that had no literary "conventions, signposts, traditions." He continued, "That is why I felt the need in the book to discuss the reality as well as the fiction . . . [to] take a fictional way and a non-fictional way of treating the same material . . . because I thought it *was* helping, it *was* providing some kind of context and some kind of extra perspective." Rushdie went on to attribute Pakistan's history of dictatorships to "a level of intellectual and moral corruption amongst the ruling elite of such intensity" that it "reads like fantasy . . . except to someone who knows Pakistan" (38).

Thus, in *Shame*, Rushdie's nonfictional commentaries also set the stage for and lead into the sordid, violent roman à clef, the Big Sharam at the center of the novel, where the magic realism becomes more realistic and the novel's tone darker. Conversely, the roman à clef goes a long way toward explaining how Pakistan got to be the way it is described in Rushdie's comments. Occupying much of the novel after the opening chapters, the roman à clef might seem to merit Aijaz Ahmad's complaint about "the infinite bleakness of *Shame*, its cage-like quality" (139) or Andrew Teverson's declaration that "*Shame*, by contrast [to *Midnight's Children*], is more obviously indebted to the darker genres of the Gothic and of tragedy," especially "classical Greek tragedy and Senecan revenge tragedy" (137). While *Shame* does have its family dynasties, revenge killings, and rulers who bring a plague on their people—even a sense of foreboding and fate building to a catastrophe—such humorless interpretations of the novel seem selective, forced, and exaggerated. Readers do not have to summon up "the ghost in *Hamlet*," like Teverson, to know that "something is rotten in the state of Pakistan" (138). Teverson himself strikes a better balance when he calls *Shame* "Rushdie's tragedy of clowns" and quotes an interview with Rushdie to the effect that the rulers in *Shame* do not measure up to tragic figures—hence, Teverson concludes, the novel's "political satire," "blackly comic effect," and "deadly banalities of corrupt uses of power" (139). In *Shame*, Rushdie gives the last word on the subject to one of his female characters, Bilquìs Hyder, who points to her husband the dictator and says, "Once there were giants. . . . Now the pygmies have taken over" (287).

The roman à clef covers the history of Pakistan from 1947 to 1982 but focuses on two main political figures, Iskander Harappa and Raza Hyder. The former is based on Zulfikar Ali Bhutto (president, 1971–73, and prime minister, 1973–77; hanged 1979), while the latter is based on General Muhammad Zia-ul-Haq (military dictator and president, 1978–88; killed in 1988 in a suspicious plane crash). A future political figure can be seen in Harappa's daughter Arjumand, who is based on Benazir Bhutto (prime minister, 1988–90 and 1993–96; assassinated 2007). While following the general course of history, Rushdie vastly simplifies, for his own fictional purposes, the careers and family lives of these historical personages. For instance, both Bhutto and Zia had sons, which is a crucial difference from the novel, and Zia lived on for years after his fictional stand-in, General Raza Hyder, is sliced to bits in the sisters' dumbwaiter. Rushdie likely focused on them not only because they were prime targets for satire but also because they were the political figures he knew best from his family visits to Pakistan. Andrew Teverson notes that Rushdie's family moved from Bombay, India, to Karachi, Pakistan, in 1964 (xv) and that "*Shame* was written at the height of this [Zia's] 'Islamisation' programme" (136). Later, in a 1988 essay collected in *Imaginary Homelands*, Rushdie summed up his views on Zia: "Pakistan under Zia has become a nightmarish, surreal land," where the "medieval, misogynistic, stultifying ideology which Zia imposed . . . in his 'Islamization' programme was the ugliest possible face of the faith" (53–54). In *Shame* itself, Rushdie expresses the anger he felt at his parents' move to Pakistan and the anger he felt again at a "senior British diplomat" who said the West could "support the dictatorship of President Zia ul-Haq" (84, 22).

The roman à clef begins abruptly at Chapter 4, after the shameless Omar has caused another case of sharam by hypnotizing and impregnating his schoolmate, the lovely Farah Zoroaster, and has gone off at age eighteen with "a scholarship at the best medical college in Karachi" (49)—not be heard of again until the age of thirty! Chapter 4 also begins with violence in Delhi just before the 1947 partition of the Indian subcontinent: Mahmoud Kemal is blown up in his movie theater, the Empire Talkies, and his queenly eighteen-year-old daughter, Bilquìs, left scorched and naked on the streets, is herded with other Muslims into the Alhambra fortress. Luckily, there she meets an army officer, another Muslim, Captain Raza Hyder, who brings her food and clothing, protects her, and soon persuades her to marry him.

After Partition, the romantic couple ends up in Karachi, Pakistan, where they experience the first difficulties of their marriage: Islamic fundamentalism as practiced by Hyder's extended family. While Captain Hyder stays at the army base, Bilquìs sleeps with forty other women crowded together in the *zenana* (women's wing) of his grandmother Bariamma's home. In the clammy darkness, all the women in their individual beds pretend to sleep while husbands slip in to make love to them: "Being married did not absolve a woman of the shame and dishonour that results from the knowledge that she sleeps regularly with a man . . . when pregnancies occurred they did so as if by magic, as if all conceptions were immaculate and all births virgin" (71).

The unmarried Rani Humayun, Raza's second cousin, makes fun of "the household sleeping arrangements" and "the forty thieves": "I tell you, Billoo, these married men and ladies are having a pretty good time in this joint family set-up. I swear, maybe uncles with nieces, brothers with their brothers' wives, we'll never know who the children's daddies really are!" (70). She concludes, "This arrangement which is supposed to be made for decency etcetera is just the excuse for the biggest orgy on earth" (70–71).

In this manner, queenly Bilquìs is introduced to a certain bizarre mentality in Pakistan, Land of the Pure (*pak*), where, it is suggested, religion, customs, and family can be smothering. Privately, Bilquìs muses, "O God. Ignoramuses from somewhere. Backward types, village idiots, unsophisticated completely, and I am stuck with them" (71–72). But to Raza she intones sweetly, "Much to be said for the old traditions," and is alarmed when he agrees (72). Her education continues when she learns that the women define "a good man" as one "who did not beat his wife" but that husbands "all hit!" (73). As the "newest arrival, the junior member" in "the empire of Bariamma," Bilquìs is "the officially designated poor-thing," lowest ranking in the zenana hierarchy (72–73). Her worst zenana experience, however, occurs when she becomes pregnant, endures her pregnancy while Raza is away fighting Indian forces on the Kashmiri frontier, and, after he returns, delivers a stillborn son: "And under Bariamma's roof little sneers and comments began to be aimed at this unnatural female who could produce nothing but dead babies" (83). The campaign of spite comes to a head when "a particularly vicious cousin named Duniyazad Begum hissed night-dark insults":

> The disgrace of your barrenness, Madam, is not yours alone. Don't you know that shame is collective? The shame of any one of us sits on us all and bends our backs. See what you're doing to your husband's people, how you repay the ones who took you in when you came penniless and a fugitive from that godless country over there. (83)

The insults result in a clawing, hair-pulling fight and the grandmother's whining expulsion of Bilquìs from the zenana: "When you leave this house your shame leaves with you" (84).

Meanwhile, Bilquìs's friend Rani Humayun does not fare any better. Eighteen-year-old Rani has "landed one of the prize catches of the marriage season" and anticipates escape from the zenana "to wed the fair-skinned, foreign-educated, sensually full-lipped young millionaire Iskander Harappa" (70). But patriotism during the Kashmiri conflict requires a delay in her wedding. At the wedding itself, the groom's procession is disrupted by a fat fellow whose horse splays under him, and the party afterward is interrupted by somber news that "the Prime Minister had been assassinated," to which the fat fellow drunkenly cries, "That bastard! If he's dead he's dead. Why does he want to come here and spoil the party?" (79). The Rabelaisian fat fellows turns out to be Omar Khayyam Shakil, who "at thirty . . . re-enters our little tale as a character with a high reputation as a doctor and a low reputation as a human being, a degenerate of whom it is often said that he appears to be entirely without shame" (79). Rani immediately recognizes Omar as her enemy, the boon companion of Iskander Harappa in a riotous life of dissipation (79). While they frequent the dens, brothels, and fancy hotels of Karachi, Rani, pregnant and later mother of Arjumand, is deposited in the "backyard of the universe" at Mohenjo, "the Harappa family estate in Sind" (93). Rani learns about her husband's dissolute lifestyle from his equally foul-mouthed cousin, Little Mir Harappa, who rides up with a gang of armed horsemen and trashes the estate in a revenge quarrel over a whore, and from Bilquìs, who by telephone confirms the fat doctor's and Iskander's playboy reputations. Rani, living on the outback estate with aging and disrespectful servants, takes to sitting on the veranda, talking to herself, and knitting shawls that graphically record Iskander's wrongs.

Rushdie's depiction of these and other women in *Shame* has taken some criticism, especially from feminists and Marxists looking for a liberation scenario, as noted by Teverson (140–41). Teverson defends Rushdie's depiction of women repressed by patriarchy as possibly motivating "oppositional movements" (142), and so does Rushdie. In their 1983 interview, Anita Phillips complained that the female characters in *Shame* "seemed to be almost entirely gossips, whores or bitches." "The men aren't that nice either," Rushdie replied, then went on to explain how Pakistani women are "repressed" and "distorted" by the "Moslem society" and by power relations with men; hence, he concludes, "a lot of women are very gossipy, bitchy and backstabbing." Rushdie quickly added that the "men have similar distortions," then connected the gender dynamics to the country's dictatorships, as if dictatorship were modeled in the household (38).

In the interview, Rushdie also says, "I'm much fonder of the women in *Shame*" than of the men, and this sentiment is echoed and reflected in the novel itself (38). Deep into the novel Rushdie confesses,

> I had thought, before I began, that what I had on my hands was an almost excessively masculine tale. . . . But the women seem to have taken over; they marched in from the peripheries of the story to demand the inclusion of their own tragedies, histories and comedies, obliging me . . . to see my 'male' plot refracted, so to speak, through the prisms of its reverse and 'female' side. (180–81)

Sure enough, the women's stories take up the larger part of the roman à clef, and the men are perceived and characterized mainly from the women's perspectives. This is because, says Rushdie, any society that "crushes its women . . . breeds repressions of other kinds as well" (181). While he hopes that "not all women are crushed by any system" and shares the common belief that Pakistan's "women are much more impressive than her men . . . their chains, nevertheless, are no fictions" (181; Rushdie's ellipsis).

Women do wield power in *Shame* but mostly of a negative, spiteful, or self-defeating kind: Rani knits her shawls, Bilquìs cheats on her husband, her daughter Naveed "Good News" Hyder commits suicide after having twenty-seven children, Arjumand "virgin Ironpants" Harappa tries to deny her femininity, and Bariamma rules her zenana and the sniping females there. All of these women seem to share some symptoms of repression and thus kinship with the allegorical character Sufiya Zinobia Hyder. Before Sufiya is born, Bilquìs and Raza Hyder embrace the illusion that the expected baby will be a son, a reincarnation of the earlier stillborn son. Instead, they suffer the second bitter disappointment of having a daughter. Thus, Sufiya Zinobia's original shame is in being born a girl, and she is never allowed to forget it. She is said to have blushed in shame at birth, and the blushing continues, with blushes so hot that she scorches people who touch her. At seventeen months, she comes down with a "brain fever" that leaves her mentally disabled (100), or the cause might have been "repeated blows to the head" (119). Regardless, her condition also leaves her "preternaturally receptive to . . . a host of unfelt feelings" around her, "emotions that should have been felt but were not," including shame, which she soaks up "like a sponge" (124–25). Inevitably these surrogate feelings build up inside Sufiya Zinobia until, at the age of twelve, she discovers "in the labyrinths of her unconscious self the hidden path that links *sharam* to violence" (144). Provoked by family tensions, the hot Loo wind, and loudly gobbling turkeys next door, the poor, frail girl attacks and kills all "two hundred and eighteen turkeys" by ripping "off their heads" and pulling "their guts up through their necks" (143).

When she is nineteen, Sufiya Zinobia has another such superhuman outburst at her sister's wedding. In the novel's most hilarious episode, Naveed creates a furor and scandalizes everyone—immediate family, extended family, and hundreds of guests—by rejecting the arranged marriage the night before and announcing a new groom. Raza Hyder gets out his gun to shoot her but cannot bring himself to do it. Instead, late-night phone calls are made, new plans hastily arranged, and "little handwritten erratum slips" created: "'Owing to circumstances beyond our control,' read the little white chitties of humiliation, 'the part of husband will be taken by Police Capt. Talvar Ulhaq'" (177). But all the sharam is too much for Sufiya Zinobia to soak up and absorb: At the wedding ceremony, she launches herself on the new groom, almost twists his head off, and bites a huge bloody chunk out of his neck.

On this occasion, as after the earlier explosion, Sufiya Zinobia also suffers some kind of autoimmune reaction in which she turns her rage inward on herself, and Dr. Omar Khayyam Shakil's services are needed. An expert in immunology, Omar works with Sufiya Zinobia for years and writes a treatise, *The Case of Miss H.*, which "becomes famous in medical circles" (147). He also falls in love with her, and, after years of agonizing, finally asks her parents for her hand in marriage. He is a fat fifty-year-old, and she is a small nineteen-year-old with a "mental age" of "about six and a half" (169). Her father is at first skeptical of the match, but Bilquìs points out that a "woman does not have to be a brainbox" and that the doctor has been the girl's best caregiver (168), so they consent to the marriage. To the narrator, the marriage seems so obscene that he pretends to have a massive headache in trying to explain and justify it, but obviously it fits right in with the novel's allegory.

As for the other men, their stories either are part of the women's or are wedged into the novel's nooks and crannies, sometimes in summary form. Upset when his rivals Raza Hyder and Little Mir Harappa are appointed ministers, Iskander Harappa, encouraged by his ambitious daughter, is roused at the age of forty to change his dissolute ways and become a politician. With his charm, sophistication, speaking ability, and astuteness, he becomes quite a successful one, getting an appointment in President A.'s government, quitting the government and forming the Popular Front when President A. becomes unpopular, and setting himself up to be elected prime minister when President A.'s government topples. He even manages to become prime minister, hold on to the position, and prosper after defeat in the election and defeat in the resulting civil war between West and East Pakistan (later Bangladesh). But his wife, Rani, has the bitter last words on his six-year reign in her series of eighteen embroidered shawls titled "The Shamelessness of Iskander the Great," which depict viciousness, domestic spying, torture, police corruption, "international shame," rigged elections, "Iskander and the Death of Democracy," and genocide in gruesome detail (203–4).

One crucial mistake Iskander Harappa makes is appointing General Raza Hyder the head of the armed forces: "This single error proved to be the undoing of the ablest statesman who ever ruled that country which has been so tragically misfortunate, so accursed, in its heads of state" (189). After becoming the hero of the Kashmiri conflict, "Old Razor Guts" Hyder is dispatched to Q. to quell unruly "local tribals" (90–91). While there, under the influence of Maulana Dawood, "the ancient divine" (98), his methods are so harsh and counterproductive—jailing the local administrator (who later disappears), replacing civil law with military rule, and hanging scores of tribals—that he is eventually replaced and assigned to a dead-end job in Karachi. Harappa should have taken warning from this premonitory alarm and from the fact that Maulana Dawood accompanies Hyder back to Karachi and begins living in Hyder's household, but Harappa thinks that rescuing and elevating Hyder to head of military will make him eternally grateful. Six years later, when another election is disputed and things become unruly in Pakistan, Commander-in-Chief Hyder takes over in a military coup. Hyder has Harappa first placed under house arrest, then charged with ordering the revenge killing of Little Mir Harappa and thrown into jail, where after two years of solitary confinement in awful conditions and under a death sentence, Harappa is both shot "through the heart" and hanged (251).

At the beginning of those eight years, the novel's setting shifts to the new northern capital of Islamabad, and during the disputed election, the roman à clef begins to merge with the allegorical ending. The mysterious deaths of four adolescent males in the slums—"their heads had been wrenched off their necks by some colossal force"—hardly make headlines (228) but in the Hyder household arouse intense suspicions. It turns out that Sufiya Zinobia is "getting worse" (248), the Beast inside her growing. This time her doctor-husband cannot help her, she briefly attacks him, and even chaining her in the bricked-up attic fails: She breaks through both chains and bricks to escape. Soon people—even Chairman Iskander Harappa just before his arrest—are hearing "about the rumoured escape of an albino panther in the wooded hills of Bagheeragali some forty miles away" (233). Apparently there is so much free-floating sharam in Pakistan that the scope of the sopping-up operation has vastly expanded.

As time goes by, "stories of the white panther" spread across the country: "From every out-of-the-way corner of the nation, it seemed, the tale of the panther was traveling to the capital," stories about "murders of animals and men, villages raided in the dark, dead children, slaughtered flocks, blood-curdling howls" (268–69). These stories coincide with Dictator Hyder's Islamization program, his growing unpopularity, and his personal mental disturbances until finally his regime topples. Hyder, Bilquìs, and Omar escape raging crowds in the streets only by donning women's burqas and taking back-road buses headed southwest—a "flight through an exploding land" (283). They hope to reach Iranian "sanctuary across the frontier, in that neighbouring country of priest-kings," but after days, they make it only as far as Q (284). Here, in Omar's crumbling ancestral mansion, Bilquìs dies of malaria and Hyder is diced to pieces in the sisters' stiletto-equipped dumbwaiter. Here, also, the long-awaited consummation of the marriage between Omar and Sufiya Zinobia, shamelessness and shame, finally takes place. In the novel's last pages she, "on all fours, naked, coated in mud and blood and shit," climbs the stairs to his bedroom, rises "on her hind legs with her forepaws outstretched" (304), twists off his head, and then explodes in a nuclear "fireball," sending up a mushroom cloud "in the shape of a giant, grey and headless man, a figure of dreams, a phantom with one arm lifted in a gesture of farewell" (305). So ends *Shame*, Salman Rushdie's "modern fairytale" about a country living, according to the Hegira (Muslim calendar) used in the novel, in the fourteenth and fifteenth centuries.

Notes

1. See Deszcz's article, cited below.
2. For a more optimistic, in-depth view of Pakistan, although it confirms some of Rushdie's harsh assessment, see Lieven.

Works Cited

Ahmad, Aijaz. *In Theory: Classes, Nations, Literatures*. London: Verso, 1992.
Deszcz, Justyna. "Salman Rushdie's Attempt at a Feminist Fairytale Reconfiguration in *Shame*." *Folklore* 115.1 (Apr. 2004): 27–44.
Lieven, Anatol. *Pakistan: A Hard Country*. New York: PublicAffairs, 2011.

Rushdie, Salman. *Imaginary Homelands: Essays and Criticism, 1981–1991*. London: Granta, 1991.

———. "An Interview with Salman Rushdie." By Anita Phillips. *Marxism Today* Sept. 1983: 36–39.

———. *Shame: A Novel*. 1983. New York: Random, 2008.

Teverson, Andrew. *Salman Rushdie*. Manchester: Manchester UP, 2007.

Shilling Postcolonial Identity: Acting, Advertising, and the Capitalist Economy in *The Satanic Verses*
Lynn Wells

Fredric Jameson describes the postmodern subject's spatial orientation as expressive of "a new and historically original dilemma, one that involves our insertion as individual subjects into a multidimensional set of radically discontinuous realities, whose frames range . . . all the way to the unimaginable decentering of global capital itself" (413). The postmodern citizen drifts through the kaleidoscopic hall of mirrors that was late twentieth-century consumer society, surrounded by prefabricated media and marketing images that furnish a series of virtual "selves" for the individual to emulate, adopt, and discard. No longer the familiar haven of the modernist flâneur, now the apotheosis of capitalism's alienating omnipresence, the city has become the scene of the postmodern subject's radical experience of perceptual vertigo and personal fragmentation. For international migrants, contemporary urban life is particularly disorienting, as they suffer both the "schizophrenia" induced by mass consumerism (Jameson 26) and the divisive effects of being torn between an old and a new culture, with neither feeling like home. In the case of migrants from formerly colonized nations, this state of displacement is exacerbated by a sense of having been "conquered" twice: first in their native lands and then again in their country of destination, often by the same cultural dominant. Within that global context, the cosmopolitan Western urban center functions as the site of the postcolonial migrants' hostile encounter with a culture that resists their integration and identification with it.

In Salman Rushdie's *The Satanic Verses*, contemporary London and Bombay serve as the primary settings for the struggle for coherent selfhood enacted by the novel's two main characters, Gibreel Farishta and Saladin Chamcha, both Indian-born men who find themselves trying to shape new identities in 1980s England. While the London in the novel is a society dominated by the ruthless self-interest of Margaret

Thatcher's right-wing capitalism, Bombay is similarly depicted as a city driven by corporate greed and superficial celebrity, manifested in the glitzy Bollywood film industry and the growing presence of American-style advertising and businesses. The international spread of American corporate power overshadows both capitalist cultures; Chamcha's friend George, commenting on the devastating industrial accident at the Union Carbide plant in Bhopal, comments: "What is Amrika for us? . . . It's not a real place. Power in its purest form, disembodied, invisible" (56).

Both Gibreel, a Bombay film star in exile in London, and Chamcha, an expatriate Indian anglophile working as a commercial voice-over artist, are affected by the ubiquity of late capitalism and the double disintegration engendered by the clashing postmodern and postcolonial conditions. In his essay "In Good Faith," Rushdie describes his protagonists' different reactions to their cultural alienation:

> *The Satanic Verses* is the story of two painfully divided selves. In the case of one, Saladin Chamcha, the division is secular and societal: he is torn, to put it plainly, between Bombay and London, between East and West. For the other, Gibreel Farishta, the division is spiritual, a rift in the soul. He has lost his faith and is strung out between his immense need to believe and his new inability to do so. The novel is 'about' their quest for wholeness. (397)

This description, however, belies the complexity of the novel's development of their identities as multiple and inherently volatile as a result of their complicity with late twentieth-century consumer society.

As actors, Gibreel and Chamcha are both skilled at assuming various roles and at exploiting the moneymaking enterprises associated with their talents—popular film, television, advertising, publicity, theater—that form part of city life. With their ability to metamorphose into different selves, Gibreel and Chamcha are exemplary citizens of contemporary culture. Douglas Kellner argues that "postmodern identity . . . is constituted theatrically through role-playing and image construction" (153). As Kellner goes on to posit, though, such multiplicity has its dangers: "It is easy to fall into, to become the roles that one plays . . . when one radically shifts identity at will, one might lose control, one might become pathologically conflicted and divided, disabled from autonomous thought and action" (153). As a result of Gibreel's tendency to serve as the projection of others' desires, particularly those of the capitalist system that has given him fame, he literally falls victim to the role of archangel that he had played in the Bombay "theological" movies. Consequently, he finds himself overwhelmed by retributive ghosts and divine visions from the personal history and Islamic heritage he thought he had neatly abandoned when leaving India. Gibreel's unstable sense of self and infiltration by the past leave him shattered, mentally precarious to the point of suicide. Chamcha, on the other hand, chooses his own role as "goodandproper Englishman" (*SV* 43), rejecting his Indian background in favor of an idealized notion of English superiority. This cultural deference leaves him vulnerable to being reconstructed by English racism, "the power of description" (168) that turns him into a devilish goat-man; the London underworld of nighttime police raids and immigrant hideouts provides the forum for his humiliation and eventual recovery. While Gibreel's perceptions of London grow manifold and increasingly phantasmagoric, Chamcha's view of the city becomes more manageable as he regains control over his splintered identity. Chamcha survives by embracing the hard-hearted tactics of self-preservation and promotion of Thatcher's policies and by manipulating for his own benefit the fluid self-image that cultural and market-driven forces had controlled.

Gibreel and Chamcha's association begins with their accidental and implausible arrival in England as the survivors of a plane crash caused by a terrorist's bomb. The two men intertwine, merging in an "angelicdevilish fall" (5) that sets the stage for their shifting and ambiguous identities to come. They are "conjoined opposites" (426) but also adversaries, with the city serving as their cosmic battleground.

The characters' habit of blending into one another suggests that their identities are equally malleable. As Aleid Fokkema contends, though, Gibreel possesses a solid "psychological core," an "original self" (58–59) of which he continues to be aware even during his most disruptive visions. In this respect, Gibreel exemplifies the Ovidian notion of selfhood, in which the soul remains constant despite outward changes ("*continuous*—that is, joined to and arising from his past"), as opposed to the Lucretian alternative embodied by Chamcha, who remakes himself entirely with each metamorphosis, shedding his own history and becoming "a creature of *selected* discontinuities, a *willing* re-invention" (*SV* 427). Because Chamcha's erratic state of being makes him "receptive to evil" whereas Gibreel's consistency gives him emotional and ethical integrity, Fokkema claims that the novel ultimately advocates the Ovidian paradigm over the Lucretian (61). Yet, significantly, it is Gibreel who dies in despair, losing the contest to the morally questionable and essentially centerless Chamcha.

One way of understanding this seeming contradiction is by looking at those elements of Gibreel's character that undermine his viability despite his fundamentally stable nature. Since his childhood as a poor boy carrying tiffins through the streets of Bombay, Gibreel has been attuned to the basic priority of the business world: to create the conditions in which buyers will want to buy what you have to sell. He himself was apparently born as the perfect commodity, for "from the beginning, it seemed, he could fulfil people's most secret desires without having any idea how he did it" (19). Before going to England, Gibreel turns this ability into a profitable movie career, bringing to life in seductive forms figures from India's many religions that correspond with his audiences' intimate conceptions of the divine. His success continues offscreen, where he enjoys an irresistible power over women. At the same time, though, he exercises almost no will over his professional affairs, relinquishing control of his fate to the producers who hold his contracts and being pushed from set to set in a wheelchair like an invalid. He soon becomes inseparable from his many movie roles, so much so that his films mysteriously stop projecting and his publicity photos all shrivel and fade after he leaves India. Gibreel's "core self" therefore becomes supplanted by projections of other people's desires, formulated by a capitalist context in which he puts himself in a position of powerlessness.

With his decision to leave India, Gibreel aims to dissolve his former identity, to "be born again" (3); he capers on the English beach after landing, ready to start again in his new nation. Yet the London that Gibreel encounters manifests his inner turmoil as he abandons himself to the disintegrative pressures that have followed him there from Bombay. Even after he accepts that the life he had planned to make for himself in England is impossible, Gibreel resists the escalating visions until he suffers a psychological and metaphysical crisis that causes him to give in to his extraordinary calling.

Gibreel's divine visions take two forms: a retelling of the founding of the Muslim religion in the seventh century and stories of contemporary tests of that faith. Much has been written about the controversial aspects of Rushdie's version of the creation of Islam, in which the prophet Muhammad is parodically renamed Mahound—"the Devil's synonym" (93)—and Archangel Gabriel is replaced by the character Gibreel, who dictates the holy verses that form the Recitation (Qur'an) but is overwhelmed with a satanic urge to tell lies. What are often overlooked are the capitalistic elements in Rushdie's account, particularly the strong correspondences between the depiction of the holy city of Mecca—renamed Jahilia—and those of the other two urban centers in the novel. Like modern-day London and Bombay, Jahilia is a highly competitive society focused on commercial gain, with its various temples vying for profits from the city's many pilgrim visitors. Mahound, frequently characterized as a "businessman" (92), introduces a threat to this profitable economy when he declares the singularity of God (Allah) and is then suspected of acting on mercenary motives when he temporarily accedes to the divinity of three goddesses in an apparent deal with the city's grandee, Karim Abu Simbel, for greater security and privileges. Even one of Mahound's close associates, pointedly named Salman, questions the ethics of his master, a former businessman who seems to have conveniently created an archangel correspondent that "handed down the management decisions of this highly corporate, if non-corporeal, God" (364).

Gibreel's contemporary visions are similarly focused on capitalistic themes. In the brief narrative of the exiled imam plotting the overthrow of the empress Ayesha, the zealous leader resorts to using a pop singer, Bilal X (modeled on Cat Stevens), to infiltrate the thoughts of his compatriots over the radio and incite a revolution against the very American consumer society that produced the singer. In the longer narrative about Ayesha, the miraculous Indian girl surrounded by clouds of butterflies, there is also a conflict between Western values and radical faith. When Ayesha convinces Mishal, the wife of a business owner, that she must make a pilgrimage to Mecca with members of her home village in order to be healed of her terminal breast cancer, her husband tries to tempt her from her plans with the comfort of his expensive car and promises of high-tech medical treatments. Yet Mishal is unshakeable in her conviction, and Ayesha moves the pilgrims relentlessly toward their doomed crossing of the Arabian Sea, the parting of which is visible only to those of steadfast faith. The march itself becomes the subject of media attention, with Ayesha transformed into a celebrity emblazoned on billboards and sponsors clamoring to have their businesses advertised along the route. In all of Gibreel's visions, the tension between Western capitalistic priorities and Eastern traditions of faith and asceticism contribute to his radically divided psyche.

Gibreel's angelic identity continues to be embroiled in the logic of the film industry. During his visions, he is likened at various points to a camera, spectator, or actor, helplessly manipulated by a higher power. Film producer Whisky Sisodia's idea to cast him as the archangel in scripts based on his own dream narratives does not help the two halves of his existence to cohere; rather, he becomes more vividly aware that there is a "splitting . . . not in him, but in the universe" (351). The division becomes intolerable when, winched up onstage for a publicity stunt, he looks out and sees people wearing rubber horns, the commodified sign of the devil. Gibreel's confusion of marketing for reality in this case leads him to choose the "left-hand," or sinister, "fork" (352) of the universe, eschewing his secular career for the path of divine retribution.

Like Gibreel, Chamcha is the product of a capitalist mindset that finds its perfect expression in the entertainment industry. His father, Changez Chamchawala, has instilled in his son the principle that identity can be bought, sold, and recreated at will. After his wife Nasreen died, Changez paid his servant to play her part. He uses his fortune to protect traditional Indian paintings from being carried away by American collectors, yet his national allegiance is secondary to his financial adventurism. "One day I will also take the dollars," he says. "Not for the money. For the pleasure of being a whore. Of becoming nothing. Less than nothing" (70–71). Chamcha's introduction to this kind of cultural prostitution came when his father "made a man" of him by humiliating him into paying for everything during his first visit to England from a billfold of pounds sterling that he had found as a boy and had had to turn over for parental safekeeping (43).

The adult Chamcha is proud to have conquered his new situation, aided by his "gift for accents" (59), which facilitated his conversion into an English gentleman in addition to providing a lucrative income. Yet his acceptance by the English requires certain compromises. On television, his Indianness has to be concealed, so that he appears either as a disembodied voice shilling products or as the heavily made-up extraterrestrial Maxim Alien. While Chamcha believes that his acting talent has given him control over his image in England, it in fact positions him to be made into the invisible alien that he is as an immigrant relative to the racially and financially dominant culture.

Whereas Chamcha's first trip to his dream city was as a legitimate immigrant with paid tuition, his journey back to England after a tour of India with his theater troupe, with its unexpected hijacking, forces him to enter without identification or money. On the flight, Chamcha gradually discerns that the England to which he is returning will be substantially different from the one he had left. The transmutation of reality is also visible on the ground, where the colors of the sky and snow suddenly appear wrong, and Chamcha surmises that he has fallen into "some other place, not England or perhaps not-England, some counterfeit zone, rotten borough, altered state" (132). Since the nation acts for Chamcha, as it does for Gibreel, as a tableau of his psychic workings, it seems that he is entering a period of crisis brought on by the destabilization of his English identity.

Once he realizes that his survival is at stake, though, Chamcha is prepared to throw off that mask without hesitation and evinces a formidable determination to remake himself. While falling, he realizes that "what had taken him over was the will to live . . . and the first thing it did was to inform him that it wanted nothing to do with his pathetic personality, that half-reconstructed affair of mimicry and voices" (9). Chamcha does not hesitate to exert his willpower over his circumstances to safeguard his own existence, even if that means casting off the English facade he has worked so hard to cultivate.

Chamcha's resolve to take charge of his situation is not enough to prevent his arrest as an illegal alien or his transmogrification into a devil because he has no access to his "*assets*" (61) that can legitimate his English citizenship. Divested of his property, Chamcha must face the police virtually naked, brutalized for his goatish characteristics. Nevertheless, he manages to turn his impotent position into one of relative strength; he tells the officer to check the computer for his personal and professional registrations, exploiting the very surveillance system covertly designed to oppress immigrants and dissidents. Once this information has been verified, Chamcha must be released, but he cannot reclaim his rightful spot in society owing to the bestial conversion that is the lasting effect of his humiliating experience.

Chamcha comes to know a different side of London under the harsh economic policies of the Thatcher government, a shadowy world in which newcomers without money live in poverty and intimidation. Although he rejects the consolation that he is now among his "own people" (253), Chamcha is reduced to a state of terrorized immobility like that of the illegal aliens hiding at the Shandaar Café. Nonetheless, despite the setbacks, Chamcha retains his commitment to remake England in the image of his new, nondeferential self. His first scheme is to seek help from the entertainment industry that had previously given him a level of security. He finds, though, that his transformation into an undesirable immigrant has extended into London proper, as he has been fired from *The Aliens Show* for being too "racial." The television mogul Hal Valance tells him that "ethnics don't watch ethnic shows.... They want fucking *Dynasty*, like everyone else" (265). The predominance of American-style cultural imperialism fits with the ethos of Thatcherite England, in which the free market replaces all other priorities. Mishal, one of the café owner's daughters, defines Thatcherism as an essentially racist undertaking: "The emphasis is on small-scale enterprises and the cult of the individual, right? In other words, five or six white bastards murdering us, one individual at a time" (284). However, the immigrant community is not exempt from the new economic thinking. Mishal, her sister, and her mother exploit poor families unable to get into public housing. Chamcha soon believes that everyone in the contemporary English reality is out to serve his or her own interests: "I am a man, Chamcha realized, who does not know the score, living in an amoral, survivalist, get-away-with-it world" (263). With this realization, he understands that his best chance at coping successfully with this abnormality rests not with others, but with himself.

Paradoxically, his strategy involves an acceptance of his metamorphosis into an enemy in his own country. He decides to play this latest part to the hilt, to become "loud, stenchy, hideous, outsize, grotesque, inhuman, powerful" (289); this voluntary submission is the first stage in a transformation that will enable him to use his monstrosity to overcome his adversity. Chamcha becomes a heroic image of racial abjection, symbolized by the rubber devils' horns worn by the oppressed immigrants. This commodification of the immigrants' suppressed rage against the national government acts as an ironic commentary on the power of capitalism, as does the ritualistic melting of a statue of Prime Minister Thatcher at the Club Hot Wax near the Shandaar Café. Despite his own experiences, however, Chamcha is not interested in serving as leader of the downtrodden, since his motivations, like everyone else's in the capitalist society, have become selfish rather than communal.

Instead, Chamcha focuses his energies on taking revenge against Gibreel, who maintains the approval of English society that Chamcha himself has lost. Gibreel never suffers the overt racial discrimination that Chamcha does since he is able to project an acceptable image of himself as a celebrity. In terms of the two kinds of "ideas" contrasted throughout the novel, Gibreel represents the first one, the sort that "compromises, does deals, accommodates itself to society, aims to find a niche, to survive" (335), the category to which Chamcha belonged before his devilish conversion. Rejected by the capitalist world he thought would sustain him, Chamcha undergoes a paroxysm of anger so intense that it restores him to human form, finally leaving him free to become the second kind of idea, the nonconformist, "bloody-minded" (335) kind that will stop at nothing to shape people and events to its own will.

Following his return to human form, Chamcha demands restitution from the society that has deprived him of his rights. He reclaims his home but not his wife, Pamela, the epitome of all things English. Yet the reclamation of property is not sufficient to satisfy Chamcha's resentment against Gibreel, "Mister Perfecto, portrayer of gods, who always landed on his feet, was always forgiven his sins, loved, praised, adored" (294). He refocuses his attention on Gibreel as the personification of the societal forces that caused his downfall.

Chamcha's obsession with destroying Gibreel preoccupies the later part of the novel and takes the form of an elaborate scheme in which Chamcha returns to his facility with mimicry to convince his adversary of his girlfriend's infidelity, thus accelerating Gibreel's descent into madness. Rejected by English society, Chamcha is desperate to define himself against it, even in negative terms, using the very skills that the capitalist system has taught him to pursue the darling of that culture: machination, exploitation, and remorseless self-interest. It is significant that, during his persecution of Gibreel, Chamcha thinks of himself as a *"confidence man"* (440) like the minor character Billy Battuta, who goes after his victims because he can get away with it.

Chamcha triumphs over his nemesis and thereby takes his symbolic revenge against the English, but this comes at the expense of regressing to the type of superficial selfhood he had sworn to renounce and of becoming like the amoral society around him. His continuous exposure to late twentieth-century media, especially television, exacerbates his sense that he has become the creature of a world in which all reality has been replaced by whirling images with no referential depth, the brainchildren of advertisers and corporate sponsors. While channel surfing before his showdown with Gibreel, Chamcha muses that "the effect of all this box-watching was to put a severe dent in what remained of his idea of the normal, average quality of the real" (406).

During this same scene, however, Chamcha takes note of one show that intimates a way for him to live in the contemporary context while constructing a more stable identity. Chamcha watches a gardening program describing a "chimeran graft" (406)—an English tree with another variety grafted onto it—and considers it a metaphor for his own situation. He intuits that he should be able to meld the foreign part of himself with his English identity, to be both Indian and English in a way that is not divisive.

His final trip to India allows him to implement this notion and to find alternative values to the ruthlessness of late capitalism. On the flight, he leaves his capitalistic self behind and recognizes the defeat of that system at its own hands in a magazine article about Hal Valance, whose "sanitized" *Aliens Show* has failed (517). The presence of Whisky Sisodia on the plane, touting the goddess of wealth as the proper deity for the times while harassing the flight attendants, shows the world of big-money entertainment in an obscene light. Chamcha perceives in him postmodern identity in its most distressingly shallow and incoherent form: "O, the dissociations of which the human mind is capable . . . O, the conflicting selves jostling and joggling within these bags of skin" (519). When Chamcha reaches India, though, he learns that having multiple aspects to one's personality need not be disorienting, so long as integration occurs around humane values that position the individual in relation to others, rather than around the priorities of self-centered acquisition central to consumer society.

Chamcha's English existence had been founded on his total break with the past. By severing ties with his father, Chamcha felt that he had become his own man, while in fact he had developed Changez's tendency to manipulate others for his own gratification. Weakened by his final illness, Changez no longer threatens his son's autonomy, and Chamcha perceives in his dying father a beneficial part of himself, his own history, that had persisted despite his denial of it. Chamcha's nascent power to accommodate these disparate facets of himself is made possible by love, which allows him to see his father as a separate being for the first time. The same kind of self-serving attitude that Chamcha had directed toward his father had characterized his other relationships as well: with his wife, with Gibreel, and with his friend Zeeny, who had encouraged him to reconcile with his heritage. On this visit, however, Chamcha accepts his Indian background and appreciates Zeeny on her own terms; he even enters into her sense of communal responsibility by participating in a human chain uniting people across the country.

In return for his altruistic feelings, Chamcha is rewarded with the kind of reformed identity he had imagined for himself during the descent from the plane: "His old English life, its bizarreries, its evils, now seemed very remote, even irrelevant . . . this looked like the start of a new phase, in which the world would be solid and real" (534). In this "new phase," Chamcha reclaims his original name and inherits some of his father's property and estate, but the contact with his personal history is not debilitating. Rather, he is able to arrive at the state of "historical immediacy" that Homi Bhabha proposes as the optimum condition for the postcolonial migrant, in which "the past dissolves in the present, so that that future becomes (once again) an *open question*" (219). Standing with Zeeny at the very of end of the novel waiting for bulldozers to demolish his family home, Chamcha faces a future in which he can live comfortably in India or elsewhere, secure in having an identity that, while multifaceted, will withstand the vertiginous effects of global contemporary living.

Gibreel, on the other hand, is never able to take control of his fractured personality and ultimately finds the postmodern world unbearable. By embracing his angelic side, he hopes to achieve the wholeness of character that he did not get by turning his back on his heritage. His design to impose "clarity, at all costs" (353) on London society ends in disaster, as each time he tries to use his delusional powers as an angel to reshape the city, it shifts under his grasp, reflecting his own unstable mental state. He vows to cleanse London of its errors, to reach into the exploitive hearts of men such as the pimps at King's Cross and burn them to purity with the fire of their own desires. Yet this effort at attaining self-unity through the single-minded exercise of his seraphic function is doomed, since he is never free from the economic taint that he seeks to purge from English society.

The interpenetration of Gibreel's commercial and divine roles becomes so profound that he loses all sense of reality. He murders both Allie and Whiskey Sisodia, then takes his own life, the ultimate act of self-abnegation, with the gun hidden inside Changez's magic lamp, a "modern spook" (546) that completes his destructive experience of contemporary life. Yet it is important to note that Gibreel's act of self-sacrifice in saving Chamcha from the fire that destroys the Shandaar Café is the act of selflessness that sets in motion Chamcha's final restorative trip to India.

With their drastically different endings, Gibreel and Chamcha represent two divergent experiences of migrants from former colonies in a late twentieth-century Western urban center. Both characters are predisposed to the shattering effects that consumer capitalism can have on identity, since they are both implicated in an industry that promotes performance over essence and places profit above all other considerations. While Gibreel apparently fares better owing to his talent for materializing others' desires, he in fact becomes the passive victim of the system that provides his success. The schizophrenia of Gibreel's mind is both bred by and projected on the social world around him. Chamcha's vision of the city, conversely, changes in accordance with his adaptation to the unscrupulous moral code of Thatcherite England in its dealings with those who do not conform to its economic and cultural program. Although Chamcha exerts his will over his situation such that he feels vindicated for his marginalization, he does not attain the reformed personality that is his actual goal until he transcends his society's superficial egotism and integrates his past and present selves in an ethically superior way. Chamcha's promising outlook at the end of the novel suggests that Rushdie means him to stand as a model of how the postcolonial wanderer can realize a level of secure self-awareness, despite the disorientation of the postmodern condition.

Works Cited

Bhabha, Homi K. *The Location of Culture*. London: Routledge, 1994.

Fokkema, Aleid. "Post-Modern Fragmentation or Authentic Essence? Character in *The Satanic Verses*." *Shades of Empire in Colonial and Post-Colonial Literatures*. Ed. C. C. Barfoot and Theo D'haen. Amsterdam: Rodopi, 1993. 51–63.

Jameson, Fredric. *Postmodernism, or, The Cultural Logic of Late Capitalism*. Durham: Duke UP, 1991.

Kellner, Douglas. "Popular Culture and the Construction of Postmodern Identities." *Modernity and Identity*. Ed. Scott Lash and Jonathan Friedman. Oxford: Blackwell, 1992. 141–77.

Rushdie, Salman. "In Good Faith." *Imaginary Homelands: Essays and Criticism, 1981–1991*. London: Granta, 1991.

———. *The Satanic Verses*. New York: Viking, 1989.

From Multiculturalism to Pop Cosmopolitanism: Transcultural Exchanges in Salman Rushdie's Children's Books

Justyna Deszcz-Tryhubczak

Haroun and the Sea of Stories (1990), a fairy tale inspired by the *fatwā* (legal ruling) but in fact begun earlier as an intimate fairy tale–autobiography dedicated to Rushdie's first son Zafar, became a fervent, if a bit didactic and naïve, apologia for freedom of artistic expression. *Luka and the Fire of Life* (2010), Rushdie's second venture into children's literature, intended as gift to his younger son Milan, was not directly occasioned by any real trauma in Rushdie's life, except perhaps fear of old age and the withering of artistic energy and talent. This might be a reason why adult readers are likely to come away from *Luka* with a sense of dilution of the typical Rushdiean commitments to freedom, hybridity, intertextuality, carnivalization, suspension of binaries through dialogic counternarratives, and reciprocity between the real and the fantastic. Nevertheless, exclusive focus on veiled allusions to Rushdie's artistic and political predicaments may in fact overshadow the books' merits as works of children's literature offering "'contact zone[s]' . . . the particular social configuration of child and adult as they read a text together" (Waller 275).[1] In particular, within children's literature studies, *Haroun and the Sea of Stories* has often been interpreted as a postcolonial fairy tale addressed to both young and adult inhabitants of the emerging global village since it celebrates two different cultural heritages without estranging either one. In its central metaphor of the Sea of Stories, the narrative unites the Indian storytelling tradition with the subversive and revisionary trend within the Western literary fairy tale.[2] Although this choice of intertextualities may seem just play with various heritages, it is in fact a conscious strategy of the novelist aimed at creating what Timothy Brennan refers to as "written orality" (139), which involves "digressions and juxtapositions of the oral storyteller" and popularization of tradition, i.e. "epic, holy book, national legend" (141–42). As Brennan points out, written orality is both a postmodern and a postcolonial narrative solution also present in Rushdie's other novels, where it constitutes a significant element of the writer's "revisionist spirit" of commitment to political issues with "a sense of human tragedy and protest" and attempts at making "the events meaningful by coming to understand their human cost" (140, 141). This revisionist spirit is also marked by "the realization of art's functional role in political and social life" (141). As Brennan argues, such commitments testify to Rushdie's status as "a Third World Cosmopolitan," like Gabriel García Márquez, Mario Vargas Llosa, Isabel Allende, or Bharati Mukherjee (viii).

Admittedly, *Luka* may seem a little trivial in comparison to the artistic and political complexity of *Haroun*. Nevertheless, in his second children's book, Rushdie goes further than just providing an intertextual fairy-tale playground and employs, albeit perfunctorily, the narrative framework of massively multiplayer online games (MMOs) to celebrate "pop cosmopolitanism." This cosmopolitanism is defined by Henry Jenkins as a set of cultural practices resulting from the global corporate and grassroots convergence of the media combining with the international flow of cultural commodities and popular culture, which has led to the evolution of "new forms of global consciousness and cultural competency" (155–56). Jenkins stresses that pop cosmopolitanism forms a salient aspect of contemporary childhood as children, in particular, are becoming global citizens who are not simply "reconfigured" by the culture industry into "consummate consumers" of commercial culture (Zipes, *Relentless Progress* 56). They also become autonomous agents transgressing their parent cultures and embracing unprecedented freedom of reference, and hence, they play "central roles as grassroots intermediaries" enabling international exchanges of popular culture (Jenkins 169).[3] Significantly, while engaging in global popular culture and participating in online communities that transcend geographical borders, young people neither abandon their backgrounds nor ignore specificities of foreign cultures; instead, they try to understand them better, thereby gaining an appreciation of their own lives and the lives of their peers all over the world. This might turn out to be a perilous adventure, however. As Jenkins puts it, "The pop cosmopolitan walks a thin line between dilettantism and connoisseurship, between orientalistic fantasies and a desire to honestly connect and understand an alien culture, between assertions of mastery and surrender to cultural difference" (164). If seen in this context, Luka's encounters with a variety of cultural materials evoke another utopian vision of globalization that may soon become real both for digital natives and for their parents, who are dependent on electronic mediation and seem to enjoy the negotiation between the lure of mass-market exoticism and a genuine desire for a broader cultural experience. Moreover, Rushdie's apparently lighthearted story may encourage reflection on the relations between children, literature, and the media, and especially on media literacy, "the ability to scrutinize the media and media contents in a critical way, to express one's own views through the media and to creatively take part in production of media contents" (von Feilitzen et al. 10).

In *Haroun*, Rushdie achieves the effect of written orality through introducing Indian storytelling as it functions in the *Kathāsaritsāgara*, the largest available collection of tales in Sanskrit verse, most probably written by Somadeva in the eleventh century CE. With the Mahābhārata, the Panchatantra, the Rāmāyana, and the Jātaka, it belongs to the Indian tradition of cyclical, episodic, and digressive storytelling. The Chinese-box pattern of the *Kathāsaritsāgara* is metaphorically represented by the idea of the ocean; its four hundred individual stories of various generic origins and from all over India "are swallowed up in story collections, and these story collections in turn are swallowed up in yet larger collections of story collections" (Irwin 67). In this, they are indeed redolent of interweaving streams and rivers that flow across boundaries of numerous lands toward their final destination, the ocean. According to N. M. Penzer,

He [Somadeva] felt that his great work united in itself all stories, as the ocean does all rivers. Every stream of myth and mystery flowing down from snowy heights of the sacred Himalaya would sooner or later reach the ocean, other streams from other mountains would do likewise, till at last fancy would create an ocean full of stories of every conceivable description. (xxxi)

Indeed, the main plot of the *Kathāsaritsāgara*, the romantic adventures of Prince Narawahanadatta and his quest for the throne, is interspersed with shorter tales. Using the terminology of Western poetics, these yarns can be categorized as fables, anecdotes, religious sermons, gothic stories, exempla, or romances, and are narrated by the characters to clarify their arguments or to both instruct and amuse the listeners.

Somadeva hoped that this skillful combination of multivocal, discontinuous, and imbricate, or overlapping, stories would not only be a source of entertainment but also make a valuable contribution to human wisdom. It can be argued that Rushdie achieves the same aim by providing his Western readers, both young and old, a less familiar Eastern reference point than *The Arabian Nights*, thereby succeeding in positing the Oriental as a defamiliarizing element. In particular, Rushdie's choice of the *Kathāsaritsāgara* prevents the reader from forming too many harmful associations with overworked and already Disneyfied tropes of "popular Orientalism" (Phillips and Wojcik-Andrews 72). Simultaneously, the *Kathāsaritsāgara* offers another, equally recondite and inspiring grasp of the frame techniques invigorating the "exotic" quality of the digressive, episodic, and circular Indian verbal tradition, and one with which readers are not yet so conversant.

Haroun can also be seen as a revisionist fairy tale, inspired by Rushdie's lifelong fascination with Frank Baum's *The Wonderful Wizard of Oz* (1900), itself an upshot of the general subversive trend within the fairy-tale genre, initiated in Victorian England by George MacDonald, Oscar Wilde, Charles Dickens, W. M. Thackeray, and John Ruskin. This new approach was aimed at expanding fairy-tale discourse beyond customary sermonizing tales intended "to mollify and apologize for broken promises of a better life as working conditions and social relations became more stressful and alienating" (Zipes, *Fairy Tales* 131). Progressive authors radically altered traditional scripts by stimulating children's and adults' imaginations through the experience of fairy-tale realms full of original images and symbols that directed the growing readership toward liberated political and social consciousness. For Frank Baum, the challenge of creating a modern fairy tale consisted not only in reappropriating old stories or conceiving innovative ones, but also in writing an Americanized fairy tale resonant with the American audience of the Gilded Age. Although critics disagree about the utopian interpretation of Baum's book, the writer's vision proved so influential that it led to the formation of the Oz cult, not to mention Baum's thirteen sequels to the first tale and numerous spin-offs by other authors.[4]

It seems that it was the potential of Baum's imaginary realm to affect reality that attracted Rushdie, so much disempowered by the dystopia of real life. As in *The Wonderful Wizard of Oz*, the subversive quality of *Haroun* is generated by the gradual empowerment of the young protagonist who learns to depend on himself instead of looking for solutions from the outside. Even though Dorothy becomes the owner of the silver shoes at the very beginning of her stay in Oz, only at the end of the book, when she has understood the meaning of her adventures, does she learn about their magical powers. For Haroun, the progression from uncertainty to self-reliance means believing in the power of the Wishwater. To make the elixir work, one needs to concentrate on one's heart's desire long enough—which initially is none too easy for the boy, depressed by the condition of the sad city and his family problems. Hence, Haroun's final success depends not so much on magical agency but on his own ability to hope for and conceive an alternative future. Moreover, despite his sympathy for the Guppees, who indulge in the comforts of binary thinking, Haroun proposes his own solution to the conflict on Kahani by making the two nations understand that they would benefit from the mutual appreciation of differences and cooperation. Haroun's development of independent reasoning and activism is all the more important as he, like Dorothy, has to cope with the despondency of his parents, who are too weak to weather the misfortunes that befall them. Finally, both protagonists develop a sense of responsibility for their companions, coupled with the awareness of what they can do for others, who in turn depend on the children for the fulfillment of their own quests.

This new sense of reciprocity is in turn related to the protagonists' realization of their own potential to create a less alienating society in which "man knows and controls the forces acting upon him" (Zipes, *Breaking the Magic Spell* 65). If the children were protagonists of a classical fairy tale, they would inevitably be denied the freedom inherent in the utopian transformation of the status quo. Dorothy could defeat the Wicked Witch, but after some time, she would most likely become as gray as Aunt Em. It is also quite possible that even though Haroun would help his father to reconnect to the Sea of Stories, the saddest of the cities would remain so. One could even conclude that all memory of the children's journeys could be erased from their minds. In other words, they would only be receivers of events enacting traditional patterns, while their homes would remain the same. Then, they could only turn into "good citizens" and define themselves, as Zipes puts it, within the "background of finite choices proposed by society" (*Fairy Tales* 100).

Nevertheless, for all their innovation, both Baum's and Rushdie's stories are based on the Western linear quest narrative of an individual seeking fulfillment of his or her own potentiality, which, even if it leads to the attainment of utopia, is likely to be annulled once the utopian solution becomes institutionalized—hence, Haroun's misgivings about the happy conclusion of his own adventures. The way to preserve the utopian energy, Rushdie suggests, is to keep telling stories about the very process of change as a means to rekindle hope whenever it is needed. Therefore, perhaps the most triumphant moment comes when Rashid recovers from aphasia and begins to tell stories again, of which the first is "Haroun and the Sea of Stories." This ideal act of storytelling is a time-gaining operation as the tale about Haroun's heroic endeavors becomes a self-begetting, self-perpetuating, and never-ending narrative that cannot be silenced. It is also at this oxymoronic point of simultaneous closure and perpetuation that the circular Indian storytelling converges with the linear narrative of the Western fairy tale. Together, they interact to create a basis for other, more fragmented and dispersed allusions to world cultures, thereby making the book a postcolonial fairy tale about tolerance and understanding that stem from the awareness and appreciation of diverse traditions interacting but never becoming obliterated into sameness.

Undoubtedly, in the aftermath of the Rushdie affair, this utopian fantasy of a Third World cosmopolitan may seem even more facile than it did in the 1990s. However, as David Harvey argues in his *Cosmopolitanism and the Geographies of Freedom* (2009), recently "cosmopolitanism has been reconstructed from . . . a variety of standpoints" (78). Although some thinkers still espouse a general concept of cosmopolitanism as "an ethos, a habit of mind, [or] a set of loyalties to humanity as a whole," he writes, "against this universal vision are ranged all manner of hyphenated versions of cosmopolitanism, variously described as 'rooted,' 'situated,' 'actually existing,' 'discrepant,' 'vernacular,' 'Christian,' 'Bourgeois,' 'liberal,' 'postcolonial,' 'feminist,' 'proletarian,' 'subaltern,' 'ecological,' 'socialist,' and so forth" (79). Harvey is far from celebrating this abundance, but the list should be completed by yet another, and relatively recent, phenomenon: popular cosmopolitanism. In the cultural exchanges encouraged by global social networks, Henry Jenkins sees the possibility for bonding semantically with "others worldwide who share the same tastes and interests" (156). This pop cosmopolitanism is developing particularly intensively within global children's and youth culture, which is becoming exceptionally dependent on the flow of cultural contents across various communal media and social software. Such an "alchemy between youth and digital media" (Ito et al. ix) is indeed revolutionary, as it suspends adult normativity, opening up a space for independence within the social group that has always been systematically controlled in relation to its access to information, self-expression, and means of social communication. To some extent, this empowerment of young people comes from their creative interactions with popular culture, which in turn often occur within what has come to be called the glocal communal spaces of fandom. An example of such a glocal platform is MMOs, graphically rich 3-D video games played in virtual worlds online and "allowing individuals to interact not only with the gaming software . . . but also with other players," Constance Steinkuehler contends. MMOs are another element of popular culture fostering the emergence of pop cosmopolitanism, since they provide spaces for "global player populations" within which "individuals enculturate one another into routine and valued practices and perspectives," as well as engaging in "the joint creation, maintenance, and transformation of shared online repositories of community knowledge and skills." In this way, Steinkuehler continues, the games contribute to the formation of "twenty-first century citizenship—a cosmopolitan disposition marked by the willingness to engage in an increasingly globalized, diverse socio-technical world and the development of intellectual practices crucial to successful navigation in it" ("Virtual Worlds").[5]

If, as Jenkins asserts, pop cosmopolitanism is "generating its own intelligentsia, its own critics, historians, translators, and educators" who are "producing their own vernacular theories of globalization . . . [and] their own explanations," it could also be argued that such accounts and "pedagogical interventions" may be produced by writers (170). In particular, these could be created by authors writing for children and wishing to reflect on young people's experiences of various cultural materials, encouraging both them and their parents to think about the influence of global convergence both on cultural specificities and on conceptions of rights, capabilities, citizenship, or governance. An interesting example of a theory embracing the nature and scope of youth media use and its influence on children's literature is the radical change theory proposed by Eliza Dresang in *Radical Change: Books for Youth in a Digital Age* (1999) and still being developed in an effort to accommodate rapid technological changes affecting the Internet generation. For Dresang and her research partner Bowie Kotrla, numerous recently published children's books reflect the following three "technology-influenced digital-age principles or characteristics" directly related to changes in how young people read books (94):

- *Interactivity* refers to dynamic, user-initiated, nonlinear, nonsequential, complex cognitive, emotional, and physical behaviors and relationships with and among components of literature.

- *Connectivity* refers to the sense of community or construction of social worlds that emerges from changing perspectives and expanded associations in the real world or in literature.

- *Access* refers to the breaking of long-standing information barriers, bringing entrée to a wide diversity of formerly largely inaccessible opinion and opportunity in society and sophistication in literature. (94)

In children's books representing radical change, the above-mentioned qualities are usually manifested in "graphics in new forms and formats; words and pictures reaching new levels of synergy; nonlinear or nonsequential organization and format; multiple layers of meaning from a variety of perspectives; cognitively, emotionally, and physically interactive formats; sophisticated presentations; and unresolved storylines" (16).

Significantly, as Dresang and Kotrla stress, these innovations correspond to a broader change both in the adult perception of children and in children themselves, caused by the fact that as children learn to use new media to carry out demanding tasks and comprehend sophisticated issues, they become partners for adults, who often struggle in their adoption of new technology.

It is hard to know whether Rushdie has read Henry Jenkins's chapter "Pop Cosmopolitanism: Mapping Cultural Flows in an Age of Media Convergence" or is familiar with the research of other academics investigating the connection between virtual worlds, popular culture, and new spaces of global social relationships that result in the emergence of pop cosmopolitanism. Still, Rushdie's use of MMOs—or, in his playful pun, "Muu" (*Luka* 9)—may be seen as his acknowledgment of their inherent narrative freedom for "excursions and digressions" and for telling stories "sideways, to give alternative possibilities that the reader can, in a way, choose between," as he said in an interview with Max Miller (Rushdie, "Interview"). It also suggests his sense of their significance as spaces fostering interaction among individuals of various cultural backgrounds, especially since his Muu is located in the same multicultural magical land as *Haroun*.

However, although Rushdie begins with an insightful conception of Luka as a contemporary boy fond of games, he fails to deploy productively the potential of this reference by ignoring the social significance of MMOs as spaces encouraging a sense of solidarity and cooperation. This neglect has not been registered in numerous online comments by MMO fans expressing their enthusiasm about Rushdie's choice, even though it becomes obvious early in the book in the depiction of Luka's pastime as a solitary activity:

> Like everyone he knew, Luka possessed a wide assortment of pocket-sized alternate-reality boxes, and spent much of his spare time leaving his own world to enter the rich, colourful, musical, challenging universes inside these boxes, universes in which . . . a life was a thing you could win, or save up for, or just be miraculously granted because you happened to bump your head into the right brick, or eat the right mushroom, or pass through the right magic waterfall, and you could store up as many lives as your skill and good fortune could get you. In Luka's room near a small television set stood his most precious possession, the most magical box of all,

the one offering the richest, most complex journeys into other-space and different-time, into the zone of multi-life and temporary death: his new Muu . . . when he stepped away from the world of mathematics and chemistry and into the Zone of Muu, he felt at home, *at home* in a completely different way to the way in which he felt *at home* in his home, but at home nevertheless; and he became, at least in his own mind, Super-Luka, Grandmaster of the Games. (12–13)

Of particular interest in this quote is the mention of an alternative home Luka actively creates for himself while playing. Rushdie has often stressed the provisionality of attachments to a specific background, but the construction of "cartographies," "solidarities and alliances" that, as David Harvey argues, "can be and are built across space, turning fixed boundaries into porous borders" (50) has never been so intense as it is in the world marked by unprecedented digitalization and transnational social movements. Hence, one should ask why Rushdie does not show Luka actively making his own "cartography" and why, although in his interview he recalls observing Milan and his friends playing together, he prohibits Haroun, or any of Luka's friends from "his gang, the Intergalactic Penguins" (6), from participating in the game and aiding him in his mission. He even makes Haroun seem strangely unconcerned about his father's coma, so that he leaves the plot with a comment directed to Luka: "'I knew it would happen soon. . . . You've reached the age at which people in this family cross the border into the magical world. It's your turn for an adventure" (6). Moreover, although Luka is accompanied by other characters—Dog the bear, Bear the dog, the Elephant Birds, or the Insultana of Ott, in whom the boy sees a strong resemblance to his mother—young readers are not very likely to identify with them, as they could with the young girl Blabbermouth of *Haroun*. This failure is even more surprising in a writer who, in this previous novel and in his other writings, assigns the utmost value to community and solidarity, especially if they are based on cultural affinities. In this light, although *Luka* may fulfill the above-mentioned criteria of interactivity and access, it paradoxically misses the chance to provide an almost too-obvious example of social connectivity that could illustrate the potential of the web to gather children in their own local communities and around the world and so enable them to become creators and communicators of culture.

Granted, young (and perhaps also adult) readers are likely to make connections with the book's plentiful and irreverently mixed-up references—to world literature (*The Chronicles of Narnia*, *A Connecticut Yankee in King Arthur's Court*, *The Discworld*, *The Cherry Orchard*, Sir Arthur Conan Doyle), to "the world's dead religions, aka mythologies" (175) in the international assembly of gods residing on the Mountain of Knowledge, and to popular culture (*Terminator*, the *Intergalactic Penguins* online game, *Ratatouille*). Even if the hunt for allusions results in the appreciation of the multitude of cultures and traditions, young readers are not very likely to feel encouraged to imagine the possibility of a direct sense of community with other young people worldwide. This lapse becomes even more evident at the moment of Luka's appeal to the gods to rebel against the Aalim. Whereas in *Haroun* it was up to the users of stories, i.e., the nations of Kahani or the inhabitants of Alifbay, to ensure the undisturbed circulation of tales, the revolt of gods seems to imply that it is stories themselves that are somehow supposed to oppose the tyranny of ideologies without any agency of tellers and listeners (201). Again, Rushdie fails to consider a possibility of imbuing Luka's success with such agency or its broader social and political implications.

And yet, despite the failure to create an example of a socially meaningful kidspace, *Luka* is not a failure as long as it is seen as a contact zone for young and adult readers within which they may reflect together on how individual children see their local lives and what meanings they associate with global cultural goods. It may also be a starting point for a discussion about children's hopes and expectations for their own future, a starting point whose importance should be particularly appreciated in times when parents' interventions in the lives of their children often matter less than the influence of peers and culture. Such a reflection is indeed of great significance in times when, as Ulla Carlsson rightly contends,

> The communication society of today has enormous potential regarding our planet, not least for those who are young today—we gain access to cultures and knowledge that used to be beyond our horizons. But in many parts of the world, there are fears that globalization poses a mortal threat to uniqueness . . . People defend their identities, and when common culture can no longer be maintained as it once could be, stockades are raised around local cultures, religious beliefs and communities. Transcendence of boundaries and defense of boundaries are twin aspects of the globalization process. Globalization processes force us not only to focus more on transnational phenomena in general, but also to highlight difference. (16)

Rushdie seems to signal the possibility of such intergenerational cooperation in the description of Rashid's interest in Luka's games and his attempts at dispelling Soraya's doubts about the beneficial influence of gaming:

> Once again it was his father Rashid Khalifa who encouraged Luka, and who tried, with comically little skill, to join him on his adventures. Soraya was sniffily unimpressed, and, being a commonsensical woman who distrusted technology, worried that the various magic boxes were emitting invisible beams and rays that would rot her beloved son's mind. Rashid made light of these worries, which made Soraya worry even more. "No rays! No beams!" Rashid cried. "But see how well he is developing his hand-eye coordination, and he is solving problems too, answering riddles, surmounting obstacles, rising through levels of difficulty to acquire extraordinary skills." (11–12)

Although Rashid focuses only on very basic skills that can be improved through gaming, one may easily imagine how Rushdie could artistically develop this family exchange toward a discussion about alternative media and the role their young users may have in initiating social change.

It might seem that the role of literature in shaping "the global imagination" has been considerably diminished by the omnipresence of the media. However, both *Haroun and the Sea of Stories* and *Luka and the Fire of Life* testify to the fact that "literature remains a significant place in which this imagination is produced and represented, and a site where it is possible to gauge the shifting valences of culture in relationship to those other political, social, and economic realities that globalization most commonly names" (O'Brien and Szeman 611–12). These two tasks also appear to constitute one of the major challenges facing contemporary children's literature, which should offer readers spaces from which they may critically assess their reality. Most important, however, it should provide them with hope for a chance to shape their own lives and the public sphere, which appears especially desirable in the context of both the possibilities and limitations of the globalized world. Rushdie's works for children reveal that children's books may indeed serve as a vehicle of utopian visions of cosmopolitan solidarity, justice, and equality that will inspire young people's activism and make them into responsible citizens. Rushdie himself expresses this intention in his plea to the Six Billionth Living Person, which could as well be directed to any child: "Live in your own time, use what we know, and as you grow up, perhaps the human race will finally grow up with you and put aside childish things" (Rushdie, "'Imagine There Is No Heaven'" 143).

Notes

1. Waller here refers to Maria Tatar's *Enchanted Hunters: The Power of Stories in Childhood* (2009), where Tatar uses Mary Louise Pratt's concept of the "contact zone" to discuss possibilities for shared cultural experience that may occur when children and adults read together.

2. See Plotz and Ellerby. For a commentary on other approaches, including the critique of the simple-mindedness of Rushdie's vision, see Teverson.
3. Although Jenkins focuses on Asian American cultural exchanges, these processes are occurring worldwide, as reflected in the research included in *New Questions, New Insights, New Approaches: Contributions to the Research Forum at the World Summit on Media for Children and Youth 2010*: "For children and youth, the many media platforms of today are often combined into the trinity of internet, television and mobile phone. They intersperse a myriad of optional applications providing increasing possibilities to engage individual users' interests and mark their activities" (von Feilitzen et al. 10). It should also be pointed out that optimistic analyses of global convergence remain alert to inequalities in consumers' access to the new media.
4. It also inspired such contemporary authors as Philip Jose Farmer, Geoff Ryman, and Gregory Maguire. For more on Rushdie's own Ozian inspirations, see Deszcz-Tryhubczak, cited below.
5. Naturally, one could object to Jenkins's and Steinkuehler's conclusions by claiming that such online activities in fact make digital youth into consumers at a very early age. Yet, as can be proved by, for example, activities of fandom communities, consumers are not passive but often engage actively with cultural products, subjecting them to critical scrutiny, which in turn often results in pushing them in new aesthetic and thematic directions.

Works Cited

Brennan, Timothy. *Salman Rushdie and the Third World: Myths of the Nation*. New York: St. Martin's, 1989.

Carlsson, Ulla. "Young People in the Digital Media Culture. Introduction to the Research Forum Plenary Session. New Questions, New Insights, New Approaches." *Contributions to the Research Forum at the World Summit on Media for Children and Youth 2010*. Ed. Cecilia von Feilitzen, Ulla Carlsson, and Catharina Bucht. Göteborg: International Clearinghouse on Children, Youth and Media, 2011. 15–18. Web. 18 May 2012.

Deszcz-Tryhubczak, Justyna. "A Writer on the Yellow Brick Road: Salman Rushdie's Ozian Inspirations." *Twice-told Children's Tales: The Influence of Childhood Reading on Writers for Adults*. Ed. Betty Greenway. New York: Routledge, 2005. 51–68.

Dresang, Eliza T., and Bowie Kotrla. "Radical Change Theory and Synergistic Reading for Digital Age Youth." *Journal of Aesthetic Education* 43.2 (2009): 92–107.

Ellerby, Janet Mason. "Fiction under Siege: Rushdie's Quest for Narrative Emancipation in *Haroun and the Sea of Stories*." *Lion and the Unicorn* 22.2 (1998): 211–20.

Harvey, David. *Cosmopolitanism and the Geographies of Freedom*. New York: Columbia UP, 2009.

Irwin, Robert. *The Arabian Nights: A Companion*. Harmondsworth: Penguin, 1994.

Ito, Mizuko, et al. Foreword. *Civic Life Online: Learning How Digital Media Can Engage Youth*. Ed. W. Lance Bennett. Cambridge: MIT P, 2008. vii–ix.

Jenkins, Henry. *Fans, Bloggers and Gamers: Exploring Participatory Culture*. New York: New York UP, 2006.

O'Brien, Susie, and Imre Szeman. "Introduction: The Globalization of Fiction/The Fiction of Globalization." *South Atlantic Quarterly* 100.3 (2001): 603–26.

Penzer, N. M. Introduction. *The Ocean of Story: Being C. H. Tawney's Translation of Sōmadeva's Kathā sarit sāgara (or, Oceans of Streams of Story)*. London: Sawyer, 1928.

Phillips, Jerry R., and Ian Wojcik-Andrews. "Telling Tales to Children: The Pedagogy of Empire in MGM's *Kim* and Disney's *Aladdin*." *Lion and the Unicorn* 20.1 (1996): 66–89.

Plotz, Judith. "*Haroun* and the Politics of Children's Literature." *Children's Literature Association Quarterly* 20.3 (1995): 100–04.

Rushdie, Salman. *Haroun and the Sea of Stories*. 2nd ed. London: Granta, 1991.

———. "'Imagine There Is No Heaven.' A Letter to the Six Billionth World Citizen." *Step Across This Line: Collected Nonfiction, 1992–2002*. New York: Random, 2002. 141–44.

———. Interview by Max Miller. *BigThink.com*. Big Think, 12 Nov. 2010. Web. 4 July 2011.

———. *Luka and the Fire of Life*. London: Cape, 2010.

Steinkuehler, Constance. "Virtual Worlds, Learning, & the New Pop Cosmopolitanism." *Teachers College Record*. Teachers College, Columbia University, 17 Nov 2006. Web. 18 May 2012.

Teverson, Andrew S. "Fairy Tale Politics: Free Speech and Multiculturalism in *Haroun and the Sea of Stories*." *Twentieth-Century Literature* 47.4 (2001): 444–66.

von Feilitzen, Cecilia, Ulla Carlsson, and Catharina Bucht, eds. Foreword. *Contributions to the Research Forum at the World Summit on Media for Children and Youth 2010*. Göteborg: International Clearinghouse on Children, Youth and Media, 2011. 9–11. Web. 18 May 2012.

Waller, Alison. "Psychic Barriers and Contact Zones: Rereading Rose and the Rupture between Child and Adult." *Children's Literature Association Quarterly* 35.3 (2010): 274–89.

Zipes, Jack. *Breaking the Magic Spell: Radical Theories of Folk and Fairy Tales*. Austin: U of Texas P, 1979.

———. *Fairy Tales and the Art of Subversion: The Classical Genre for Children and the Process of Civilization*. 2nd ed. New York: Routledge, 1991.

———. *Relentless Progress: The Reconfiguration of Children's Literature, Fairy Tales, and Storytelling*. London: Routledge, 2008.

Rushdie as Artist, Migrant, and Humanist in *Imaginary Homelands* and *Step Across This Line*
Lydia Forssander-Song

Salman Rushdie's reputation rests primarily on his fiction, especially his Booker Prize–winning 1981 novel *Midnight's Children* and his 1988 novel *The Satanic Verses*, prompter of the *fatwā* (legal ruling) issued by Ayatollah Khomeini of Iran on February 14, 1989. So far, he has also written nine other novels, including two for children, and one short-story collection. However, Rushdie is also a very avid reader of both fiction and nonfiction as well as a highly engaged and engaging commentator on his art and his society. In addition to his fiction, he has published a travel memoir, *The Jaguar Smile: A Nicaraguan Journey* (1987); a personal introduction to the movie *The Wizard of Oz* for the British Film Institute (BFI) Film Classics series (1992); and two collections of essays, criticism, interviews, speeches, and columns entitled *Imaginary Homelands: Essays and Criticism, 1981–1991* (1991) and *Step Across This Line: Collected Nonfiction, 1992–2002* (2002). This essay will focus specifically on *Imaginary Homelands* and *Step Across This Line* and highlight Rushdie's journey as an artist, migrant, and humanist.

Imaginary Homelands

Imaginary Homelands (*IH*) encompasses the period immediately after *Midnight's Children* through Rushdie's initial reactions to the fatwā. The collection contains twelve sections. The first section deals with Rushdie's responses to reactions to *Midnight's Children*. It opens with the title essay and closes with a consideration of the state of India forty years after its independence from the British. The second section covers Rushdie's observations of Indian and Pakistani politics. In particular, he discusses Indian and Pakistani censorship, Indira Gandhi's assassination, the Nehru-Gandhi dynasty in Indian politics, the rule of Pakistan's General Zia ul-Haq, and Benazir Bhutto—subjects and characters he treats fictionally in *Midnight's Children*, *Shame*, and *The*

Satanic Verses. The third section consists of Rushdie's insights on Indian literature and language and includes his controversial claim that "'Commonwealth literature' does not exist," as well as discussions of the work of Anita Desai and Rudyard Kipling. The fourth section contains Rushdie's thoughts on movies, especially Hollywood movies set in India. He reveals his love for Satyajit Ray's movies, his criticisms of the films *Handsworth Songs* and *Gandhi*, and his admiration for the film *Brazil*. The fifth section includes Rushdie's comments on British immigrant experiences, on V. S. Naipaul's novel *The Enigma of Arrival*, and on the "discovery" of a Russian American abstract expressionist painter (from the West) by an Indian professor (from the East). The next section consists of Rushdie's views on British politics, especially the general election of 1983 and Charter 88. This section also includes Rushdie's interview of Edward Said.

Sections 7 to 11 hold Rushdie's criticism of literature arranged according to geographical regions. Thus, section 7 is on African fiction by Nadine Gordimer, Rian Malan, and Nuruddin Farah, as well as Ryszard Kapuściński's *Another Day of Life* about Angola. The following section, on British fiction, examines works by John Berger, Graham Greene, John Le Carré, Julian Barnes, and Kazuo Ishiguro, and recounts Rushdie's travels in Australia with Bruce Chatwin. Section 9 treats fiction by Michel Tournier, Italo Calvino, Umberto Eco, Günter Grass, Heinrich Böll, Siegfried Lenz, Peter Schneider, Christoph Ransmayr, Maurice Sendak, and Wilhelm Grimm. The tenth section focuses on the South American magic realist fiction of Gabriel García Márquez and Mario Vargas Llosa, with which Rushdie's own has often been compared. His reviews of American fiction in section 11 include discussions of E. L. Doctorow, Richard Ford, Raymond Carver, Isaac Bashevis Singer, Philip Roth, Saul Bellow, Thomas Pynchon, Kurt Vonnegut, and Grace Paley. This section also includes Rushdie's impressions of America from his trip there in "Travels with a Golden Ass."

The final section of this collection explores Rushdie's opinions about religion. It incorporates essays on Naipaul's *Among the Believers*, a piece of nonfiction about Islam in various parts of the world, and responses to the fatwā: "In God We Trust," on his own religious background and views of religion in the public sphere; "In Good Faith," a defense of *The Satanic Verses*; and "Is Nothing Sacred?" the Herbert Read Memorial Lecture for 1990, delivered by Harold Pinter while its author was in hiding. The essay "One Thousand Days in a Balloon," on Rushdie's reflections after more than a thousand days of living in hiding due to the fatwā, appears in the 1992 revised paperback edition in place of the earlier essay "Why I Have Embraced Islam."

Step Across This Line

Step Across This Line (*SATL*) consists of four sections. This collection covers the remaining period of Rushdie living in hiding under the fatwā, the new millennium when he is finally a free man, and the new age of "Terror versus Security" (the title of a January 2000 column Rushdie wrote for the *New York Times*). Part 1 includes a wide-ranging series of essays on subjects such as *The Wizard of Oz* and movie titles, British novelists, the influence of Italian literature on his writing, adapting *Midnight's Children* for the screen, the sixties, rock music, acting, leavened bread, photography, soccer, journalism, religion, Indian literature, politics, icons, and a long-awaited visit to India in 2000. Part 2, entitled "Messages from the Plague Years," contains speeches, correspondence, and articles written while Rushdie was in hiding. Part 3 encompasses monthly columns Rushdie wrote for the *New York Times* between December 1998 and March 2002. These columns deal with topics such as national and international politics, the millennium, the tenth anniversary of the fatwā, globalization, Islam, terrorism, American immigrants, Edward Said, J. M. Coetzee, human rights, evolution, abortion, and non-Hollywood and independent movies and reality television. Part 4, entitled "Step Across This Line," explores the ideas of the frontier and borders and is a talk that Rushdie delivered as part of the Tanner Lectures on Human Values at Yale in 2002.

Rushdie as Artist

The contents of his nonfiction collections demonstrate that Rushdie is not only a prolific writer but also an avid reader of world literature—of fiction, nonfiction, and the news. He is also an interested and interesting citizen of the world. His writings about his readings reveal some of the key influences on his fiction: in particular, the works of Italo Calvino, Gabriel García Márquez, and Günter Grass. In "Influence," Rushdie states that "by using what is old, and adding to it something of our own, we make what is new" (*SATL* 66). He describes "the world of the imagination" as "not so much a continent as an ocean." Continuing this metaphor, he elaborates, "The writer must find the trick of weaving the waters together until they become land . . . if he fails, of course, he drowns. The fable is the most unforgiving of literary forms" (*SATL* 62–63). He adds elsewhere, "The fable is now the central, the most vital form in Western literature; and it should be read by anyone who takes pleasure in entering a world so beautifully and completely realized that, for all its apparent alienness, it rapidly becomes our own" (*IH* 287).

Rushdie's interest in the old stories, and specifically in the fable, keeps him in good company with Calvino, Márquez, and Grass. He describes Calvino in *If on a winter's night a traveller* as "joyously playing with the possibilities of fiction, of story-telling, which is, after all, also a nursery euphemism for lying" (*IH* 258–59). Saleem Sinai in *Midnight's Children* and Rashid Khalifa in *Haroun and the Sea of Stories* are examples of such fabulous storytellers. Rushdie reveals that "Saleem Sinai is not an oracle; he's only adopting a kind of oracular language. His story is not history, but it plays with historical shapes." He then explains:

> History is always ambiguous. Facts are hard to establish, and capable of being given many meanings. Reality is built on our prejudices, misconceptions and ignorance as well as on our perceptiveness and knowledge. The reading of Saleem's unreliable narration might be, I believed, a useful analogy for the way in which we all, every day, attempt to "read" the world. (*IH* 25)

Saleem uses an old story, the history of India, and makes it new. Rushdie highlights, through Saleem, the fabulous subjectivity of the storyteller.

In a similar vein, Rushdie writes of Márquez's *One Hundred Years of Solitude*, "In the world he describes, impossible things happen constantly, and quite plausibly, out in the open under the midday sun. It would be a mistake to think of Márquez's literary universe as an invented, self-referential, closed system. . . . Macondo exists. That is its magic" (*IH* 302). Rushdie describes Márquez's use of magic realism as "a development out of Surrealism that expresses a genuinely 'Third World' consciousness. It deals with what Naipaul has called 'half-made' societies, in which the impossibly old struggles against the appallingly new" (*IH* 301). These fabulations are a development of the contest over reality. Rushdie explains that "the damage to reality in South America is at least as much political as cultural. In Márquez's experience, truth has been controlled to the point at which it has ceased to be possible to find out what it is. The only truth is that you are being lied to all the time" (*IH* 301).

Rushdie explores this connection between art and politics in his own writing as well as in Grass's writing. In the title essay of *Imaginary Homelands*, he states:

> As Richard Wright found long ago in America, black and white descriptions of society are no longer compatible. Fantasy, or the mingling of fantasy and naturalism, is one way of dealing with these problems. It offers a way of echoing in the form of our work the issues faced by all of us: how to build a new, "modern" world out of an old, legend-haunted civilization, an old culture which we have brought into a newer one. (19)

Consequently, Rushdie writes of Grass, "A writer who understands the artificial nature of reality is more or less obliged to enter the process of making it. . . . And since to argue about reality is to be at once creative and political, it is not surprising that when Grass writes about literature he finds himself writing about politics" (*IH* 281). Like Grass, who became a politician in addition to being a writer, Rushdie believes in the strong connection between art and politics and is not only an artist but also an activist, especially for freedom of speech. Furthermore, Rushdie comments, "Reality is an artefact . . . [that] does not exist until it is made, and that like any other artefact . . . can be made well or badly . . . be unmade. What Grass learned on his journey across the frontiers of history was Doubt. Now he distrusts all those who claim to possess absolute forms of knowledge" (*IH* 280).

Grass's suspicion of "absolute forms of knowledge" parallels Rushdie's wariness of religious absolutism. In his Herbert Read Memorial Lecture, Rushdie quotes Read, "Change is the condition of art remaining art." He then adds, "Art, too, is an event in history, subject to the historical process. But it is also *about* that process, and must constantly strive to find new forms to mirror an endlessly renewed world" (*IH* 418; emphasis in orig.). Rushdie's fiction strives to reflect "the dance of history in our age: slow, slow, quick, quick, slow, back and forth and from side to side, [as] we step across these fixed and shifting lines" (*SATL* 365). For Rushdie, frontier and border crossings are best illustrated in the condition of the migrant. However, in spite of his best efforts, Rushdie also points out after the fatwā, "Art can look after itself. Artists, even the highest and finest of all, can be crushed effortlessly at any old tyrant's whim" (*IH* 293).

Rushdie as Migrant

Rushdie says, "I see Grass . . . as a double migrant: a traveller across the borders in the self, and in Time. And the vision underlying his writing, both fiction and non-fiction, is, I believe, in many ways a migrant's vision." He also describes Grass as "the man who migrated across history" because, as he puts it, "Nazi Germany was, in some ways, another country" (*IH* 280). "This is what makes migrants such important figures," Rushdie explains, "because roots, language and social norms have been three of the most important parts of the definition of what it is to be a human being. The migrant, denied all three, is obliged to find new ways of describing himself, new ways of being human" (*IH* 278). This migrant condition becomes the new reality that art must reflect.

Rushdie attempts to portray this migrant condition in *The Satanic Verses*. He claims in the essay "In Good Faith" that *The Satanic Verses* is "a migrant's-eye view of the world. It is written from the very experience of uprooting, disjuncture and metamorphosis . . . that is the migrant condition, and from which, I believe, can be derived a metaphor for all humanity" (*IH* 394). Rushdie clarifies this by insisting that "we all cross frontiers; in that sense, we are all migrant peoples" (*IH* 279). "'The past is a foreign country,' goes the famous opening sentence of L. P. Hartley's novel *The Go-Between*, 'they do things differently there,'" Rushdie observes, adding that for him, "it's my present that is foreign, and that the past is home, albeit a lost home in a lost city in the mists of lost time" (*IH* 9). Consequently, instead of sinking into despair over a migrant's losses (despite accusations that *Midnight's Children* is pessimistic), Rushdie declares:

> *The Satanic Verses* celebrates hybridity, impurity, intermingling, the transformation that comes of new and unexpected combinations of human beings, cultures, ideas, politics, movies, songs. It rejoices in mongrelization and fears of the absolutism of the Pure. *Mélange*, hotchpotch, a bit of this and a bit of that is *how newness enters the world*. It is the great possibility that mass migration gives the world, and I have tried to embrace it. *The Satanic Verses* is for change-by-fusion, change-by-conjoining. It is a love-song to our mongrel selves. (*IH* 394)

Unfortunately, not everybody shares his sense of the transgressive migrant condition as something to celebrate. Witness the fatwā. Nor do all Indian writers think alike on the definition of Indian literature: Indians within India do not always embrace Indian writers who have emigrated or who write in English. For all of these reasons, Rushdie's work has not always been welcomed in India.

The use of English can be problematic for those who want to divest themselves of the vestiges of empire, so Rushdie has had to defend his choice of language: "Those of us who do use English do so in spite of our ambiguity towards it, or perhaps because of that, perhaps because we can find in that linguistic struggle a reflection of other struggles ... between the cultures within ourselves and the influences at work upon our societies. To conquer English may be to complete the process of making ourselves free" (*IH* 17). Rushdie speaks for Anglo-Indian writers who "in the forging of a British Indian identity [find that] the English language is of central importance.... Having been borne across the world, we are translated men. It is normally supposed that something gets lost in translation; I cling, obstinately, to the notion that something can also be gained" (*IH* 17). Rushdie's optimism about the migrant (and postcolonial) condition and his determination to reflect that reality in a postmodern world through his fiction make him an important voice in an increasingly globalized world, where the migrant condition is becoming more normative.

Additionally, Rushdie muses, "It may be that when the Indian writer who writes from outside India tries to reflect that world, he is obliged to deal in broken mirrors, some of whose fragments have been irretrievably lost. But there is a paradox here. The broken mirror may actually be as valuable as the one which is supposedly unflawed" (*IH* 10–11). This "broken mirror" reflects the reality of the migrant condition that is an increasingly common experience in the modern world. It also portrays Rushdie's own personal situation. Consequently, in his introduction to the movie *The Wizard of Oz*, Rushdie elucidates, "So Oz finally *became* home [in the book series]; the imagined world became the actual world, as it does for us all, because the truth is that once we have left our childhood places and started out to make up our own lives, armed only with what we have and are ... there is no longer any such place *as* home: except, of course, for the home we make (*SATL* 29–30; emphasis in orig.). So the Technicolor Oz of the imagination becomes the preferred space compared to the gray Kansas of the movie's reality.

This optimistic and new reading of the movie's famous line "There's no place like home" coincides with Rushdie's own positive reading of the migrant condition. As Rushdie points out:

> To migrate is certainly to lose language and home, to be defined by others, to become invisible or, even worse, a target; it is to experience deep changes and wrenches in the soul. But the migrant is not simply transformed by his act; he also transforms his new world. Migrants may well become mutants, but it is out of such hybridization that newness can emerge. (*IH* 210)

Rushdie clings to this hope of newness. Like Grass, he believes that "while there is yet life, there must be analysis, struggle, persuasion, argument, polemic, rethinking, and all the other longish words that add up to one very short word: hope" (*IH* 281).

Rushdie as Humanist

Rushdie expresses this hope and his belief in the human succinctly in the conclusion to his 1996 commencement address at Bard College: "Do not bow your heads. Do not know your place. Defy the gods. You will be astonished how many of them turn out to have feet of clay. Be guided, if possible, by your better natures" (*SATL* 140). Rushdie also eschews religion in "In Good Faith," where he states, "I have spiritual needs, and my work has, I hope, a moral and spiritual dimension, but I am content to try and satisfy those needs without recourse to any idea of a Prime Mover or ultimate arbiter" *(IH* 405). Here, Rushdie clearly dissociates himself from God and religion.

Drawing from his Indian background, Rushdie nevertheless concedes the importance of religion to others in "In God We Trust":

> If one is to attempt honestly to describe reality as it is experienced by religious people, for whom God is no symbol but an everyday fact, then the conventions of what is called realism are quite inadequate. . . . A form must be created which allows the miraculous and the mundane to co-exist

at the same level—as the same order of event. I found this to be essential even though I am not, myself, a religious man. (*IH* 376)

Religion cannot be ignored. Furthermore, its association with "the miraculous" supports Rushdie's own view of art as portraying an alternative version of reality. Consequently, Rushdie speculates, "Perhaps I write, in part, to fill up that God-chamber with other dreams. Because it is, after all, a room for dreaming in" (*IH* 377). He continues, "Politics and religion, both in theory and in practice, are, I would suggest, manifestations of our dreaming selves," and this emphasis on the imagination, on "dreaming," is very important to his fiction (*IH* 378).

Rushdie also admits the importance of the idea of God as an answer to humanity's questions about origins and morality. He concedes in "Is Nothing Sacred?":

> The idea of god is at once a repository for our awestruck wonderment at life and an answer to the great questions of existence, and a rule book, too. The soul needs all these explanations . . . the language of secular, rationalist materialism has failed to answer these needs. . . . and we must concede that it is not only [communism in Central Europe] that has failed, but the idea that men and women could ever define themselves in terms that exclude their spiritual needs. . . . art was repressed as viciously as was religion. . . . The challenge of literature is to . . . find a way of fulfilling our unaltered spiritual requirements. (*IH* 421–22)

So, Rushdie recognizes the importance of humanity's spiritual needs and hopes that his work has a moral and spiritual dimension.

His argument with religion lies in religion's insistence on only one version of reality. This religious dogmatism manifests itself most clearly in the fatwā. Rushdie further explicates the difference between religion and literature, asserting,

> Whereas religion seeks to privilege one language above all others, one set of values above all others, one text above all others, the novel has always been *about* the way in which different languages, values and narratives quarrel, and about the shifting relations between them, which are relations of power. The novel does not seek to establish a privileged language, but it insists upon the freedom to portray and analyse the struggle between the different contestants for such privileges. (*IH* 420)

Literature's insistence on freedom leads Rushdie to believe that art can be "the third principle that mediates between the material and spiritual worlds" (*IH* 420). He claims, "If religion is an answer, if political ideology is an answer, then literature is an inquiry; great literature, by asking extraordinary questions, opens new doors in our minds" (423). Since this free inquiry relies on freedom of speech in order to work, he passionately believes in freedom of thought and speech.

Nonetheless, in asking the question "Is Nothing Sacred?" Rushdie ends up opposing "secular fundamentalism" as well (*IH* 418). Even literature is not sacred. He finds himself "backing away from the idea of sacralizing literature," because, he says, "We must not become what we oppose. The only privilege literature deserves—and this privilege it requires in order to exist—is the privilege of being in the arena of discourse, the place where the struggle of languages can be acted out" (*IH* 427). Rushdie is careful to grant freedom to opposing voices. Through literature, this "struggle of languages" that he values most, he finds hope in the human. As he explained in his 2002 Tanner Lecture on Human Values at Yale, "In our deepest natures, we are frontier-crossing beings. We know this by the stories we tell ourselves; for we are storytelling animals, too," and "stories are the tracks we leave" (*SATL* 350, 359). Consequently, fiction is humanity's legacy.

These "tracks" can also be in the form of news. In a speech to the American Society of Newspaper Editors, Rushdie proclaims,

> The news has become a matter of opinion. And this puts a newspaper editor in a position not at all dissimilar from that of a novelist. It is for the novelist to create, communicate, and sustain over time a personal and coherent version of the world that entertains, interests, stimulates, provokes, and nourishes his readers. It is for the newspaper editor to do very much the same thing with the pages at his disposal. In that specialized sense—and let me emphasize that I mean this as a compliment!—we are all in the fiction business now. (*SATL* 132)

In this "fiction business," freedom of speech is a prerequisite, as Rushdie pronounces in "A Declaration of Independence," written for the International Parliament of Writers in February 1994:

> The creative spirit, of its very nature, resists frontiers and limiting points, denies the authority of censors and taboos. For this reason it all too frequently is treated as an enemy by those mighty or petty potentates who resent the power of art to build pictures of the world that quarrel with, or undermine, their own simpler and less open-hearted views. (*SATL* 250–51)

Once again, the "struggle of languages" produces powerful fiction that is potentially threatening to those who are in power.

In spite of his activism for freedom of speech, Rushdie observes in the case of the release from jail of the Bulger killers (juvenile murderers of a two-year-old in Britain) that "the behavior of the British tabloids makes the free-speech argument harder and harder to sustain—that a cherished democratic principle is being destruction-tested by yellow journalists" (*SATL* 330). He remarks that "the feedback loop between events and their reporting is now so tight, so fast, that the media are major protagonists in the stories they report; and in this story they are working to subvert all civilized principles of justice and creating in their readers a lynch-mob mentality that may actually get people killed" (*SATL* 330). In the area of justice, Rushdie espouses a vision of Britain "in which restraint is valued more highly than melodrama, compassion is better than revenge, and dignity is worth keeping" (*SATL* 331). Freedom of speech and technology-aided prompt reporting can make "protagonists" out of journalists. In such cases, the journalists' sense of justice must supersede their rights to freedom of speech.

Concerning freedom and justice, Rushdie further notes in response to the September 11, 2001, terrorist attacks on the United States:

> The fundamentalist believes that we believe in nothing. . . . To prove him wrong, we must first know that he is wrong. We must agree on what matters: kissing in public places, bacon sandwiches, disagreement, cutting-edge fashion, literature, generosity, water, a more equitable distribution of the world's resources, movies, music, freedom of thought, beauty, love. These will be our weapons. Not by making war but by the unafraid way we choose to live shall we defeat them. (*SATL* 338)

Rushdie advocates fearlessly believing in and determinedly agreeing on the things that matter, and he provides us with a long list of such things. Finally, he concludes, "If terrorism is to be defeated, the world of Islam must take on board the secularist-humanist principles on which the modern is based, and without which their countries' freedom will remain a distant dream" (*SATL* 341). This appeal to "secularist-humanist principles" to defeat religious fanaticism from within "the world of Islam" requires freedom of speech. While hiding due to the fatwā, Rushdie wrote in "One Thousand Days in a Balloon," he reminded himself that "Islam doesn't have to mean blind faith. It can mean what it always meant in your family, a culture, a civilization, as open-minded as your grandfather was, as delightfully disputatious as your father was, as intellectual and philosophical as you like. Don't let the zealots make *Muslim* a terrifying word, I urged myself; remember when it meant *family* and *light*" (435). Unfortunately, his idea of converting to Islam in order to transform Islam from within—after proclaiming "*I am not a Muslim*" in "In Good Faith" (*IH* 405)—did not work for him, and he ended up renouncing the Muslim faith again. He continues to call for "the world of Islam" to transform itself from the inside, although he found that he could not operate from within that context himself.

Conclusion

Ultimately, Rushdie's earlier hopeful vision became a little less assertive in the aftermath of September 11, 2001. He wants to read *The Conference of the Birds* by the Sufi Muslim poet Farid ud-Din Attâr as saying that "by crossing those frontiers, conquering those terrors and reaching their goal, they [the birds] themselves were now what they were looking for. They had become the god they sought," and concludes that "the idea of overcoming, of breaking down the boundaries that hold us in and surpassing the limits of our own natures, is central to all stories of the quest" (*SATL* 351, 352). Since September 11, Rushdie has also realized that "those who spend their time on guard, waiting for the barbarians to arrive, in the end don't need any barbarians to come. In a dark variation of the ending of the 'Conference of the Birds,' they themselves become the barbarians whose coming they so feared. And then there are no solutions" (*SATL* 358). In the new age of "Terror versus Security" that Rushdie first highlighted in his January 2000 column for the *New York Times*, this potential darkness is now a greater possibility. Then, Rushdie confidently asserted, "In a choice between security and liberty, it is liberty that must always come out on top" (*SATL* 290). In the 2002 Turner Lecture on Human Values at Yale, however, Rushdie confesses,

> Like every writer in the world, I am trying to find a way of writing after September 11, 2001, a day that has become something like a borderline. Not only because the attacks were a kind of invasion but because we all crossed a frontier that day, an invisible boundary between the imaginable and the unimaginable, and it turned out to be the unimaginable that was real. (*SATL* 375–76)

Although Rushdie is a strong believer in the imagination, this new reality still proves challenging. He closes his Turner Lecture with this question, comment, and tentative hope: "Will we become the suits of armor our fear makes us put on, or will we continue to be ourselves? The frontier both shapes our character and tests our mettle. I hope we pass the test" (*SATL* 381). Rushdie's new uncertainty about the future and his shaken belief in the human is part of a journey that is not over yet—for him or his readers—and he is certain to continue to explore this new frontier and much else in both the fiction and nonfiction he has yet to write.

Works Cited

Chauhan, Pradyumna S., ed. *Salman Rushdie Interviews: A Sourcebook of His Ideas*. Westport: Greenwood, 2001. Print.

Herwitz, Daniel, and Ashutosh Varshney, eds. *Midnight's Diaspora: Critical Encounters with Salman Rushdie*. Ann Arbor: U of Michigan P, 2008.

MacDonogh, Steve, ed. *The Rushdie Letters: Freedom to Speak, Freedom to Write*. Dingle: Brandon, 1993.

Reder, Michael, ed. *Conversations with Salman Rushdie*. Jackson: UP of Mississippi, 2000.

Rushdie, Salman. *Imaginary Homelands: Essays and Criticism, 1981–1991*. London: Granta, 1991.

_____. *The Jaguar Smile: A Nicaraguan Journey*. 1987. Toronto: Vintage, 1997.

_____. "One Thousand Days in a Balloon." *Imaginary Homelands: Essays and Criticism, 1981–1991*. Rev. ed. London: Granta, 1992. 430–39.

_____. *Step Across This Line: Collected Nonfiction, 1992–2002*. Toronto: Vintage, 2003.

_____. *The Wizard of Oz*. London: British Film Institute, 1992.

Sawhney, Sabina, and Simona Sawhney. "Reading Rushdie after September 11, 2001." *Twentieth-Century Literature* 47.4 (2001): 431–43.

One and Many in *The Moor's Last Sigh*
Dohra Ahmad

Since September 11, 2001, commentators have rushed to offer their interpretations of radical Islam, the "clash of civilizations," jihad, and other purportedly relevant phenomena, but rarely turn to literary sources. Much contemporary fiction would in fact have proved valuable, from Hanif Kureishi's "My Son the Fanatic" (1994) and Zadie Smith's *White Teeth* (2000), both of which present fundamentalism as a modern, metropolitan, late-capitalist invention, to Kamila Shamsie's *Burnt Shadows* (2009), which traces the role of the CIA in shaping Afghanistan's retrogressive mujahideen. But the most obvious novelistic source on fundamentalism would be the work of Salman Rushdie. While *The Satanic Verses* anticipated many of the themes that later played out in his own history, Rushdie's best work on fundamentalism and hybridity—the two worldviews that, according to Rushdie, distinguish all culture—came in his 1995 novel *The Moor's Last Sigh*, which brilliantly represents the two as not only competing modes of expression but competing forms of historiography. Through one or the other, Rushdie asserts, all thinking people organize their ideas of art, love, and politics and their pictures of past, present, and future. Ultimately, Rushdie reveals the apparent opposites as distorted versions of each other. *The Moor's Last Sigh* contains several forms of fundamentalism, and as the novel progresses, it becomes clear that they are all modern, artificial phenomena. Conversely—and less palatably to his cosmopolitan readership—Rushdie shows hybridity, too, to be its own brand of fundamentalism.

An investigation of these two warring modes of expression may begin with Rushdie's apparent elision of Islam in *The Moor's Last Sigh*. When the novel first appeared, many readers wondered whether and where Rushdie would represent Ayatollah Khomeini and his militant followers. The question was easy to answer with the earlier *Haroun and the Sea of Stories*: The ayatollah became the despotic Khattam-Shud, "the Arch-Enemy of all Stories" (39). In *The Moor's Last Sigh*, Rushdie employs metaphor and association rather than allegory, thus taking his study of Islam in a more interesting and useful direction and breaking the simple equivalence between Islam and fundamentalism. Therefore, we can enter the novel through its conspicuous absence of Islam.

I. Fundamentalisms

A year after Khomeini's *fatwā* (legal ruling), Rushdie effectively, if obliquely, forswore Islam as a literary subject. In a 1990 review of Philip Roth's memoir *The Facts*, Rushdie retells Roth's story of his experience following the publication of *Goodbye, Columbus*. Vilified by Jewish readers, whom he had previously identified as his constituency, Roth responded, in Rushdie's summary, "'I'll never write about Jews again!'" On that score, Rushdie declares portentously, "He seems to speak directly, profoundly, not only to, but *for*, me"—the implication, of course, being that Rushdie would never write about Muslims again (*Imaginary Homelands* 347; Rushdie's emphasis).[1] However, Rushdie's ambition would hardly allow him to limit himself so categorically. Announcing that Roth "speaks for" him even as he himself speaks for Roth is a careful and unusual maneuver. As he both swears and does not swear a parallel vow to Roth's, he both obeys and disobeys it in *The Moor's Last Sigh*.

For while the novel travels as far south as one can go in India in order to shake off the presence of Islam and while its cast of hundreds includes almost no Muslim characters, it still addresses reductive, fundamentalist Islam through its portrayal of many other types of fundamentalism. Islam lingers in two ways: on a literal level through the protagonist's hidden ancestor and on a symbolic level through the other faiths that separately dramatize its minority and majoritarian incarnations. As Aamir Mufti and others have pointed out, "fundamentalism" is a shifty and unreliable term, subject to abuse as an all-purpose pejorative or more perniciously as a synonym for Islam. Writing on *The Satanic Verses* and its fallout, Mufti sets out to "use the term . . . in a very specific sense," usefully historicizing and contextualizing a particular public discourse of Islamism (52, 59–60). In *The Moor's Last Sigh*, Rushdie responds to the same problem but through an entirely different tactic. Rather than narrowing the term, he widens it to show that fundamentalist mindsets infect not only Islam but also Hinduism, Christianity, Marxism, modern art, and for that matter, even the doctrine of hybridity that many would prefer to view as redemptively flexible. Within his novel, Islam is only one of many rigid, totalizing visions that claim to rely on an eternal truth. Rushdie places all of these totalizing visions in the same category; hence, my own topic of not merely fundamentalism but the plural, fundamentalisms. Furthermore, the novel portrays Islam not as synonymous with fundamentalism but rather as two utterly separate phenomena in its minority and majoritarian versions.[2]

Though the story is practically devoid of Muslim characters, Islam pervades the novel in the form of the hidden, illegitimate ancestor, one namesake of the doubly referential title. *The Moor's Last Sigh* shares the basic structure of *Midnight's Children* (as well as Ralph Ellison's *Invisible Man* before it) with a beleaguered first-person narrator delving into his ancestry and autobiography from a hidden and threatened location. But whereas the narrator of *Midnight's Children* quite simply represents India (having been born at the exact moment of independence), the titular Moor embodies all the nation's minorities. Moraes "Moor" Zogoiby is "a jewholic anonymous, a cathjew nut, a stewpot, a mongrel cur"—to be precise, the son of a Catholic and a Jew (104). As in *Midnight's Children*, the narrator must go back three generations to begin his story, first chronicling the dissipation of his mother's Portuguese Indian spice-baron clan. Only after six chapters does Moor's mother, Aurora, then a young and insouciant heiress, fall in love with her penniless employee Abraham Zogoiby—at which point Rushdie races through a quick detour on the several millennia of Jewish migration to India. As though the mix were not historically and literarily rich enough, Abraham soon confronts his mother, Flory, with the possibility that his family descends from Boabdil, the last Arab ruler of Spain.

From here on, Flory's, Abraham's, and thus Moor's questionable descent reverberates throughout the text as Rushdie continually equates Jews and Muslims. Among the many associations, Rushdie reminds us that both groups became Indian at the same time, upon their shared expulsion from Spain in 1492.[3] Further, Rushdie uses literary sources to justify the association, quoting passages from *The Merchant of Venice* that disparage Arabs and Jews as well as Indians. In Rushdie's summary of Shakespeare, "Moors, Indians, and of course 'the Jew' . . . are waved away" and thus become functional equivalents (114–15). Dismissed from European literature as well as from Europe, the Muslim and the Jew find refuge, if not peace, in India and in Rushdie's hybrid literature.

The tie between "the dispossessed Spanish Arab and the ejected Spanish Jew" is so strong that Rushdie hardly needs Abraham to insist on the coupling of Boabdil and Abraham's own nameless Jewish foremother (82). The sixteenth-century liaison parallels a twentieth-century connection as Indian Muslims and Jews struggle for survival as minorities, finding self-determination only in Bombay's underworld. In Abraham's own estimation, his negotiations with a decadent Parsi shipping-magnate family are like "when the armies of Islam thundered in" (182). Writing on *The Satanic Verses*, Gayatri Spivak points to another tie between Indian Islam and Indian Judaism: "Islamic India is another theme of migrancy . . . For Islam as such has its head turned away from the subcontinent, across the Arabian Sea, perpetually emigrant toward Mecca" (110). If Indian Islam is definitionally migrant, Judaism has been historically migrant, as the community historian Flory continually reminds her son.

Hillel Halkin, reviewing *The Moor's Last Sigh* for *Commentary*, characterizes Rushdie's use of Jewish characters as a gesture of "cowardice" and "surrender" (59). Here, he is supported by Norman Rush in the *New York Times Book Review*, who finds Abraham's identity "off-putting" (7). Yet Halkin himself notes that Abraham's Jewishness serves a literary purpose, since "Abraham, the original Jew and the original monotheist, is in Islamic tradition the first Muslim." While hinting that Rushdie has used Judaism as a figure for Islam, Halkin stops short of registering the value of that association. In fact, the history of Jews in India serves Rushdie's purposes remarkably well. His own justification for the apparent marginality of his subject is that Indian Jews represent the ultimate test of Indianness to absorb diverse subjects. "Majority, that mighty elephant, and her sidekick, Major-Minority, will not crush my tale beneath her feet. Are my personages not Indian, every one?" his narrator exclaims (87). Jews are important both in their own right and as symbolic of a more generalized minority existence in India.

In order to test the capacity of Indian identity to absorb difference, Rushdie has carefully chosen the smallest religious minority in India as well as one of the oldest, present in India even before the birth of Islam or Sikhism. After centuries of untroubled dual identity, two modern developments endowed the deeply Indian community with a new sense of difference. The first was the arrival of British colonialism, with its classifying tendencies and obsession with race. Along with the newly created ethnic minority of Anglo-Indians, the historically Indian Jews oscillated in census, civil service, and army classifications between the general categories of Indian and European. No arbitrary titles, such classes determined government pay scales and employment quotas, rendering it beneficial for Jews to be classified as European (Roland 40–41). Second, Zionism during its height in the 1930s brought Indian Jews for the first time into an international religiously based political movement, highlighting their difference from Indians organizing for independence (Roland 128–70). Thus, Indian Jews, mirroring Rushdie's relationship to both India and Islam, found themselves in a position simultaneously inside and outside India. Without referring directly to these two historical factors, Rushdie creates a sense of the dual pressures of insularity and assimilation bearing down on the small Cochin community. The choice of Judaism as a subject was a challenging and fruitful one, not cowardly, as Halkin claims.

Even as migrant Islam surfaces as minority Judaism in the novel, the statist, authoritarian version of modern Islam appears in Rushdie's satiric portrait of monotheistic Hinduism. Invisible Islam then is split into two components: Migrant Islam, the minority religion of banished Boabdil, becomes a struggling Judaism, and fundamentalist Islam, majority religion and statist ideology, becomes a warped, dishonest monotheistic Hinduism. Just as minority Judaism both symbolizes other minority religions and carries its own genuine history, majority Hinduism too both functions as a figure for majority Islam elsewhere and carries its own context and meaning. Indeed, Rushdie had identified Balasaheb Thackeray and his Shiv Sena party (transmuted here into Raman Fielding and Mumbai's Axis) as a danger to multicultural India and as a target of his own pen, even before he himself became a target of another brand of fundamentalism. It was in 1987, writing on India's fortieth anniversary, that Rushdie reluctantly introduced his readers to the Shiv Sena and "its leader, Bal Thackeray, a former cartoonist," whose objectives directly oppose Rushdie's ideal of a hybrid India (*Imaginary Homelands* 31–32).

In transforming the Shiv Sena into the fictional Mumbai's Axis (MA), led by another vicious cartoonist, Rushdie emphasizes the group's sectarian outlook at the expense of its regionalism. According to Thackeray himself, the Shiv Sena was founded primarily to safeguard the economic interests of Marathi-speaking Maharashtrians against other residents of Mumbai, including Hindu "outsiders" (Katzenstein 18). That particular form of exclusivism—linguistic and regional rather than religious—drops out of Rushdie's consideration in his fictional portrayal of Mumbai's Axis. Within *The Moor's Last Sigh*, the greatest tragedy of Hindu fundamentalism, as represented by Raman Fielding and his MA, is that it denies its own diversity. To make this point, Rushdie uses Zeenat Vakil (who had previously appeared in *The Satanic Verses*) as a mouthpiece. To Zeenat, MA betrays the "many-headed beauty" of Hinduism with its insistence on "a single, martial deity, a single book, and mob rule" (338). Again, the rigidity of institutionalized Hinduism holds true in its own right but also functions as an oblique criticism of Islam, which Rushdie believes ought to have the capacity to engage criticism productively from within.

As he turns his novelist's eye on Indian Judaism and Hinduism, Rushdie's interest is in how majority and minority faiths function differently and how in shifting contexts they often come to resemble each other. Within Flory's tiny Cochin enclave, Judaism is a majority religion and, accordingly, has established its own set of lies and hypocrisies, such as denying the illegitimate Muslim ancestor. Hinduism, on the other hand, while technically a majority religion, splinters into castes and regional deities. Appearing rigid and fluid by turns, minority Judaism and majority Hinduism take on each other's characteristics. The history of minorities in India bears out Rushdie's artistic assertions: For example, Jewish communities in India have come to conform to Hindu social structurings, as one analysis of the division of Cochin and Bombay Jews into hierarchized, ancestral, caste-like subgroups attests (Schermerhorn 242). As if to remind the reader that Islam lurks between the lines of his text, Rushdie shifts interreligious influence in an unlikely direction. Over centuries, South Indian Judaism began gradually to take on attributes of the surrounding Hindu majority, such as vegetarianism and Nayar symbolism, whether through coerced or respectful assimilation (Katz and Goldberg). For Rushdie's fictional Jews, though, the only concrete syncretic adaptation is Flory's insistence that synagogue-goers remove their shoes, a "positively Moorish practice" (*Moor's* 75). Even though he has set his action in a region with a relatively minor Muslim presence, Rushdie dictates, ahistorically, that Cochin Jews adopt Muslim conventions.

Rushdie's exploration of the various forms of religious faith finds parallels in his portrayal of competing philosophies of art. In *The Moor's Last Sigh*, art is another kind of faith: a vehicle for organizing and expressing experience and an undertaking with internal orthodoxies and schisms. In treating art as a secular expression of faith, Rushdie revisits Aadam Aziz's "god-shaped hole" from *Midnight's Children*.

Struck by an agnostic epiphany, Aadam finds his new irreligion has left him with "a vacancy in a vital inner chamber" (4). As Rushdie himself has described (Appignanesi and Maitland 62), he shares such a vacancy and fills it with writing; in that sense, the novelist's proxy within this work is not Moor, but his mother, Aurora, who conveys both the power and the possible shortcomings of an aesthetic that celebrates hybridity. Describing Aurora's painting, Rushdie could be speaking of his own writing. It is Aurora's father, Camoens, who first notices the vacancy in his young daughter's paintings, in which "only God was absent" (60). Later, Aurora's paintings attempt to make up for that absent god as she creates a secularist art by borrowing from many religious traditions.

Diametrically opposed philosophies of art find their expression in the novel's two artists, who are also the two women who compete for Moor's love and loyalty: his cruel but straightforward mother, Aurora, and his deceptive, chameleon-like lover, Uma. Aurora's painting and Uma's sculpture neatly represent two opposing modes of artistic expression. Aurora's painting, with the exception of her brief realist phase, is teeming, surreal, and multivalent. As Camoens exclaims over her first painting, "it is the great swarm of being itself"—specifically, "being" rendered as contradictory, hyperabundant, oppositional, and historically grounded (59). Here, on the other hand, is Uma's art: "The centrepiece of the show was a group of seven roughly spherical, metre-high stone pieces with a small hollow scooped out at the top and filled with richly coloured powders—scarlet, ultramarine, saffron, emerald, purple, orange, gold . . . entitled *Alterations in/Reclamations of the Essence of Motherhood in the Post-Secularist Epoch*" (261). Uma's sculpture also purports to convey "being," but in a purified, unitary, and essentialist form.

Uma's art, Raman Fielding's monotheism, and the late ayatollah's fundamentalist Islam find their kin among the various species of fundamentalism explored in the novel's central opposition. Rushdie sets up his dialectic as early as his first page, when Moor recalls Uma and Aurora punningly presenting the two possibilities for literary expression. Uma says, "in fondness, 'Oh, you Moor, you strange black man, always so full of theses, never a church door to nail them to'"; Aurora responds, "quick as snakebite, 'So full, you mean, of faeces'" (3). This opening pairing of theses versus feces gives us an opposition that structures the entire novel. Theses are pure, transcendent truths, a category that reappears as various singular beliefs from founding myths of nations and religions to the Word as brought by the Prophet in the Judeo-Christian milieu of the book to the figure of Ram in the overlayered Hindu milieu. Feces, their opposing category, are stories told and retold, filtered through the human body like a breath or a sigh. This category reappears as paintings painted over, evolving nations and subjects, and a polytheistic universe. The theses/feces duality guides the book's later dualities: racial purity opposed to miscegenation; legitimacy opposed to illegitimacy; the name opposed to multiplicitous and continually evolving nicknames; definitive analyses opposed to provisional analyses; and authoritarianism opposed to tolerance.

The opening paragraphs of *The Moor's Last Sigh* pretend to assert that the book will be organized according to the simple duality represented by the characters of Uma and Aurora. We are given a string of simple oppositions: godly/ungodly, Christian/un-Christian, "'Amrika' and 'Moskva' . . . the two great super-powers," and "here I stand" / "here I sit" (3). Yet throughout the book, the two overarching opposing categories of theses and feces, or the definitive and the provisional, implicate each other in innumerable ways. In the most obvious and intellectually appealing sense, Rushdie shows that the category of feces more accurately reflects reality and thus implicates the category of theses as false constructions. Berating Uma for her false self-construction, Moor articulates the distinction between provisional expression, which contains truth, and definitive expression, which necessarily obfuscates. "It wasn't a metaphor, Uma," he says in response to her falsified family narrative. "It was a lie. What's scary is, you don't know the difference" (270). Rushdie allies multiplicitous, polytheistic Hinduism and "its many-headed beauty" with the now-ascendant category of the provisional, using Zeenat Vakil to point out the inappropriateness of Hindu nationalism's construction of a singular, quasi-monotheistic Cult of Ram. It is Zeenat who articulates the view of fundamentalism as a human construction that manufactures its own history. In her succinct and ironic expression, "This fundo stuff is really something new" (338).

This may be Rushdie's most important observation on fundamentalism in *The Moor's Last Sigh*, and other novelists have joined social historians in bearing it out. In her 2000 blockbuster *White Teeth*, Zadie Smith presents modern religious fundamentalism as a hybrid form itself, as well as a highly historically determined development. Here, she describes her young rebel Millat's "Raggastani" crew in 1989, on their way to burning copies of the (unnamed) *Satanic Verses*:

> Raggastanis spoke a strange mix of Jamaican patois, Bengali, Gujarati, and English. Their ethos, their manifesto, if it could be called that, was equally a hybrid thing: Allah *featured*, but more as a collective big brother than a supreme being, a hard-as-fuck *geezer* who would fight in their corner if necessary; kung fu and the works of Bruce Lee were also central to the philosophy; added to this was a smattering of Black Power . . . but mainly their mission was to put the Invincible back in Indian, the Badaaaass back in Bengali, the P-Funk back in Pakistani. (192)

Above all else, in Smith's portrayal, this is a late-capitalist phenomenon: "Everything, everything, everything was *Nike*™; wherever the five of them went the impression they left behind was of one gigantic swoosh, one huge mark of corporate approval" (193). Rushdie, like Smith, reveals that in terms of fundamentalism and hybridity, the reality is reversed, and fundamentalism is a manufactured and hybrid construction. That inversion holds true with the other incarnations of the theses/feces dichotomy, such as racial purity and miscegenation. As Moor's father, Abraham, says in confronting his exclusivist mother, Flory, "*My mother who insists on the purity of our race, what say you to your forefather the Moor?*" (82). Miscegenation, Abraham insists, is reality, and racial purity a lie. By association, apparently benign fundamentalisms lose the ability to inspire faith. Rushdie experiments with various utopian theories and grand unified theories, showing them to be rigid, codified, institutionalized modes of organizing and expressing reality. Moor himself points out to Zeenat the parallel nature of her Marxism and the fundamentalism she deplores. His grandfather, Camoens, fifty years earlier, had also fallen victim to Marxism's doctrinal rigidity. A still unluckier grand unified theory is great-grandfather Francisco da Gama's widely ridiculed *Towards a Provisional Theory of Transformational Fields of Conscience*, or "dynamic networks of spiritual energy similar to electromagnetic fields," which brings the poor visionary ignominy and finally death (20). Here, Rushdie parodies Anton Mesmer, whose eccentric, quasiscientific theories he incorporated into his 1994 short story "The Harmony of the Spheres." That story documents a search for ways to organize experience in absolutely comprehensive terms—a search that ends in madness and suicide.

If art successfully fills the vacancy left by the loss of faith, then utopias and grand unified theories represent a failed attempt to locate a secular definition of spirituality. Utopias are particularly doomed to failure since they both rely upon newness and aspire to timelessness. A utopian structure demands fixity and therefore threatens the process of movement that is art. Where utopias point toward an ahistorical, fixed future, origin myths refer back to an ahistorical past. In undermining a series of origin myths, Rushdie plays out Edward Said's distinction between fundamentalist origins and fluid beginnings. Rushdie traces the illegitimate roots of every family history, a starting point that falls into the category of Said's secular, open beginnings. Young Aurora, for one, vocalizes the project of debunking origins, deriding Anglicanism as "this Church that only startofied because some Piss-in-Boots old king wanted a sexy younger wife" (94). Religion, family, and nation receive the same disillusioning treatment.

Rushdie is fascinated by the process through which beginnings become origins, the same process through which his own prose in *The*

Satanic Verses crystallized into what Spivak calls "a disposable container of blasphemy" (116). Through both direct and indirect means, Rushdie effectively breaks down fundamentalisms in all their related, often hidden forms. Perhaps the only grand unified theory to survive the rigors of the text is the artist Vasco Miranda's "'Indian variation' upon the theme of Einstein's General Theory":

> Everything is for relative. Not only light bends, but everything. For relative we can bend a point, bend the truth, bend employment criteria, bend the law. D equals mc squared, where D is for Dynasty, m is for mass of relatives, and c of course is for corruption, which is the only constant in the universe—because in India even speed of light is dependent on load shedding and other vagaries of power supply. (272)

While uniting East and West, physics and sociology in parodic formula, Vasco identifies nepotistic corruption as the only reliable constant.

II. Hybridities

With fundamentalisms undermined, hybrid art—the art of feces, breath, and bastard—apparently must triumph. This is the simple and palatable inversion, conventionally viewed as Rushdie's political and aesthetic program: Pure corruption overthrows corrupt purity. If purity is a corrupt and false construct, then only corruption has integrity. Within the structure of this inversion, Aurora's art (and, by extension, Rushdie's writing) triumphs as the only possible art for India or indeed for the world. Aurora's painting dispels the notion that modernity cannot survive in India, a notion that haunts the novel's early chapters. Riffing on Le Corbusier's visits to Ahmedabad in the 1950s, Rushdie rewrites history to bring the yet-unknown architect to India even earlier, commissioned by Francisco da Gama to build experimental structures on his ancestral property. Anachronism follows anachronism as "foreign artists came to stay and left behind strange mobiles that looked like giant metal coathangers twirling in the breeze, and pictures of devil-women with both eyes on the same side of their noses, and giant canvasses that looked like an accident had befallen with the paint" (16). However, India cannot absorb the likes of Calder, Picasso, and Pollock, and Le Corbusier's "follies" eventually go down in flames. A generation later, Francisco's equally visionary son Camoens experiments with another modernist import—Leninism—with as little success. Granted special permission by the Moscow authorities, Camoens trains a troupe of actors to impersonate the top comrade and declaim his great words. After months of toil, a "genuine" Lenin visits Cochin to inspect Camoens's effort toward the propagation of radicalism but finds the actors "too tall, too short, too fat, too skinny, too lame, too bald, and that one has no teeth," and departs with the pronouncement that "this country of yours . . . gives to him the shits." Camoens must conclude reluctantly that communism "was not 'the Indian style'" (30–31). Those aesthetic and political modernities may fail, but after independence, Aurora creates an alternative modernity. Several chapters and one generation later, her art emerges to reclaim "the shits" as a proud characteristic of Indian national life.

Like fundamentalism, hybridity appears in many guises, including the mythical land for whose loss the original Moor sighed. Rushdie based the novel's title (and that of a series of Aurora's paintings) on the legend that Arab Andalusia's last sultan, the weak and quixotic Boabdil, wept upon being forced from Granada, where, as Rushdie puts it elsewhere, a "composite culture" thrived with "Christians and Jews and Muslims living side by side for hundreds of years" (*Conversations* 202). As his namesake cried for Andalusia, our Moor and his creator both mourn the loss of a tolerant, multicultural India whose demise Rushdie dates at the rise of the Hindu Right in the 1990s. Elsewhere, the same ideal becomes Moor's vision of love:

> the blending of spirits, as mélange, as the triumph of the impure, mongrel, conjoining best over what there is in us of the solitary, the isolated, the austere, the dogmatic, the pure; of love as democracy, as the victory of the

no-man-is-an-island, two's-company Many over the clean, mean, apartheiding Ones. (289)

What begins as an apparent prescription for art and culture metamorphoses into a comprehensive philosophy of every aspect of life.

For Rushdie, a proper art must not only embrace elements of divergent traditions, but do so outside the law. "I am a bastard child of history," he gleefully declared in his 1990 essay "In Good Faith" (*Imaginary Homelands* 394). Throughout the novel, he explicitly connects the bastard with the work of feces-art. "*Bastard:* I like the sound of the word," Moor exclaims. "*Baas*, a smell, a stinky-poo. *Turd*, no translation required. Ergo, *Bastard*, a smelly shit; like, for example, me" (104). With the gloss of Rushdie's bilingual pseudoderivation, the single epithet neatly encapsulates linguistic mongrelization, both in itself and as a figure for racial and religious miscegenation, along with illegitimacy: in other words, the three elements essential to literary expression.

Through his (provisional) valorization of legal, artistic, linguistic, and philosophical hybridity, Rushdie suggests a utopia of universal illegitimacy. Moor and Rushdie yearn for Abraham's world of the miscegenated, where no one can claim legitimacy; Bombay is its urban exemplar. The city is "the bastard child of a Portuguese-English wedding, and yet the most Indian of Indian cities. In Bombay all Indias met and merged" (350). Rushdie's artistic project demands that Moor and his miscegenated siblings be illegitimate. In the novel, Abraham and Aurora never marry, since neither bishop nor rabbi will marry them. In fact, colonial India operated under three distinct law codes, English, Hindu, and Mohammedan. Miscegenated children, whether Portuguese Catholic, Anglican, or Hindu, were subject to Mohammedan law, a simplification that Anglo-Indians protested in an 1830 Petition of Grievances to the British parliament (Abel 23; Hawes 143). The majority of interracial and interreligious children were indeed illegitimate, being the product of rape, prostitution, or concubinage, rather than marriage, but even those who escaped circumstantial illegitimacy were definitionally illegitimate in the sense of existing outside the law. Their tenuous position mirrored that of the Christian converts whom, Gauri Viswanathan shows, colonial law had placed into a "liminal existence" (185). For Rushdie and for Moor, that liminality provides a source of artistic power. Moor's permanent outsider status lends a new meaning to Uma's opening quip: He never has a church door on which to nail his theses because he has never had a church.

Rushdie initially appears to endorse a hybrid art—the art of the feces—through the linked sets of associations enumerated above: illegitimacy, miscegenation, pluralism, linguistic play. In all its many forms, bastardization causes a breaking down of legal fundamentalism that is in keeping with the Moor's tentative, poignant, self-affirming vision of love. According to standard readings of Rushdie, feces must triumph over theses. We have come to view Rushdie as the champion par excellence of a hybrid art; thus many critical treatments of *The Moor's Last Sigh* see the novel as responding single-mindedly to the fundamentalist excesses of the *Satanic Verses* firestorm (Baker; Weiss; Glage and Kunor).[4] Indeed, to claim otherwise is to go against the grain of Rushdie scholarship, and Rushdie himself provides plenty of evidence for a "pro-hybridity" understanding of his novel. However, the novel itself undermines such a sanguine conclusion: For by the time of Moor's exile from India, Rushdie chooses to annihilate his illegitimate, mongrel city. The positive productive vision of hybridity cannot sustain itself through the entire narrative. Like fundamentalism, hybridity has its own shortcomings, difficulties, and hypocrisies, and as both Aurora's art and Moor's love demonstrate, it carries with it the seeds of its own destruction. Even Aurora must reluctantly conclude that "the ideas of impurity, cultural admixture, and mélange which had been, for most of her creative life, the closest things she had found to a notion of the Good, were in fact capable of distortion, and contained a potential for darkness as well as light" (303).

What are the shortcomings of a guiding philosophy based on principles of hybridity? For one, Rushdie shows that, since fundamentalism will still be the dominant mode, a hybridity-based art will necessarily be bound by the logic of fundamentalism. Even a work that contains numerous impermanent meanings will be vulnerable to reductive readings when brought into the public sphere. The reception of Aurora's painting *The Kissing of Abbas Ali Baig*—a Breughalesque "state-of-India painting" whose contents range from Tantric paintings to cartoons to real-life celebrities—illustrates this process, as Raman Fielding and his followers insist that it must be interpreted as an anti-Hindu political work.

If we engage in so tedious a decoding as to locate a figure for *The Satanic Verses* anywhere in *The Moor's Last Sigh*, it would certainly be this painting. Like Rushdie's own maligned work,

> it became, however, an albatross, and I witnessed both her ennui at having endlessly to defend it, and her fury at the ease with which this 'teapot monsoon' had distracted attention from the body of her real work. She was required by the public prints to speak ponderously of 'underlying motives' when she had had only whims, to make moral statements where there had been only ('only'!) play, and feeling, and the unfolding inexorable logic of brush and light. (234)

The controversy surrounding the painting marks the moment at which Aurora "becomes" a Christian artist, just as *The Satanic Verses* transformed Rushdie from a secular British Indian into a blaspheming Muslim.

Here, the fear is that hybridity art will be subject to the rules of the fundamentalist world, with only two possible outcomes: Either the work of art will be absorbed into the rubric of fundamentalism, or it will be held out as a *definitive* counterattack on fundamentalism. In either case, the art loses its provisional character and thus its power. *The Kissing of Abbas Ali Baig* illustrates the latter outcome; Aurora's ill-fated protest dance illustrates the former. As J. M. Coetzee observes in his review of *The Moor's Last Sigh*, when "a show of 'Hindu fundamentalist triumphalism' passes by their house, she dances in view of the celebrants, dancing *against* the god, though, alas, her dance is read by them as part of the spectacle" (13), demonstrating fundamentalism's capacity to absorb its opposite.

A related fear regarding hybridity art is that it defines itself in relation to fundamentalisms. The very derivation of illegitimacy, after all, implies law, just as "hybridity" implies pure strains, and the metaphor of the masala implies its own component spices. The project of blasphemy, in other words, depends upon orthodoxy. Such definition by opposition may imply an attraction to fundamentalism: This potential attraction underlies Moor's obsessive curiosity as to whether his artist-mother is in bed with Raman Fielding. Borrowing at once from Freud and thermodynamics, Moor describes the ongoing relationship between Aurora and Fielding—and, by extension, between hybridity and fundamentalism—as a "strange dance of attraction and repulsion" (230).

Finally, Rushdie documents the possibility of the institutionalization of hybridity art, a possibility that surfaces in his novel in figures of state galleries and retrospective shows. These figures dramatize Rushdie's fear of crossing from low to high and therefore from blasphemy to orthodoxy. Luther's theses, the overarching structural figure for the text, themselves evolved from heretical pronouncements into established religion. Rushdie fears that the trope of a world of miscegenation has become a cliché and that pidgin, creole, and hybrid literatures lose their power when crystallized into a written form. If hybridity derives its critical stance from its newness, it may be a stance that cannot be sustained. In this novel's terms, the inherent danger is that the miscegenated child may cease to be a bastard.

If Uma and Aurora are the two artists who embody definitive and provisional artistic expression, Aurora's unctuous lover Vasco Miranda represents the moment of hybridity's institutionalization. Introducing himself to Aurora, he claims kinship on the basis that both are "exponents of Epico-Mythico-Tragico-Comico-Super-Sexy-High-Masala-Art" (148–49). Unlike Aurora, he courts and receives massive commercial success; here, Rushdie briefly and guiltily acknowledges the profit motive behind magic realism.[5] Rushdie almost allows Vasco to appear as a benign character, consistently identifying him with cartoons from his physical appearance to his first mural painting to his last words, "That's all folks!" One cannot forget, however, that a cartoon, the parody imam of *The Satanic Verses*, almost killed Rushdie. Vasco too engages in a parody of fundamentalism, even as he parodies hybridity elsewhere. In response to India's annexation of Goa, Vasco looses a reflexive battery of protonationalist practices, cooking coconut curries and recounting apocryphal stories of Portuguese explorers, "his fishy Goan tales" (156). The ultimate palimpsest, Vasco finally bursts. Rushdie's always difficult—and sometimes failed—task is to wrest control of the novel from Vasco Miranda and thereby to prevent it from becoming "High-Masala-Art."

III. (In)conclusion

Rushdie's final thesis is that all previous assumptions must be inverted. He ultimately presents fundamentalism as a historically grounded construct and hybridity as a rigid and institutionalized doctrine. The incessant inversions may disappoint readers who prefer to believe that Rushdie simply celebrates hybridity and will certainly disorient any reader, but they serve a further purpose as well. By obviating any facile conclusions, they allow Rushdie to reclaim his text from the possibility of misreading. The history of Rushdie's writing, after all, is a history of violence following from a reductive, literalist reading. In *The Moor's Last Sigh*, he enacts the only way to win against such reductivism: namely, to throw multiplicity in its face by taking ownership of all possible interpretations—ideally, even the utterly contradictory ones.[6]

Rushdie's writing, like the fundamentalist festival, manages to contain its own opposite. Orthodoxy and blasphemy, theses and feces, the definitive and the provisional, coexist within his pages—which is why

Uma and Aurora, mouthpieces for fundamentalist art and hybridity art, must continually be identified with each other. Only by asserting complete inversion may Rushdie both close his writing to the possibility of misinterpretation and leave open the possibility of further writing. Only thus can he pull his work out of the matrix of fundamentalism and hybridity that defines human experience.

Notes

1. See David J. Zucker's essay in this volume for a complete exploration of the parallels between Rushdie and Roth.
2. See Ian Almond's essay for an excellent study of the "not one but several Islams in [Rushdie's] work, a polyphony of different Islams which many commentators have overlooked" (1138).
3. For more on this topic, see Mona Narain's chapter in this volume.
4. A notable exception is Rachel Trousdale's essay, which carefully outlines the failures of cosmopolitanism in *The Moor's Last Sigh*.
5. Laura Moss argues that *The Moor's Last Sigh*'s primary mode is parody—specifically, of magic realism. I would add, however, that *The Moor's Last Sigh* operates on so many registers at once that its purpose cannot be classified simply as parody.
6. For an expanded discussion of how *The Moor's Last Sigh* depicts the process of interpretation, see my essay "'This Fundo Stuff is Really Something New': Fundamentalism and Hybridity in *The Moor's Last Sigh*."

Works Cited

Abel, Evelyn. *The Anglo-Indian Community: Survival in India*. Delhi: Chanakya, 1988.
Ahmad, Dohra. "'This Fundo Stuff Is Really Something New': Fundamentalism and Hybridity in *The Moor's Last Sigh*." *Yale Journal of Criticism* 18.1 (2005): 1–20.
Almond, Ian. "Mullahs, Mystics, Moderates, and Mughals: The Many Islams of Salman Rushdie." *ELH* 70.4 (2003): 1137–51.
Appignanesi, Lisa, and Sara Maitland, eds. *The Rushdie File*. London: Institute for Contemporary Arts, 1990.
Baker, Stephen. "'You Must Remember This': Salman Rushdie's *The Moor's Last Sigh*." *Journal of Commonwealth Literature* 35.1 (2000): 43–54.
Coetzee, J. M. "Palimpsest Regained." *New York Review of Books* 43.5 (1996): 13.
Glage, Liselotte, and Ruediger Kunor, eds. *The Decolonizing Pen: Cultural Diversity and the Transnational Imaginary in Rushdie's Fiction*. Trier: Wissenschaftlicher Verlag, 2001.

Halkin, Hillel. "Salman Rushdie Surrenders." *Commentary* 1 July 1996: 59.
Hawes, C. J. *Poor Relations: The Making of a Eurasian Community in British India, 1773–1833*. Sussex: Curzon, 1996.
Katz, Nathan, and Ellen S. Goldberg. *The Last Jews of Cochin: Jewish Identity in Hindu India*. Columbia: U of South Carolina P, 1993.
Katzenstein, Mary Fainsod. *Ethnicity and Equality: The Shiv Sena Party and Preferential Policies in Bombay*. Ithaca: Cornell UP, 1979.
Moss, Laura. "'Forget Those Damnfool Realists!': Salman Rushdie's Self-Parody as the Magic Realist's 'Last Sigh.'" *ARIEL* 29.4 (1998): 121–39.
Mufti, Aamir R. "Reading the Rushdie Affair: 'Islam,' Cultural Politics, Form." *Critical Essays on Salman Rushdie*. Ed. M. Keith Booker. New York: Hall, 1999.
Roland, Joan. *Jews in British India: Identity in a Colonial Era*. 2nd ed. New Brunswick: Transaction, 1998.
Rush, Norman. "Doomed in Bombay." *New York Times Book Review* 14 Jan. 1996: 7.
Rushdie, Salman. *Conversations with Salman Rushdie*. Ed. Michael Reder. Jackson: UP of Mississippi, 2000.
_____. "The Harmony of the Spheres." *East, West*. New York: Pantheon, 1994.
_____. *Haroun and the Sea of Stories*. London: Granta, 1990.
_____. *Imaginary Homelands: Essays and Criticism, 1981–1991*. London: Granta, 1991.
_____. *Midnight's Children*. New York: Penguin, 1980.
_____. *The Moor's Last Sigh:* New York: Pantheon, 1996.
Said, Edward. *Beginnings: Intention and Method*. New York: Basic, 1975.
Schermerhorn, R. A. *Ethnic Plurality in India*. Tucson: U of Arizona P, 1978.
Smith, Zadie. *White Teeth*. New York: Random, 2000.
Spivak, Gayatri C. "Reading *The Satanic Verses*." *What Is an Author?* Ed. Maurice Biriotti and Nicola Miller. Manchester: Manchester UP, 1993.
Trousdale, Rachel. "City of Mongrel Joy: Bombay and the Shiv Sena in *Midnight's Children* and *The Moor's Last Sigh*." *Journal of Commonwealth Literature* 39.2 (2004): 95–110.
Viswanathan, Gauri. "Coping with (Civil) Death: The Christian Convert's Rights of Passage in Colonial India." *After Colonialism*. Ed. Gyan Prakash. Princeton: Princeton UP, 1995. 183–210.
Weiss, Timothy. "At the End of East/West: Myth in Rushdie's *The Moor's Last Sigh*." *Jouvert* 4.2 (2000): 47.

Disorientation and Double Vision in *The Ground Beneath Her Feet*

Bernard F. Rodgers, Jr.

Anyone who has read *Midnight's Children* or *The Satanic Verses* will find *The Ground Beneath Her Feet*—another five-hundred-plus-page Rushdie extravaganza—familiar territory. While it lacks the focus that *Midnight's Children* gains from having its main actor as its narrator and Indian history as its frame, or the ferocious force that subversive political and religious satire gives to *The Satanic Verses*, Rushdie's eighth novel offers more than enough to engage his admirers and annoy his critics. It too overflows with characters and caricatures, secret sharers and solitaries, pop and high culture, deep thoughts and silly puns, multicultural literary and mythological references, frequent digressions, metafictional twists and turns, philosophical asides, and various other narrative hijinks. It too reflects his affection for the outsider, the outcast, and the nonbeliever. While it echoes his earlier characters and themes, *The Ground Beneath Her Feet* expands Rushdie's notion of migration into an exploration of the even more widespread conditions of disorientation and outsideness, introduces double vision as a new variation on duality and multiple identities, and shifts the setting to New York and the Americas, midway from East to West.

The book was widely described as a rock-and-roll version of the Orpheus and Eurydice myth, and it is, among other things. Rushdie is one of the international generation of post–World War II baby boomers who grew up to the soundtrack of that music, which he described to Peter Kadzis as "the first globalized cultural phenomenon" (219). In the multiethnic Bombay neighborhood where he was raised in the 1950s and 1960s, his playmates were not only Hindu and Muslim, but also Australian, Japanese, and American. Like tens of millions of others, these teenagers sang, strutted and swayed, bounced and boogied, to the same American and English beats. Since All-India radio was forbidden to broadcast Western popular music, those beats first reached him via Radio Ceylon and records that his Western friends brought with them when they came to the city. Like that of his hero, Ormus Cama, Rushdie's world was shaken when he bought his first single, "Heartbreak Hotel," at the Rhythm House record store in Bombay (Kadzis 219). The novel is his homage to the R&B legends of his youth. A year after *The Ground Beneath Her Feet* appeared, the book also gave him the chance to live out a rock fan's fantasy when U2 lead singer Bono asked permission to set the novel's title song to music, included it on the band's *Million Dollar Hotel* album, and gave Rushdie a cameo in the song's music video.

"There are so many stories to tell," Saleem Sinai says at the beginning of his saga, "too many, such an excess of intertwined lives events miracles places rumours, so dense a commingling of the improbable and the mundane! I have been a swallower of lives; and to know me, just the one of me, you'll have to swallow a lot as well" (*Midnight's Children* 8). This time, Rushdie's usual themes of home, exile, migration, freedom, unity, and fragmentation are rooted in a love story. The lovers are Ormus Cama and Vina Apsara, known worldwide as leaders of the supergroup VTO, and the narrator of their story is their friend and third wheel, photographer Umeed "Rai" Merchant, who has loved Vina too. To know *three* of them in a Rushdie novel, of course, involves a host of characters, plots and subplots, and "too many" stories. The tale spans more than sixty years, the history of four families in Bombay, corruption, urban renewal, the emergency rule, a fateful cricket accident, arson, a serial killer, homicides, suicides, earthquakes, and assassinations. It also includes pirate radio and witches in mod 1960s London; a blind Indian record producer named Yul Singh; an impresario named Mull Standish who started off as a long-haul trucker and Las Vegas street hustler; instructions from and sexual encounters with characters from another dimension; numerous twins (alive, dead, and imaginary); resurrections through the power of love; and hundreds of pop culture allusions.

The novel's epigraph, a quote from Rainer Maria Rilke's *Sonnets to Orpheus*, reminds us of its center:

> it is Orpheus. His metamorphosis
> into this and that. We should not trouble
>
> about other names. Once and for all
> it's Orpheus when there's singing.

The Ground Beneath Her Feet's Orpheus is Ormus, a Bombay Parsi composer and musician, who is an amalgam of Elvis Presley, Mick Jagger, John Lennon, Bob Dylan, and Miles Davis. Its Eurydice is Vina, a part-Indian and part-Greek American, who becomes a diva like Tina Turner, Janis Joplin, Diana Ross, Joni Mitchell, and Madonna and whose death produces an outpouring of feeling rivaling that expressed at Princess Diana's untimely passing. "He glittered, he shone," while "people loved her . . . for making herself the exaggerated avatar of their own jumbled selves," and their love and deaths are what prompt Rai to tell the story (181, 339). Hers, announced in the book's first words, occurs when she disappears into the underworld in an earthquake in Mexico on February 14, 1989—the same day that the ground fell apart beneath Salman Rushdie's feet and plunged him underground for more than a decade.

Rushdie chose to have Vina die on that date and to make it the opening of *The Ground Beneath Her Feet* because, as a goodbye to Bombay, a hello to New York and America, and a portrait of three artists who left India for the West, the impulses behind this sprawling novel are profoundly autobiographical. His decade underground clearly created a shift in his perspective that is most obvious in the changes the book rings on the meaning of the word "disorientation." Before the *Satanic Verses* affair, Rushdie saw himself as a voice for the millions of exiles and migrants who, like him, left their homes to create new lives in new lands. His fictions and essays were focused especially on the experience of migrants from the South Asian subcontinent, on memories of India and Pakistan, and on those who had lost that "ground beneath their feet." After the initial shock and confusion caused by the *fatwā* (legal ruling)—which at one point led him to try to make peace with his pursuers by professing his faith in Islam, a statement he retracted shortly thereafter—he became less connected to that audience but even more adamant about his lack of religious belief and his right to express unpopular ideas. He also began to see the issues involved in his conflict with fundamentalist and radical Islam as emblematic of a larger, more essential division among people everywhere. While he was writing *The Ground Beneath Her Feet*, he expressed this realization in a 1996 commencement address at Bard College that foreshadows the ideas he pursues in the novel. "In the years to come," he told the graduates, in words that they and all of us who heard them that day will not easily forget,

> you will find yourselves up against gods of all sorts, big and little gods, corporate and incorporeal gods, all of them demanding to be worshipped and obeyed—the myriad deities of money and power, of convention and custom, that will seek to limit and control your thoughts and lives. Defy them; that's my advice to you. Thumb your noses. For, as the myths tell us, it is by defying the gods that human beings have best expressed their humanity. (*Step Across This Line* 139)

"Disorientation [means] loss of the East," Rai notes in the first pages of the novel and repeats several times afterward (*Ground* 5). He soon expands the meaning of this word, however, to encompass the rejection of conformity and refusal to know one's place that Rushdie recommended to Bard's students and their guests. In the late 1930s, he recounts, Ormus's father, Sir Darius Xerxes Cama, joined his fellow Freemason William Methwold in an investigation of comparative mythology, explored relationships between Homeric and Indian mythological traditions, and concluded that all the ancient myths of

Proto-Indo-European or Aryan cultures have common roots. He was particularly drawn to the ideas of a Frenchman, Georges Dumézil, and his theory that all Aryan cultures are based on the concepts of religious sovereignty, physical force, and fertility—that is, until he realized that these three parts are not enough, that there had to be a fourth: "What about *outsideness*," Sir Darius asked his friend. "What about all that which is beyond the pale, above the fray, beneath notice? What about outcastes, lepers, pariahs, exiles, enemies, spooks, paradoxes? What about those who are remote?" Looking out of his library window at the Arabian Sea, he decided that "the only people who see the whole picture . . . are the ones who step out of the frame" (42–43).

Outsideness and stepping out of the frame become synonyms in the novel for disorientation, converting a word that usually carries negative connotations into a positive force. Rai elaborates on this idea when he later tells us that he has long believed that "in every generation there are a few souls, call them lucky or cursed, who are simply *born not belonging*, who came into the world semi-detached, if you like, without strong affiliation to family or location or nation or race" and that

> the phenomenon may be as 'natural' a manifestation of human nature as its opposite, but one that has been mostly frustrated, throughout human history, by lack of opportunity. And not only by that: for those who value stability, who fear transience, uncertainty, change, have erected a powerful system of stigmas and taboos against rootlesssness, that disruptive, anti-social force, so that we mostly conform, we pretend to be motivated by loyalties and solidarities we do not really feel, we hide our secret identities beneath the false skins of those identities which bear the belongers' seal of approval. But the truth leaks out in our dreams . . . we soar, we fly, we flee. And in the waking dreams our societies permit, in our myths, our arts, our songs, we celebrate the non-belongers, the different ones, the outlaws, the freaks. (72–73)

He returns to this subject when he again refers to the root meaning of disorientation and then challenges it. "Lose the east and you lose your bearings, your certainties, your knowledge of what is and may be, perhaps even your life," he observes. But he goes on to say:

> What if all of it—home, kinship, the whole enchilada—is just the biggest, most truly global, and centuries-oldest piece of brainwashing? Suppose that it's only when you dare to let go that your life begins? When you're whirling free of the mother ship, when you cut your ropes, slip your chain, step off the map, go absent without leave, scram, vamoose, whatever: suppose that it's then, and only then, that you're actually free to act! To lead the life nobody tells you how to live, or when, or why. In which nobody orders you to go forth and die for them, or for god, or comes to get you because you broke one of the rules . . . Suppose you've got to go through the feeling of being lost, into the chaos and beyond; you've got to accept the loneliness, the wild panic of losing your moorings, the vertiginous terror of the horizon spinning round and round like the edge of a coin tossed in the air.
>
> You won't do it. Most of you won't do it. The world's head laundry is pretty good at washing brains. . . .
>
> Vina was the first one of us to do it. Ormus jumped second, and I, as usual, brought up the rear. And we can argue all night about why, did we jump or were we pushed, but you can't deny we all did it. We three kings of Disorient were. (176–77)

The last paragraph of this excerpt from a page-long exposition of the ideas in Rushdie's commencement address hardly makes it seem less personal, less its author's self-defense and cri de coeur rather than his character's. Rai is meant to be a somewhat unreliable narrator, but in passages such as this, he sounds very much like a mouthpiece for his creator. Rushdie links similar thoughts to his tale when, nearly halfway through the book, he has Rai interrupt the flow of his narrative once again to remind both himself and us of what the novel is supposed to be about:

> Death is more than love or is it. Art is more than love or is it. Love is more than death and art, or not. This is the subject. This is the subject. This is it.
> What deflects us from the subject is loss. Of those we love, of the Orient, of hope, of our place in the book. Loss is more than love or is it. More than death or is it. More than art, or not. Darius Cama's "fourth function" added . . . the necessary additional concept of the existential outsider, the separated man . . .
> *The only people who see the whole picture are the ones who step out of the frame.* If he was right then this is the subject also. (202–3)

Then there is this: "Certain patterns occur, seem inescapable. Fire, death, uncertainty. The carpet whipped out from under us to reveal a chasm where the floor should have been. Disorientation. Loss of the East" (313). The novel is peppered with sentences, paragraphs, and whole pages devoted to such elaboration on the meanings it attaches to "disorientation." Unfortunately, Rai does not express any of his ideas just once. However, the theme that separation from a single place, a single set of standards and points of reference, a single frame for viewing the world, is an essential—if dangerous—way to live is perhaps most effectively expressed through Rushdie's multifarious use of variations on the metaphor of "double vision."

Here, as in his other novels, there are frequent references to metamorphosis, a form of disorientation and transformation from one condition and identity to another. Shadows, another form of doubles, also recur throughout the book. Even the Partition and renaming of Bombay—"Forget Mumbai. I remember Bombay" (158), Rai insists—becomes an occasion for his confronting and, in this case, refusing to accept a double vision of his city (164). When Sir Darius sees the study of comparative mythology perverted by the Nazis' use of the term

Aryan, this darker vision overshadows his original one and causes him to abandon his studies and begin a life of dissipation.

At another level, the metaphor of double vision is evident in Rushdie's naming of his central characters. Umeed "Rai" Merchant's middle name means prince, desire, and will, and is also the name of a musical style; his given name means hope. The conflict between his conflicting visions of desire, will, and hope are central to his character. Ormus's parents are Parsis, as Indian Zoroastrians have long been called. His father, Sir Darius Xerxes, is named after Persian kings who conquered much of the Mediterranean world at a time when Zoroastrianism was still their empire's religion. His mother, Lady Spenta, is named after the six Amesha Spentas (Bounteous Immortals), angels who are "divine sparks" of Zoroastrianism's non-created creator god, Ahura Mazda, and the emanations through whom all subsequent creation was accomplished. Ahura Mazda's creation—*asha*, or truth and order—is the antithesis of chaos; Angra Mainyu is the creator of evil—*druj*, or falsehood and disorder. As Parsis, the elder Camas have a view of the world built on this particular double vision of order and disorder, good and evil. Furthermore, their last name is Indian and links them to Kama, the Hindu god of love, doubling their religious connections.

Ormus is one of his parents' second set of twins, the smaller of the two babies, whose existence was concealed from the doctor's examinations during his mother's pregnancy by his larger brother, who was stillborn. His parents had named the child they expected Gayomart, after the first created man. Sir Darius was familiar with the semidivine children whom the Olympians inserted into a womb that was bearing a human child. So the miraculous birth of Ormus and fear for his safety lead his mother to want to name her surviving baby—the dead baby's shadow—after a god; she chooses local variants of Ahura Mazda, Hormuz or Ormazd, which Sir Darius latinizes to Ormus. Premature, with a small purplish bruise "like the shadow of an eyeball," Ormus Cama is therefore named after two gods and born to be a mythic hero (35). With a first name from Latin—which also suggests the Greek singer

Orpheus—and a surname from Hindi, he is also born to step across boundaries, blend traditions, and attempt to conquer death.

Although her name is mythic, Vina's origins are anything but lofty. Born Nissa Shetty, she is renamed Nissy Poe when her father abandons her family and her mother remarries; Diane Egiptus when relatives take her in after her mother murders her stepfather and two sisters and then commits suicide; and briefly called Nissa Doodhwala when she is shunted off to live with her father's relatives in India. Soon after, however, having begun to read about India and its myths, she runs away from her family and renames herself Vina Apsara. Vina, Sanskrit for longing, wishing, or hoping for something that has been taken away from you, is an Indian feminine given name and the name of an Indian stringed instrument. Apsara, also Sanskrit, refers to a group of beautiful, supernatural women, nymphs, and dancers who are caretakers of fallen heroes. Vina also suggests Venus, the Greek goddess of love, as well as the Latin word *vita* (life) and the diva Tina. Through their names, the stage is set for the god and goddess of love—both with double heritages, one with a symbol for what will become actual double vision on his eyelid—to meet and reenact the myth of Orpheus and Eurydice. In Rushdie, though, this is not yet enough doubling. Vina and Ormus will also reenact an inversion of the Greek tale: the Hindu myth of Kama and Rati—in which *he* dies and *she* brings *him* back from the dead.

The most pervasive image of doubling in the novel is its use of twins. Sir Darius and Lady Cama's first two boys were also twins, the precocious and willful Cyrus and the slow-witted Virus; one fails to kill his little brother Ormus but succeeds in becoming a serial murderer, the other becomes a kind, musically gifted mute. Ormus's dead brother, Gayomart, becomes his companion from another world. Rai establishes his reputation as a war photographer by developing the film he discovers in the shoe of another photojournalist he finds hanging in a hut where he is imprisoned—whom he refers to as "the dead twin I did not know I had" (243). Even the Gemini 4 astronauts are mentioned and described as twins. In London, Ormus thinks of Vina, whom he has not seen for more than a decade, and imagines she has become the "unknown twin" of the girl he knew (296). After Vina dies in the earthquake, Ormus refuses to believe he cannot find her and discovers a young Vina impersonator who seems to be her twin, named Mira (not only a name that slant rhymes with Vina's but a pun: "mirror" in New York pronunciation).

The novel's most elaborate use of double vision to suggest outsideness, stepping beyond the frame, and disorientation is its "otherworld." This otherworld has several components, none of which is wholly successful. In a scheme whose rationale is never made clear, Rushdie mixes historical and fractured people, works of art, and events in the "real" world of the novel. Jesse Garon Parker, who is managed by "Colonel" Tom Presley, sings "Heartbreak Hotel" and stars in a film called *Treat Me Tender*. Carly Simon and Guinevere Garfunkel, Uncle Meat and the Plastic Ono Band, and Jack Haley and the Meteors have hit records. John Lennon tops the charts with "Satisfaction." Lou Reed is a woman and Laurie Andersen is a man. Nathan Zuckerman, Sal Paradise, John Yossarian, Oskar Mazerath, and Stephen Dedalus are novelists; John Slade writes poetry, Kilgore Trout writes science fiction, Pierre Menard wrote *Don Quixote* and F. Alexander, *A Clockwork Orange*; Nick Carraway and Jay Gatsby are literary critics who appear on television talk shows. The New York arts scene in the early 1970s is presided over by Amos Voight from his studio/factory named Slaughterhouse-22. Small countries in Europe such as Illyria and Arcadia choose not to join the European Union; one of the post-Soviet republics is Nadezhda-Mandelstan. India wins a war with Pakistan. Lee Harvey Oswald's gun jams in Dallas and his conspirator on the grassy knoll, named Steel, is knocked over the head with his eight-millimeter camera by an amateur cameraman named Zapruder who is filming the scene. A popular fantasy thriller called *The Watergate Affair* imagines a future president Richard Nixon who has to leave office when he is caught bugging the offices of the Democratic National Committee. After he has served two terms and drawn us into the Vietnam War with our ally Great Britain, John F. Kennedy is succeeded in the presidency by his brother Robert; both are then killed in a Los Angeles hotel by a Palestinian gunman. President Sukarno survives a communist coup in Indonesia. Ormus Cama is murdered with a Giuliani & Koch automatic pistol outside his Manhattan apartment building by a woman who may be from another dimension. Bad weather in California is blamed on a Hispanic handyman named Elvis Nino. Rai goes into the mountains and finds himself at the Wainganga River of Kipling's *The Jungle Book*. Yet, at the same time, the novel references Madonna, Tina Turner, Janis Joplin, and Joni Mitchell; Randy Newman, John Lennon, and Mick Jagger; the Righteous Brothers, the Temptations, the Miracles, the Searchers, and the Who. It also includes lines from writers such as Aristotle, Karl Marx, Susan Sontag, Kurt Vonnegut, Joan Didion, and Robert Frost and mentions actual books, movies, operas, and historical events.

These jumblings of the real and imaginary are outdone by Rushdie's creation of a parallel world to which usually only Ormus has access. In the beginning, this consists of a dreamworld, in which Gayomart leads Ormus to see movies that have yet to be produced and hear songs that have yet to be written or issued. Except in leap years, exactly 1,001 nights before these records arrive in the real world, Ormus clearly hears the tunes but gets only a scrambled transmission of the lyrics. As he flies to England in 1960, he passes through "a membrane" and begins to receive visits from a beautiful young woman named Maria who claims that they have been lovers and are meant to be together, while an older woman who appears to be her chaperone asks him if Maria is telling the truth. Later, after he is put in a three-and-a-half-year coma by an auto accident, Maria begins to appear in the bedroom where he is recuperating and attempts to have intercourse with him; in this case, others in the house see her and chase her away. She continues to return, and ultimately, they do begin to have sex. In rather elaborate dialogues, Maria and the woman explain to Ormus that they are from another world that is in conflict with this one and that "our" world is about to be destroyed by earthquakes and superseded by theirs. When this does not happen, they return to say that, in fact, their world must fade away.

Ormus explains most of this to Vina as they fly to America. He has been living in two worlds since he awoke from his coma, he says. As he explains, "It could just be that I found a way of stepping outside the picture.... You have to break the rules, deny the frame story, smash the frame.... It could be I found the outsideness of what we're inside." When she asks what the other world is like, he says, "The same only different. John Kennedy got shot eight years ago . . . Nixon's President. East Pakistan recently seceded from the union . . . And the British aren't in Indochina, imagine that.... Charles Manson's a mass murderer, and Allen Konigsberg never directed a picture and Guido Anselmi doesn't exist. Nor do Dedalus or Caulfield or Jim Dixon, by the way, they never wrote any books, and the classics are different too" (350–51).

All of these explanations leave us with a "real world" in which some characters and facts match the ones we know and some do not and an "otherworld" in which some characters and facts do not match the ones we know and some do. This is certainly disorienting, certainly steps out of the frame, and, in some ways, entertains. If it is meant to suggest that our world is as fictional as the world of a novel, however, and that the world of dreams is more real than the one in which we live from day to day, it neither convinces nor coheres. Perhaps expecting coherence is just another frame that Rushdie means to push us beyond; or, perhaps, this version of an otherworld simply does not work.

The final element that distinguishes *The Ground Beneath Her Feet* from Rushdie's earlier novels is the move it makes to New York in its second half. Here, the book seems to suggest that outsideness makes you one of the crowd and stepping out of or changing the frame *is* the norm. As Vina describes it when she tries to convince Ormus to leave England for America with her:

> You get to be an American just by wanting, and by becoming an American you add to the kinds of American it's possible to be, that's in general I'm

talking about?, okay?, and New York City in particular. However you get through your day in New York City, well then that's a New York kind of day . . .

You'll say things all wrong but they'll at once become American ways of saying things. You won't know shit but it'll right away become an American type of ignorance. Not belonging, that's an old American tradition, see?, that's the American way. (331)

It does not really turn out that way for Ormus. He and Vina have a fantastic ride as rock royalty: She becomes VTO's voice and personality, and he becomes a withdrawn control freak, encased on stage in a glass booth while she is in nonstop motion. They play their last concert in the summer of 1987, and he then retreats into seclusion. She goes out on her own and is swallowed up by the earthquake. He refuses to accept this and becomes obsessed with the idea that she escaped. In his Howard Hughes–like Manhattan aerie, he sets up hundreds of screens to monitor all of the world's Vina impersonators, convinced that she will appear again. Instead, he finds Mira, who saves his life as Vina once did, and together they reconstitute VTO and go on a worldwide *Into the Underworld* tour. Without Vina, however, he longs for death, which finally comes.

For Salman Rushdie, however, the move to America has turned out to be liberating. Vina's description of what America—especially New York—can be to a migrant is echoed in comments he has made in television and newspaper interviews. In *The Ground Beneath Her Feet* and the other novels he has written since settling in New York City—*Fury, Shalimar the Clown, The Enchantress of Florence,* and *Luka and the Fire of Life*—he has continued to test the boundaries of his talent and vision, while openly engaging with the literary, art, and political worlds. Having stepped out of the frames of India and England, accepted and embraced the disorientation this involved, he has chosen to put the ground of New York City beneath his feet and added to the kinds of American writer it is possible to be.

Works Cited

Kadzis, Peter. "Salman Speaks." *Conversations with Salman Rushdie*. Ed. Michael R. Reder. Jackson: UP of Mississippi, 2000. 216–27.

Rushdie, Salman. *The Ground Beneath Her Feet*. New York: Holt, 1999.

_____. *Midnight's Children*. New York: Knopf, 1995.

_____. *Step Across This Line: Collected Nonfiction, 1992–2002*. New York: Random, 2002.

Repetition and Listing in *Fury*

Robert C. Evans

When Salman Rushdie's novel *Fury* appeared in 2001, its reception was decidedly mixed. Some praised it, but many dismissed it, often disdainfully. One problem may have been its timing: It was reviewed immediately after the terrorist attacks of September 11, 2001. The book, which simultaneously satirizes and reflects the trivial, hedonistic materialism of the pre–September 11 era, thus ran the risk of seeming trivial itself, since its often unsympathetic central character, Malik Solanka, has been seen as Rushdie's alter ego. Of course, Rushdie's depiction of Solanka's privileged life and jet-setting lifestyle may have been intended as self-mocking. In any case, many readers have found Solanka unappealing, and contempt for the character has sometimes blown back on his creator.

As the novel opens, Solanka—a one-time Oxford don—has abandoned his second wife and their small son to live the self-indulgent life of a highly prosperous, middle-aged, single man in New York City. Solanka made his original fortune by inventing a doll named Little Brain, now a popular television star and center of a worldwide merchandising franchise. Yet Solanka, despite his wealth and fame, is full of mysterious furies. At one point, while still in England, he stands, drunk and holding a knife, over the bed where his wife and child are sleeping.

Afraid of harming his family, he heads to New York, where his furies, if anything, intensify. Indeed, he even briefly suspects that he may be responsible for a string of serial killings that he cannot precisely recall. Eventually these worries prove unfounded, but in the meantime, he becomes sexually involved with a beautiful, much-younger woman. Later, he takes up with a stunningly attractive but slightly older woman whose beauty literally stops traffic. Both women are also highly intelligent and extremely articulate. Why either woman should find the dumpy Solanka so sexually appealing seems unclear. Neither seems motivated by greed. Whatever the explanation, Solanka's involvement with them often creates highly improbable complications. *Fury* will strike some readers as evolving from a relentless social satire into a farfetched political melodrama. Ultimately, Solanka is back in England, observing his wife and toddler from a distance in a park—an ending that can be read either as movingly tender or as cloyingly sentimental.

Throughout *Fury*, Rushdie habitually repeats "fury" as both a key word and central theme. By one count, the word "fury" appears forty different times (every six or so pages), often as the subject of lengthy philosophical reflections. Moreover, various *kinds* of personal, political, social, or mythological furies are mentioned. References to the Greek Furies appear at least eight times, and the word "furious" appears four times as well.

Yet repetition of "fury" is just one of many kinds of repetition Rushdie employs in this book. Repetition of various sorts—of letters, words, sounds, phrases, clauses, names, and practically every imaginable part of speech—is a major feature of *Fury*'s style, syntax, and structure. Rushdie's love of repetition and lists often contributes greatly to the book's energy, verve, and vitality. *Fury* is worth reading, in part, simply as a display of Rushdie's skill in manipulating words, no matter how one responds to its larger plot, characters, and themes. The repetitions and listings contribute variously to whatever successes the book achieves but also to its flaws. Since repetition and listing are notable features of other works by Rushdie, examining the rhetoric of repetition and listing in *Fury* may be relevant to his methods of writing in general.

I.

Rushdie's habits of repetition have been touched on by others when discussing novels other than *Fury*. Thus, Bernard Rodgers refers to Rushdie's "spendthrift imagination," noting that in general his is "an esthetic of excess," in which "episode [is] piled on episode, character on character, plot on plot, pun on pun, comic name on comic name, digression on digression" (214). Likewise, Ambreen Hai comments that one sentence by Rushdie "grows and bends under the weight of its accumulating catalog" (206), and Sara Suleri also mentions the unfolding, in another work, of a "comically breathless catalog" (179). Ian Baucom discusses yet another of Rushdie's lengthy lists found in *The Satanic Verses* (211), and Robert J. Forman has noted similarities to Homeric catalogs elsewhere in Rushdie's writings (2805). Some readers find Rushdie's penchant for listing or cataloging occasionally unfortunate. Thus, Nico Israel condemns as "childish" a list in one work of "four Russian generals": "Pissov, Sodov, Bugrov and Phukov" (214). Yet few readers will deny that cataloging, listing, and repetition—whatever their successes or failures—are major features of Rushdie's fiction in general and of *Fury* in particular.

By examining the types and functions of repetition and listing in *Fury*, one can better appreciate the varied contributions those methods make to this specific book as well as to Rushdie's broader oeuvre. If repetition and cataloging are recurrent features of his style, as indeed they seem to be, then discussing them here may have implications much broader than for *Fury* alone.

II.

Rushdie's use of cataloging in *Fury* involves just about every kind of listing one can imagine. Even the very first sentence of the novel contains a small list of sorts, but one of the book's truly bravura listings appears a bit later on the very first page, as the narrator describes the material riches of life in New York at the start of the new millennium:

> Stores, dealerships, galleries struggled to satisfy the skyrocketing demand for ever more recherché produce: limited-edition olive oils, three-hundred-dollar corkscrews, customized Humvees, the latest anti-virus software, escort services featuring contortionists and twins, video installations, outsider art, featherlight shawls made from the chin-fluff of extinct mountain goats. (3)

This catalog is typical of many in *Fury*. It does not simply suggest but actually depicts—in highly efficient and very specific detail—the abundance of an exceptionally pleasure-seeking and even decadent society. Some items listed here are clearly believable ("customized Humvees"), some are unremarkable ("the latest anti-virus software"), and some seem whimsical to the point of improbability (the "featherlight shawls"). Some references are fairly funny, such as the one to "contortionists and twins," while others are almost scandalous in their suggestions of monetary waste, such as the reference to "three-hundred-dollar corkscrews." Catalogs like this one suggest not only the wealth and diversity of the society Rushdie describes but also the precision and inventiveness of the narrator's mind. Merely to *list* many of these items is to satirize them, but the list also implies the narrator's intimate familiarity with the society he mocks as well as the variety of tones one might adopt in describing that society.

Clearly, in compiling this list, the narrator is having some creative fun, but other lists are wholly serious. Thus, a later comment notes that "there were waiting lists for baths, doorknobs, imported hardwoods, antiqued fireplaces, bidets, marble slabs" (3). Here the list seems unexaggerated and completely credible; the mockery used earlier has now given way to basically trustworthy reporting. Lists then can sometimes contribute to the realism and reliability of Rushdie's prose, but they can at other times exemplify his sense of fun, irony, and satire. Strings of words and terms help give each item maximum individual emphasis while also making the reader feel nearly overwhelmed by the sheer number of details listed. One senses, about both of the lists just cited, that the narrator could easily have made them twice or thrice as long. The trick, as scholars of literary catalogs such as Robert Belknap have suggested, is to make a list long enough so that it seems interesting and representative but not so long that it seems monotonous or boring.

The lists in *Fury* are almost invariably clear, efficient, and emphatic. They help give the novel a sometimes forceful energy and rapid pace. It is easy to imagine how Rushdie could make the same points in much more labored and stilted ways. Instead, his lists are often swift, surprising showpieces. They tend to stand out from the prose around them, calling attention to themselves and thus contributing in especially memorable ways to Rushdie's statements of theme and development of characters. His lists demonstrate vividly his control over his prose. They rarely ramble, and often they display clever inventiveness. Sometimes the pleasure they offer is simply the pleasure of listening to a skilled writer playing with sounds and rhythms: Often the lists would sound musical even to someone who knew no English. Some of Rushdie's lists are extremely simple in structure; often, however, their organization is complex and baroque.

Sometimes the energy the lists contribute to *Fury* derives from their strong metrical emphasis on key words. Thus, early on, the narrator presents a key character by writing that "she was breaking a rule of big-city life, breaking it brazenly, sure of her power, confident of her turf and posse, fearing nothing" (4). Here the verbs "breaking," "breaking," and "fearing" are all heavily stressed, as are the synonymous adjectives "sure" and "confident." Rushdie also uses alliterative *b* sounds to stress key words, just as he employs the assonance of long *a* sounds in "breaking," "breaking," and "brazenly"—words that also happen to share an opening emphasis on *br*. The very phrasing of this sentence conveys some of the force and power the narrator attributes to the character being described. The sentence is as strongly memorable as the person it depicts.

In addition to using lists to offer memorable descriptions of specific persons, Rushdie also often uses them to convey striking impressions of particular moments and milieus. Early in the novel, for instance, the narrator notes,

> In New York, too, there were circuses as well as bread: a musical about lovable lions, a bike race on Fifth, Springsteen at the Garden with a song about the forty-one police gunshots that killed innocent Amadou Diallo, the police union's threat to boycott the Boss's concert, Hillary *vs.* Rudy,

a cardinal's funeral, a movie about lovable dinosaurs, the motorcades of two largely interchangeable and certainly unlovable presidential candidates (Gush, Bore), Hillary *vs.* Rick, the lightning storms that hit the Springsteen concert and Shea Stadium, a cardinal's inauguration, a cartoon about lovable British chickens, and even a literary festival; plus a series of "exuberant" parades celebrating the city's many ethnic, national and sexual subcultures and ending (sometimes) in knifings and assaults on (usually) women. (6)

Here, in a single sentence packed with 124 separate words, the narrator manages to convey both the overwhelming diversity and the monotonous predictability of life in New York. By one count, the list above contains twenty-five distinct items, organized in a variety of ways. Sometimes the narrator stresses simple pairings. Sometimes the list includes fairly long separate clauses. Sometimes repetitions suggest the tedious predictability and triviality of popular culture, as in the references to "lovable" lions, dinosaurs, and chickens. At times a single phrase or word receives unusual emphasis because it intrudes unexpectedly, as in the references to "even a literary festival" and, in the catalog's final word, the reference to "women."

Like many others one might cite, this list demonstrate that Rushdie's catalogs are often far more than merely predictable litanies, with one thing tediously following another and with no principle of selection or organization involved. Instead, often his catalogs are little set pieces, variously structured and crafted so that they achieve maximum effectiveness, both as pieces of rhetoric and as simple experimentations in sound and rhythm. Yet the list just cited raises another question highly relevant to *Fury* in particular—a question very germane to debates about the novel's overall merits: Is *Fury* so inextricably linked to a particular era that it will rapidly seem dated? Do lists such as the ones just quoted start growing stale almost as soon as they are concocted? Is *Fury* the kind of book likely to have (or continue to have) any resonance for readers beyond a small subset of jet-setters living in New York City at the turn of the twenty-first century? Twenty years hence, will anyone really know or care who Amadou Diallo, Rudy, or Rick were? In other words, are Rushdie's lists often catalogs that will someday seem woefully irrelevant and perhaps even literally meaningless to most readers?

One answer to such questions is that the items Rushdie lists are often sufficiently general, or "archetypal," that they are likely to seem recognizable even after years and decades have passed. Thus, the references to musicals, movies, and cartoons about lovable animals will probably make sense and seem current even when the particular works alluded to have receded from memory, while Rushdie also gives us enough information about the general identity of Amadou Diallo, and the controversy surrounding him, that we need not know more. The political references are likely to "date" more quickly (who, people may wonder, was Rick?), but the context makes the general identities of the politicians mentioned seem clear enough. In fact, it seems part of Rushdie's satirical point that particular politicians come, go, and fade, but that archetypal political contests are perennial. We need not know that Rick was Rick Lazio in order to sense that he was a New York politician with a populist-sounding first name. Likewise, the other names suggest an election in which everyone else had also adopted populist personas.

Most items in this list are general enough that we can sense their symbolic significance, yet they are specific enough to give Rushdie's prose a flavor of historical precision. Also, through a strange accident of history, his book happens to convey a sense of life in New York just before what will surely always remain an exceptionally important event in American (if not world) history: the terrorist attacks of September 11, 2001. Any future reader wanting to know how it felt to be a New Yorker, or at least a privileged, upper-class New Yorker, right before September 11 could do far worse than to peruse Rushdie's novel. Like many notable satirists, especially Ben Jonson, Rushdie gives us enough specific details to root his satire in a credible social milieu while also making most of his references general enough that we can sense their symbolic significance.

III.

Whether or not Rushdie's novel comes to seem dated, many of its lists are likely always to fascinate. Simply as talented displays of how words can be organized in interesting ways, the lists are worth reading and help contribute to the aesthetic pleasure *Fury* can provide.

The lists in *Fury* tend to be variously structured. Many, for instance, tend to emphasize vigorous verbs. Thus, at one point, the narrator wonders about "the digits that encode beauty, the number-fingers that enclose, transform, transmit, decode, and somehow, in the process, fail to trap or choke the soul of it" (8). Even a list as short and apparently straightforward as this reveals Rushdie's love of linguistic game-playing, as in the play on the words "digits" and "number fingers," the similarities of "transform" and "transmit," and the long *o* sounds of "encode," "enclose," "decode," and "choke." Such sentences almost beg to be read aloud or at least listened to carefully in one's mental ear. Rushdie enjoys exploring ideas, but he also enjoys playing with the sheer sounds and rhythms of language.

Consider, for instance, the following list, which heavily emphasizes verbs but in which the final phrase nicely—and very abruptly—contradicts the one before it: "Professor Solanka never grew accustomed to the barbs [of academic conversation], often received terrible injuries from them, always pretended he saw the funny side, never once saw it" (18). Inserting the word "but" before "never" would have made the rhythm smoother, yet Rushdie clearly wants to disrupt the predictable rhythm here. This is a small detail, to be sure, but it exemplifies the frequent subtlety of Rushdie's phrasing. In another catalog, the sheer cascade of verbs mimics Solanka's speed and fear as he seeks to avoid a violent confrontation: "Then he hurried into his apartment, shut the door with his heart pounding, leaned against the wall, closed his eyes, gasped, and shook" (36). Here the phrases become shorter and shorter as the sentence proceeds, thus conveying Solanka's growing excitement and fright.

At times, though, Rushdie's lists of verbs—like some of his other lists—can seem forced and artificial, especially when they are actually voiced by characters. Nearly everyone in this novel is extraordinarily articulate. Characters often speak not as if they were thinking on the spot but as if they were delivering rehearsed and perfectly polished speeches. Many characters therefore tend to sound alike and a lot like Rushdie, the highly skilled and very self-conscious writer. Thus, late in the book, the exceptionally beautiful Neela speaks to Solanka of a mutual friend: "I set out everything I knew, half knew, intuited, and suspected, piled it all up in front of him" (155). Even later, Mila (the very young woman who somehow falls in love with Solanka) tells him, "This new world is my life, Malik, it's the thing of my time, growing as I grow, learning as I learn, becoming as I become" (179). Do real people actually speak this way? Do real people actually deliver the kinds of huge, uninterrupted monologues that Solanka unloads on Neela late in the novel? One speech goes on for two-and-a-half tightly printed pages and includes such sentences as this: "I believe you came here tonight to find out the answer, to see if you could conquer your fury as you helped me conquer mine, to find out if you could find a way of coming back from the edge" (249). The novel's spoken lists, such as this one, often sound stiff and contrived. In fact, much of the novel's dialogue is not really dialogue at all but exchanges of speeches. In general, Rushdie's lists of verbs, like his other catalogs, tend to work best when they emanate from the narrator rather than from individual characters. It is the narrator, for instance, who offers the following catalog:

> Everywhere you looked, in gyms, clubs, galleries, offices, on the streets, and on the floor of the NYSE, at the city's great sports stadia and entertainment centers, people were readying themselves for the new season, limbering up for action, flexing their minds, bodies, and wardrobes, setting themselves on their marks. (213)

Here and elsewhere, the narrator's voice reflects Solanka's perspective. Such passages therefore inevitably help characterize Solanka and his perceptions, but such lists sound far more convincing coming from the narrator than they ever do coming out of the mouths of the protagonist or other characters. These lists help characterize Solanka because they reflect his point of view, but they would (and sometimes do) sound quite artificial if spoken by Solanka himself.

As the catalog above reveals, the lists in *Fury* often heavily emphasize verbs (such as "readying," "limbering," "flexing," and "setting"), but they also often strongly stress nouns as well (as in the reference to "gyms, clubs, galleries, offices"). Sometimes lists of nouns can be used to characterize the mental scope of characters. Thus, Solanka, after visiting a doll exhibition, imagines "back rooms in the museum filled with giant heaps of the miniature dead: birds, animals, children, servants, actors, ladies, lords" (16). Sometimes the lists of nouns can convey historical change very rapidly and efficiently. Solanka, for instance, having created his own world-famous doll, Little Brain, later recalls her various transformations: "first a doll, later a puppet, then an animated cartoon, and afterward an actress, or, at various other times, a talk-show host, gymnast, ballerina, or supermodel, in a Little Brain outfit" (96). Solanka is bothered by many of these adaptations of his creation. This transformed Little Brain, he thinks, is "an imposter, with the wrong history, the wrong dialogue, the wrong personality, the wrong wardrobe, the wrong *brain*" (98; Rushdie's emphasis).

As the foregoing catalog amply demonstrates, Rushdie often lists combinations of adjectives and varied nouns. Here the listing emphasizes the sheer "wrongness" of what has happened to Little Brain. The relentlessly repeated word "wrong" underscores the point. Sometimes, instead of listing the very same adjective, Rushdie lists related adjectives as synonyms. Elsewhere, however, lists of adjectives convey variety and complexity, as in this description of the wife Solanka has abandoned: "She was faultless: the tenderest, most attentive of lovers, the most extraordinary mother, charismatic and imaginative, the easiest and most rewarding of companions, not a big talker but a good one" (12). In lists such as this, Rushdie can convey a character's key but complicated traits very quickly, at the same time characterizing Solanka's own complicated mind. And the list just quoted also displays Rushdie's own skill in the sheer *arrangement* of adjectives—some listed in sublists before the noun ("the tenderest, most attentive of lovers, the most extraordinary mother"), some listed after or by themselves ("charismatic and imaginative"), some listed as parts of balanced phrases ("not a big talker but a good one"). For anyone who reads novels partly to appreciate the sheer skill of an author's rhetoric, *Fury* has much to offer, as in the reference, nicely delayed by three distinctive adjectives, to New York's "magic, invisible, hybrid heart" (86).

Rushdie's love of listing sometimes extends to whole phrases, as when Solanka thinks of Little Brain, "his hip, fashion-conscious, but still idealistic Candide, his Valiant-for-Truth in urban-guerrilla threads, his spiky-haired girl-Bashō journeying, mendicant bowl in hand, far into the Deep North of Japan" (17). Such lists, with their varied cultural allusions and love of paradoxes, not only describe the ostensible objects of their attention (in this case, Little Brain) but also imply the wit and cleverness of Solanka, of the narrator, and, of course, of Rushdie himself. The inventive minds of all three are on display again when the book later uses phrases to describe the life of Little Brain, including "its humble beginnings, its years of struggle, its triumphant overcomings; and, O, her dauntlessness in the face of poverty and cruelty! O, her joy when Fate chose her to be one of its Elect!" (97). In lists such as this, we see and hear Rushdie's pure joy in what he can do with language, a joy also suggested when the narrator later describes "our boundarybreaking, rule-disproving, shape-shifting, transgressive, trespassing shadow-self, the true ghost in our machine" (128). Such catalogs imply a love of listing for listing's sake, and indeed, whole pages of *Fury* are simply consumed by lists, including page 87 (with its heavy use of anaphora, i.e., reference to preceding terms), page 101 (with its lists of exclamatory phrases), and page 107 (where the listing becomes almost an example of surrealistic stream-of-consciousness). Hardly a page goes by in *Fury* that fails to offer some kind of list, thus making cataloging by far one of the most significant aspects of this novel's rhetoric. Sometimes Rushdie creates lists within lists within lists. Thus, at one point, the narrator describes the wealthy young women who function as the novel's serial murder victims:

> They were nobody's dolls, but their own women, playing with their own appearance, their own sexuality, their own stories: the first generation of young women to be truly in control, in thrall neither to the old patriarchy nor to the man-hating hard-line feminism that had battered at Bluebeard's gate. They could be businesswomen and flirts, profound and superficial, serious and light, and they would make those decisions for themselves. They had it all—emancipation, sex appeal, cash—and they loved it. (74)

IV.

Why is there all the listing in this book? Several answers have already been suggested, but various others seem relevant as well. A catalog of explanations might include the following:

- Often lists emphasize the novel's focus on abundance and decadent excess.

- Often lists implicitly characterize Solanka, suggesting his fertile mind but also his egotism—his love of his own thoughts as well as his tendency to order, in his own way, everything he perceives.

- Sometimes lists help highlight the central theme: "Life is fury, he'd thought. Fury—sexual, Oedipal, political, magical, brutal—drives us to our finest heights and coarsest depths. Out of *furia* comes creation, inspiration, originality, passion, but also violence, pain, pure unafraid destruction, the giving and receiving of blows from which we never recover." Fury helps make man "the exalted, transcendent, self-destructive, untrammeled lord of creation" (30–31).

- Sometimes lists help stress subsidiary themes, as when the narrator notes that "everyone was an American now, or at least Americanized: Indians, Iranians, Uzbeks, Japanese, Lilliputians, all. America was the world's playing field, its rule book, umpire, and ball" (87–88).
- Sometimes lists contribute humor: "Matter clumped with other matter, the primal soup grew lumpy. Then came stars, planets, single-cell organisms, fish, journalists, dinosaurs, lawyers, mammals" (116–17).
- Often lists offer quick sketches of characters, as when one is described as "a hunter, fisherman, weekend driver of very fast cars, marathon runner, gym rat, tennis player, and, lately, thanks to the rise of Tiger Woods, an obsessive golfer too" (54; see also 18, 21, 30, 72, and 126). As it happens, nearly all the main characters are extraordinarily and perhaps unbelievably accomplished, and so Rushdie often lists their achievements with brisk efficiency.
- Lists involving then-current cultural allusions sometimes help give the book historical specificity, as when one character notes that she and her friends are currently creating websites for "Steve Martin, Al Pacino, Melissa Etheridge, Warren Beatty, Christina Ricci, and Will Smith. Yeah. *And* Dennis Rodman. And Marion Jones and Christina Aguilera and Jennifer Lopez and Todd Solondz and 'N Sync" (119; see also 34, 35). Notice how the list stops, restarts, stops again, and then restarts once more—further evidence of Rushdie's compulsive listing.
- Listing can also allude to pop culture of the distant past, as when, referring to obsolete dance movements, Neela says that another character will "swim and hitchhike and walk the dog, he'll do the mash, the funky chicken and the locomotion all night long" (150; see also 86). Sometimes such lists also contribute to the book's historical depth (101).

- Occasionally the lists are strikingly balanced, as when Solanka's wife lists differences between her views and his views: "Malik, you say you want to forget yourself. I say you have already forgotten yourself. You say you don't want to be ruled by your anger. I say your anger has never ruled you more. I remember you though you have forgotten me" (83–84). Here the balanced listing stresses stark alternatives in points of view; elsewhere, similarly balanced listing suggests the complexity of an individual character (12, 19), conflicts between groups (57), or opposed impulses (165).

- Sometimes lists end with sudden, surprising twists, as when Solanka thinks of a friend with "a lantern jaw, a wardrobe full of loud tweedjackets, a drum kit, a fast car, no girlfriend" (18). Twists such as this contribute further irony to an already heavily ironic novel.

- Sometimes lists emphasize Solanka's obsessions with other people, as in the long list involving his son, Asmaan, whose name is repeated eight times in a few sentences on page 105, or the similarly obsessive list about his wife on page 107.

- Occasionally listing of an especially disordered kind can suggest chaos, confusion, madness, and rage (107–8). Yet similarly disordered lists can also suggest enthusiasm, vitality, and youthful excitement (111).

- Lists of verbs can suggest the disruptions caused by Neela's beauty (149). Lists of exclamations can imply panic (85). Lists of questions can imply uncertainties about marriage (77), about Americans (87), or about the causes of America's decline (87).

- Sometimes lists stress strange, unfamiliar aspects of alien cultures (135–36), but sometimes they can suggest a tedious monotony and sameness (55–56).

- Sometimes key words, terms, or names are stressed (34, 55–56, 58, 69, 83, 99, 152, 164); at others, sentences with distinct lists are juxtaposed (59).

- Sometimes lists are used to convey comprehensiveness (56), sometimes to seem oppressive or overwhelming (38, 42), and sometimes to suggest slight variations within mind-numbing similarity (34, 58, 102).

- Sometimes Rushdie offers lists within lists, lists after lists, and lists of lists, and sometimes he offers all these variations in one long passage, as in the massive tangle of lists on page 74.

Perhaps Rushdie filled this novel with lists to provide lively contrasts with what are termed "the great heaps of . . . slow, obscure sentences" found in the "dour pages" of such writers as "Sarraute, Robbe-Grillet, and Butor" (31). Perhaps Rushdie, in writing his first "American" novel, wanted to parody or pay tribute to the kind of listing characteristic of such notable American writers as Walt Whitman, Herman Melville, and Carl Sandburg. Certainly this latter possibility is suggested at one point (on a page brimming with lists of all kinds), when the narrator exclaims, "O ye Yankee Galahads, ye Hoosier Lancelots, O Parcifals of the stockyards, what of the Table Round?" (87). Indeed, at one point, there even seems to be a direct allusion to the following famous passage from Whitman's *Song of Myself*: "Do I contradict myself? / Very well then I contradict myself, / (I am large, I contain multitudes.)" (lines 1321–23). Surely Rushdie is echoing these words when he writes, "A *sanyasi* in New York, a *sanyasi* with a duplex and credit card, was a contradiction in terms. Very well. He would be that contradiction" (82). Rushdie, in short, may have considered listing an especially appropriate method for this novel because he knows that listing is a common feature of some major American writing—a feature that allowed previous writers to suggest the complications and complexities of such an enormous and diverse society.

Listing, however, may have seemed appealing to Rushdie in this novel for other reasons as well, including the book's (and the central character's) tendency to make literally sweeping judgments. These judgments are often buttressed by lists that can seem to support the generalizations offered by various characters, but especially by the narrator and Solanka. *Fury*, despite its geographical breadth (moving from London to New York to Asia and back) and despite the sheer range of topics it covers, is ultimately a portrait of the mind of Malik Solanka. Most of the lists it offers are, by far, lists that implicitly characterize both the narrator and Solanka, no matter what else they happen to describe. In a book that revolves so much around the thoughts, feelings, perceptions, and preoccupations of one central character, the lists help add to our sense of his complexity, his society, and his era. This seems part of their main purpose.

Yet perhaps the most important aspect of all the listing and cataloging in *Fury* involves its contribution to the linguistic richness of the book—its interest as a piece of language and rhetoric. The lists that appear on practically every page almost invariably call attention to themselves simply as strings of words, phrases, clauses, and sentences. They never let us forget that this book reflects its author's complicated mind. They constantly remind us that this book's author is a writer obsessed with words and with what he can make words do.

Works Cited

Baucom, Ian. *Out of Place: Englishness, Empire, and the Locations of Identity.* Princeton: Princeton UP, 1999.

Belknap, Robert E. *The List: The Uses and Pleasures of Cataloguing.* New Haven: Yale UP, 2004.

Forman, Robert J. "Salman Rushdie." *Critical Survey of Long Fiction.* Ed. Frank N. Magill and Carl Rollyson. 2nd rev. ed. Vol. 7. Pasadena: Salem, 2000. 2799–2809.

Hai, Ambreen. *Making Words Matter: The Agency of Colonial and Postcolonial Literature.* Athens: Ohio UP, 2009.

Israel, Nico. *Outlandish: Writing Between Exile and Diaspora.* Stanford: Stanford UP, 2000.

Rodgers, Bernard F., Jr. *Voices & Visions: Selected Essays.* Lanham: UP of America, 2001.

Rushdie, Salman. *Fury.* New York: Random, 2001.

Suleri, Sara. *The Rhetoric of English India.* Chicago: U of Chicago P, 1992.

Shalimar the Clown: Love, Betrayal, and the Myths of Colonialism
Patrick Colm Hogan

Anticolonial nationalism is almost always bound up with a myth. In this myth, European powers were the colonizers and largely non-European countries were simply colonized. Thus, colonialism ends once the non-European countries throw off the political rule and escape the economic exploitation of the European countries. A successful break with European domination, then, successfully ends colonialism. This is the myth of *postcolonial emancipation*.

In fact, however, after successfully creating a new nation, a former colony is all too likely to establish its own colonies, its own forms of domination over regions or over minority populations. This *postcolonial colonialism* may be more localized when compared with the global reach of the European powers, but it need not be any less brutal.

Salman Rushdie has been sensitive to this point for many years. But, in its depth of analysis, *Shalimar the Clown* goes well beyond his earlier treatments of postcolonial colonialism, beginning to suggest that colonialism is always complex, recurrent, multiple. It is found reiteratively, at level after level, like the old story from the American South of the slave owner who beat his wife, who beat her slave, who beat the horse.[1]

Mythic Kashmir: The Loss of Eden
Of course, *Shalimar* is not a treatise about colonialism generally. It is about Kashmir. Indeed, the novel is pervaded by Kashmiri history. A central idea shared by writers on Kashmiri history is that Kashmiri culture was marked by an unusual degree of intercommunal harmony. Hindus and Muslims loved and respected one another and lived together without religious conflict. The idea is expressed in the poetry of medieval mystic poets who opposed the sectarianism of Hindu and Muslim, favoring instead the unity of all in devotion to God. In this

account, the ethnocultural category of *Kashmiriyat* (Kashmiriness) superseded and rendered innocuous the categories of religion.

This standard idea is, of course, also a myth, one created around history. The converse of emancipation, it is the myth of a lost paradise. For Kashmir, the great historical hero of this history is the fourteenth-century ruler Zain-ul-Abidin. Before his reign, the ruling "officials seized the wealth of Hindu temples, broke idols, imposed the hated jiziya [poll] tax" on non-Muslims. At this time, there was "a vicious anti-Hindu policy" including "forcible conversion" and a ban on the wearing of distinctive Hindu symbols (Akbar 24). Hindus fled, but Zain-ul-Abidin brought the Hindus back, abolished the poll tax, and practiced reconversion (27–28).

Rushdie, it seems, accepts the myth of Kashmiriyat. As he puts it, in the voice of Shalimar, "In the valley these words [*Hindu* and *Muslim*] were merely descriptions, not divisions" (57). Moreover, he points toward Zain-ul-Abidin as a model of Kashmiriyat. Indeed, in his novel, the anticommunal orientation of the indigenous Kashmiri theater group is manifest in part through their performance of the story of Zain-ul-Abidin (83).

There is undoubtedly some basis for this view in history. Yet, even so, it remains a myth. Why would mystic poets have had to denounce sectarianism if it were simply absent? Why did Zain-ul-Abidin have to call Hindus back and allow reconversion if they had not been driven away or forced to convert initially?

Rushdie, with his characteristic sensitivity to historical complexity, recognizes that the stories we tell about history involve selection and arrangement. We choose where to begin and where to end, what to see as characteristic and what to see as an exception. Indeed, when communal violence spreads in the valley, the Hindus in *Shalimar* begin to question this myth of longstanding communal harmony (239). Nonetheless, Rushdie clearly wishes to maintain this myth of a lost Eden— an Eden that persisted even into the modern period.

Emplotting Modern Kashmiri History

This modern period is, of course, a period where the details of history matter as well, and it is important to sketch a few of these first. For centuries, Kashmir was ruled, with greater or lesser incomprehension and exploitation, by non-Kashmiris. For purposes of the novel, the key transition point in this history came in 1846: The British took control of Kashmir but did not desire to continue directly controlling the territory. They therefore sold it to a Hindu ruler, Gulab Singh, who had aided them at key points (Akbar 57, 59). Despite this purchase, the maharajas were not entirely autonomous, particularly after 1889 (Bamzai 626–31). Insofar as they were autonomous, Gulab Singh and his successors were not particularly enlightened rulers, as is evidenced by the fact that, in 1924, Muslims were agitating for, among other things, "abolition of forced labour and the restoration of all mosques seized by the state government" (Akbar 69).

The story of the Nomans and the Kauls begins during the reign of the Singhs. It is significant that this period is encompassed in Rushdie's romantic vision of the lost Eden. Part of that Eden is the *panchayat* system, the system of local self-government in Indian villages. The panchayat system was praised by writers such as Farooq Abdullah as a way "to ensure the political participation of masses" (vii). Rushdie maintains this highly benevolent view of panchayats through his representation of Pachigam's panchayat, with its multiethnic, multireligious membership, including Muslim, Hindu, and Jewish members (138), its deep rationality and compassion (as shown by its decision regarding the interfaith marriage of Boonyi and Shalimar), and its healthy and productive relation to the society at large.

Here, as elsewhere, Rushdie's account appears to have been overly positive. Riyaz Punjabi reports that panchayats were "comprised of the lower level functionaries of the Maharaja," which is to say, "village heads, landlords and other influential people." Far from being autonomous, they were "manipulated by autocratic rulers." Moreover, state manipulation of panchayats continued into the period of independence (37–38, 42).

Why, then, is Rushdie adopting a romantic myth of a fall from paradise? It seems unlikely that he was unaware of the complexities and contradictions in Hindu-Muslim relations in the past, since he explicitly notes that one might take communal conflict to be the norm and harmony to be the deviation (239). It is perhaps more possible that he simply thought too well of panchayats, but this too seems unlikely—if for no other reason than the deep naïveté of such a view. Rather, it seems that Rushdie is trying to create an effective story, and the story effect he wishes to produce is horror at the ongoing devastation of Kashmir. Virtually all politically engaged writers try to do something along these lines. Most do so by increasing the evil of the enemy, making them into demonic hordes that perpetrate unspeakable evil. That option is not open to Rushdie, whose humane view of the Kashmir conflict recognizes the humanity of the Indian soldiers and the militants as well as that of civilians—Hindu, Sikh, or Muslim. In order to communicate the hell of present-day Kashmir, he does not populate it with demons but contrasts it with heaven.

Again, this happy view of Kashmiriyat is not simply made up, but it is highly selective. This sort of selection is part of the "emplotment" of history, which is to say, the creation of a story out of historical events. In such emplotment, it is not uncommon for historians and novelists to shape conflicting social tendencies by reference to a few weighty characters—for example, political leaders whose personal confrontations come to stand in for (and perhaps partially explain) larger social oppositions. In the case of modern Kashmir, this emplotment commonly involves two figures—Hari Singh and Sheikh Abdullah.

Hari Singh was the maharaja of Jammu and Kashmir when India and Pakistan became independent from Britain. At the time of independence, there were several semi-independent, "princely" states, such as Kashmir. They had a choice of joining Pakistan or India. One would expect that a Muslim ruler of a predominantly Muslim state would opt for Pakistan while the Hindu ruler of a predominantly Hindu state would opt for India. The complication in this case was that Singh was Hindu, while the state of Jammu and Kashmir was primarily Muslim, if with a significant Hindu minority.

Roughly two months after the birth of India and Pakistan, Singh had not signed the articles of accession to either nation. At this time, a "tribal uprising" occurred in western Kashmir, with at least some involvement from Pakistan. Akbar reports that the militants followed "a trail of horror . . . raping and abducting women, looting, and murdering civilians" (106). This led Singh to accede to India, with provisions for partial autonomy. Kashmiri nationalists have often remarked that the deal struck by Singh with the Indian government bears a striking resemblance to the agreement struck by his ancestor with the British.

These events are recalled in *Shalimar*. For dramatic effect, they are collapsed into a single night—the night Shalimar and Boonyi are born. This is, in effect, the moment when the new Kashmir is allegorically born—with the violence of the uprising, accession to India, and partition of Kashmir (since Pakistan retained control in part of western Kashmir). In other words, these events are what define the difference in the novel between the old Kashmir of Abdullah Noman and Pyarelal Kaul, on the one hand, and the new Kashmir of their children on the other. Indeed, Boonyi's mother—the freest and most defiant spirit in the novel—cannot survive that night.

The mention of Abdullah leads us to the other weighty character in this political drama—Sheikh Abdullah. Sheikh Abdullah was undoubtedly the most popular leader in the valley. He was known for his progressive politics (for instance, with respect to land reform and women's rights) and his opposition to religious communalism. His prominent role in the history of the valley—and his close semi-allegorical[2] relation to Abdullah Noman—are articulated directly by Rushdie: "There were two lions in Kashmir. One was Sheikh Abdullah, of course, Sher-e-Kashmir himself, the unquestioned leader of his people. Everyone agreed that Sheikh Abdullah was the valley's real prince, not that Dogra maharaja"

(59). Though Sheikh Abdullah headed the first government of Indian Kashmir, he vacillated in his relations with India over the years. As Rushdie summarizes, the Indian government kept imprisoning Sheikh Abdullah, "then doing secret deals with him, then reinstalling him in power on the condition that he supported the union with India, then getting irritated all over again when he started talking about autonomy in spite of everything" (247). Rushdie presents a similar, if more consistent, change in Abdullah Noman and his wife, Firdaus (131).

Despite Sheikh Abdullah's periodic cooperation with the Indian government, there was widespread feeling in Kashmir that Singh had simply and illegitimately sold Kashmir to India. There was a promise of a plebiscite to let the people decide their own fate (Akbar 136). However, as the years passed, that became less and less likely. Spontaneous popular discontent was no doubt exacerbated by the regional power rivalry of India and Pakistan, leading to Pakistani involvement in Kashmiri politics. Unsurprisingly, independence movements arose, some militant. Incidents such as the 1971 hijacking of an Indian airliner show the seriousness of these groups (Malik 282).

Rushdie presents such separatist acts as part of a developing spiral of violence: The presence of the military spurs greater resentment and resistance among Kashmiris, spurring greater suspicion among the military, thus motivating greater intrusion into Kashmiri lives, giving rise to increased resistance, generating violent incidents from the military, driving Kashmiris themselves to violence, and so on. The idea of such a cycle may seem obvious to the point of banality. What is remarkable about Rushdie's account, however, is that there is no single, definitive start to the cycle. It is, in fact, a wholly unnecessary spiral. In this way, it is not like classical colonialism. India's colonial occupation of Kashmir did not begin with rational greed—as in the desire to access gold, oil, or other precious resources—that then necessarily led to militarism, which in turn led to rebellion. Indian colonialism in Kashmir is, in that sense, an instance of "pure" colonial occupation—colonialism for the sake of colonialism. The occupation is justified simply by the fact that it is. Thus, in the novel, Kachhwaha rationalizes his crackdown on Kashmiris by reference to the territorial integrity of India (96), but that logic is circular. Kachhwaha claims that Kashmir is an integral part of India—thus repudiating claims for popular autonomy—simply because it has already been claimed to be part of India. The utter irrationality of such an occupation is perhaps more horrifying than the more standard forms of colonialism in which there is some straightforward motive.

This pure pursuit of control is perhaps more comprehensible in the realm of politics, when it is a matter of individual power. Unsurprisingly, the growing discontent among the Kashmiris and the increasing rigidity and harshness of the Indian political elite eventually reached a tipping point. Due to numerous political frustrations over the preceding decades and following the death of Sheikh Abdullah, the populace shifted their electoral support away from Abdullah's India-aligned party. The 1987 elections were virtually certain to favor the Muslim United Front, which would then be free to pursue a policy independent of India. However, there was massive vote fraud, and the government refused to investigate complaints and accusations. According to a number of writers, the resulting sense of complete disenfranchisement was crucial to the transformation of the insurgency (see, for example, Widmalm 77–83). What had formerly been a relatively small group of activists now swelled to a vast popular movement. Although this was far from the first case of vote rigging (Talbot and Singh 136), its scale and the context in which it occurred made it a critical moment.

The 1987 elections appear in *Shalimar*. As Rushdie explains, "Unofficially, as the results came in, it became plain that the wrong man was winning. So the election was rigged" (276). That is not all; "supporters" of the Muslim United Front "and electoral agents were seized and tortured." As a result, "thousands of previously law-abiding young men took up arms and joined the militants, disillusioned by the electoral process." Of course, here as elsewhere, there was not a single cause. "Pakistan was generous," Rushdie continues, explaining, "There were AK-47s for everyone" (276).

The Descent into Hell

Before she dies, the prophetess Nazarébaddoor explains that "the age of prophecy is at an end . . . because what's coming is so terrible that no prophet will have the words to foretell it" (68). Just as one would expect from Rushdie's analysis, the increased militancy of resistance to Indian colonialism inspired further brutality by the occupation forces. This too reached a transition point. A particularly brutal regime began in 1990. This was marked by numerous forms of state terror, including destructive house-to-house searches and the use of rape as a way of controlling and humiliating the population (Malik 308–9). Firing on crowds became a recurring practice, sometimes combined with arson, as in the 1993 burning of parts of the capital city, Srinagar, "during which [the Indian military] set fire to buildings and shot civilians trying to flee the flames" (Gossman 7). Needless to say, conditions have been no better for those arrested, however slight the justification; according to Amnesty International, "The brutality of torture in Jammu and Kashmir defies belief" (2).

These practices were made possible by the Indian government's decision to take up laws left over "from the days of colonial rule" (Malik 306). Further legal provisions only enhanced state colonial power. These included the 1990 Disturbed Areas Act, which "forbade the assembly of more than five people; authorized relatively low-ranking personnel to shoot anyone they suspected of disturbing public order; and permitted the destruction of any building thought to be an arms dump or providing shelter to militants." By the 1990 Special Powers Act, "officers were entitled to fire upon anyone contravening any law or order in force, in the disturbed area . . . arrest people without warrant . . . enter and search any premises without warrant" (Malik 307). In keeping with this, Amnesty International estimated in 1991 that some fifteen thousand detainees were being held without trial (Talbot and Singh 137). Rushdie refers to these acts, explaining that "the political echelon's decision to declare Kashmir a 'disturbed area'" meant that "search warrants were not required, arrest warrants ditto, and shoot-to-kill treatment of suspects was acceptable" (290).

Rushdie sets out the acts of terror committed by the Indian military. The most significant instances of these acts concern the characters we know and care for. Among the many devastating passages in the book, we find the description of the "retributive" murder of Abdullah and Firdaus Noman. Because Anees was a member of the Jammu and Kashmir Liberation Front (JKLF), the army murdered his father, after first breaking his hands—the hands that metaphorically held together the village of Pachigam, protecting its people and traditions. Because Anees was a militant, they raped his mother before and after killing her—to humiliate, disgrace, and dishearten anyone who knew or cared for her or her husband.

Of course, the tens of thousands dead in the following decade were not all killed by the Indian armed forces (Widmalm 131). Kashmiri militants contributed as well, even if they seem to have killed at only about half the rate of the army (Talbot and Singh 136–37). These groups received a great increase in support due to brutality of the Indian armed forces and due to the involvement of Pakistan. Moreover, they underwent a change in these years. The early militants, who developed into the JKLF, were largely secular nationalists. In Rushdie's account, these were violent but principled revolutionaries, represented by Anees Noman. Rushdie contrasts them sharply with the other militant groups that rose in importance at this time—the Islamists.

The Islamists were driven by antagonism toward infidels and were often closely associated with Pakistan. As Talbot and Singh explain, after the disintegration of the Soviet Union, Pakistani intelligence services "engage[d] some of the *jihadis*" from Afghanistan "in the militancy that had broken out in Kashmir" (167). In *Shalimar*, the Islamist groups include the terror squad of the Gegroo brothers, who raped Zoon Misri. They were part of "the most 'Afghan'" of the Islamist groups, "the Lashkar-e-Pak or Army of the Pure." This group ordered "all Muslim women to don the burqa and adhere to the dress and behavioral principles laid down by the Taliban in Afghanistan" (277).

Relations among these secular and Islamist militant groups were generally poor, often hostile. Rushdie rightly sets them against one another, both in their general aims and strategies and in their interpersonal relations. As he puts it, the "liberation-front-wallahs were nationalist subversives rather than religious fanatics and between them and the iron mullahs there was little love lost" (122). This split is encapsulated in the growing conflict between Anees and Shalimar (259).

Rushdie also nicely represents another phenomenon that recurs in colonial and revolutionary or other militarized conflicts. When violence becomes legitimated—either by the state or by antistate agents such as militants—it is very likely that these new, socially acceptable forms of violence will attract those already prone to violence or habituated to violence in other contexts. In other words, both the military and the revolutionary groups are likely to attract sociopathic and victim-seeking agents as well as criminals. The case of rape is perhaps the most obvious instance of this. If rape is accepted as a tool of domination for a given organization, it seems likely that such groups will attract rapists. This is just what we find with the Gegroo brothers. Trapped in a mosque after raping Zoon Misri, they reappear as Islamic militants. The suggestion is that they not only have literally taken refuge in a holy place, but have metaphorically taken refuge in religion.

Why Violence?

This last point is worth dwelling on, for it is crucial to Rushdie's novel. How does it happen that a rapist can justify his act by appeal to religion, or nation, in the case of the Indian military? In part, of course, this is simple hypocrisy. That is the case with the Gegroo brothers. By contrast, Kachhwaha seems to believe fully in the justice of his cause. More generally, each side claims it is responding to the cruelty of the other, but some individuals seem to believe more fully in the rightness of their response and in their own innocence. In addition to

Kachhwaha, the other obvious case of this is the Iron Mullah, Bulbul Fakh. In short, the two characters who are most committed to ideals are not those who behave most humanely. Rather, they are the characters who most fully enable inhumanity. How can this be?

Rushdie hints at an explanation when he has Pyarelal Kaul claim that "man is ruined by the misfortune of possessing a moral sense" (91). The problem is that, for Kachhwaha and the Iron Mullah, something is higher than the truth and human feeling that might have prevented violence. For the Iron Mullah, it is God and revelation, a hidden "truth" that belies apparent empirical truths; for Kachhwaha, it is the nation. Thus, according to the former, only "the infidel speaks of universal truth," whereas the believers "know that the universe is an illusion" (267). Similarly, Kachhwaha reflects, "When the truth and integrity [i.e., the national integrity of India] conflicted it was integrity that had to be given precedence. Not even the truth could be permitted to dishonor the nation" (96).

The suppression of truth by doctrine—religious or national—is neither the only source of violence nor even an adequate source, however. Perhaps even more important is the suppression of feeling. It is common for us to recoil from the suffering of others—say, people consumed in flames (as when Indian troops burned areas of Srinagar) or people driven from their homes into refugee camps (such as the Hindus who fled Kashmir). Despite this, we can engage in processes of thought that limit those feelings. This is one key place where norms enter, for norms establish something higher than human feeling. Commonly that higher principle is either national or religious. The Indian Army must suppress not only truth in the name of the nation, but empathy as well. The Iron Mullahs are even more extreme. They are so denatured by divine principle that they have only "machine parts" where they should have a heart (316).

The suppression of truth and the suppression of feeling are closely related. It is, after all, our sense of what is true (e.g., that some suspect's mother has been raped by soldiers) that provokes our fellow feeling and, ideally, our beneficence. To suppress the truth of the "enemy's" suffering is to inhibit compassion. Adding an appeal to principle only compounds the suffocation of our natural empathy.

Even so, human beings are so robustly lethargic that even the suppression of truth and the moral rationalization of cruelty are not sufficient to produce violence. Two other conditions are necessary. First, since we do nothing without motivation, the agents of violence must be motivated to inflict pain. One obvious possibility here is devotion to the nation—Kashmir or India—or the religious community or God. Interestingly, Rushdie has very few characters who are genuinely motivated by social or political aims.[3] Anees Noman may be one. Generally, in *Shalimar*, even the most vigorous nationalist or communalist actions are initiated and sustained by personal feeling. Personal relations are, to use Firdaus Noman's words, the "low-grade cause of all discontent on earth" (113). The case of Shalimar himself is obvious, given his quest for revenge against Max Ophuls, but the point also extends to others, such as Kachhwaha. Kachhwaha's entire military career is in effect a struggle against the demeaning attitude of his own father. His particular animosity toward Kashmiri Muslims derives from Boonyi's rejection—"Pachigam would suffer for Boonyi Kaul's insulting behavior" (101).

Generally, the humane social actions in the novel are based on attachment and trust. We see this in, for example, the panchayat's affirmation of Kashmiriyat in the marriage of Boonyi and Shalimar. In contrast, violence is commonly based on betrayal and humiliation, as in the cases just mentioned—Shalimar and Kachhwaha. Moreover, this personal motivation suggests why certain sorts of "principles" come to be invoked with such frequency and force—prominently, principles of group pride and honor. For Shalimar, "honor ranked above everything else" (258). The invocation of these principles is a way of rationalizing violent responses to shame.

Personal motivation is not enough either. Even with motives and rationalizations, people cannot simply go out and fight wars. Some complex of social activities must be aligned with personal motivations. In other words, some relevant institutions, some socially regularized practices, must be congruent with the actional outcomes of the relevant motives. If the actional outcome of feeling attachment-inspired good will is beneficence, there must be agencies and social policies that allow individuals to engage in beneficence. If the actional outcome of feeling shame-provoked rage is murder, there must be agencies and social policies that allow individuals to engage in murder. In both cases, the agencies and policies do not provoke the initial motivation, but rather orient and coordinate the individual motivations. Kachhwaha on his own would not have turned his shame before his father into the murder of Abdullah Noman. The Indian military and governmental policies—along with the diverse personal motivations of other individuals in the Indian army—led his motivation to that outcome.

It should be clear why this account of violence works particularly well with Rushdie's treatment of the Kashmir conflict developing through cycles of provocation and intensifying harm and cruelty. In a sense, the initial hostilities are incidental—personal experiences of shame and rage at betrayal. These begin the cycle, which then refocuses and often intensifies the prior feelings. For example, Kachhwaha's attempt to overcome his shame before his father leads him to the situation where he can be humiliated by Boonyi. The social context of India in conflict with Kashmir itself orients how Kachhwaha categorizes Boonyi (as a Kashmiri Muslim) and provides an outlet for his anger, which is then generalized to other members of her category.

The Future of the Nation: Critical Anticolonialism, Despair, and the Bhand Pather

The relatively benevolent treatment that Rushdie gives to the JKLF—not to mention his searing condemnation of Indian military actions in Kashmir—indicates that *Shalimar* is an anticolonial novel. The usual teleological and emancipatory myth is the standard result of such anticolonialism. Moreover, Rushdie's use of a romantic emplotment for the history of Kashmir—making it into a story of a tragic fall—lends itself readily to emancipatory mythologizing. Commonly, the lost Eden is precisely what the national anticolonial movement is seen as potentially reproducing. Indeed, part of the reason for most appeals to a past national utopia is precisely to claim that the future, independent nation might hope to reestablish that utopia. In *Shalimar*, Rushdie presents an alternative, a romantic but *critical* anticolonialism, one heightened by the imagination of paradise lost but not rendered cruel and triumphalist by the imagination of paradise regained.

There is one difficulty with having only a romantic myth and no emancipatory fantasy: It can lead to a sort of political despair. Where does one go with a situation in which all the political sides and all political options appear to some degree cruel and wrong? Where does one go when the only apparently fair option, "Kashmir for the Kashmiris," is reduced to an "old fairy tale" (291), its mythic status made unquestionable? One might expect a novel about Kashmir to end with some suggestion about the author's solution to the crisis. Yet, in *Shalimar*, we are faced with two people in a dark room poised to kill one another, and the haunting final sentences—"There was no second chance. There was no India. There was only Kashmira, and Shalimar the clown" (398)—suggest not only a loss of hope for India, but a sort of global condition, a standoff between innocent victims and cruel victims. Of course, Kashmira is innocent, but Shalimar, though far from innocent, is himself the product of past suffering, both personal and political. I suspect that, like me, almost all readers strongly wish for the survival of Kashmira. Yet, if she kills this victimized victimizer with her bow, what system has been defended, what exactly has triumphed?

More broadly, what does Kashmira represent? Is she simply the individual victim of terror? If so, training in archery—or the use of other, more modern weapons—hardly appears to be a solution; more Americans with guns seems an unlikely way of resolving the world's current crises. And what about Shalimar? Does he simply represent terrorists or militancy? If so, it seems clear that killing him will, at best, produce temporary security for one endangered target, not a general solution. Moreover, this killing will in no way address the political structures and military routines that created and sustain the nightmarish conditions in Kashmir.

The deeply tragic vision of the novel may be highlighted by contrasting it with the Bhand Pather, the traditional performing art of Kashmir, which features prominently in Rushdie's novel as the profession of the Nomans. M. K. Raina explains that the Bhands themselves have a "secular outlook" and are deeply anticommunalist—for example, Muslims perform "in honour of this goddess [Shiva Bhagvati]." Moreover, the purposes of their plays historically involved exposing "the injustice that the people suffered," typically including elements of legend and satire (Raina, "The *Bhand*"). More precisely, these plays often feature "the figure of a ruler from outside who is exploiting the natives" (Raina, "Humour"). A key figure in overcoming this exploitation is the *maskhara* (jester), a "rebel . . . who does not cow down to the oppressor" (Raina, "The *Bhand*").

The links between Rushdie's novel and the Bhand Pather are obvious. They share the same political purposes, the same opposition to non-Kashmiri oppression of Kashmir, the same focus on the jester—or "clown," as Rushdie prefers—and the same genuine anticommunalism, a real respect across communities, not a mere tolerance. The differences are equally striking. In the Bhand Pather, "the local character is . . . victorious in the end" (Raina, "The *Bhand*"). Moreover, that victory comes when the "the jesters fool" the outside ruler and "bring him to some kind of an understanding" (Raina, "Humour"). This is precisely what is absent from *Shalimar*. The clown is not victorious. Or, if he is, then his victory is as cruel as the oppression he is opposing. This is because the extent of the brutality is so great that even the clown wields a sword; he can no longer trick the oppressor but rather aspires to repeat the oppression. Moreover, even if the clown could maintain the role of ironic trickster, the oppressors are now too various and too filled with rage and shame to gain human understanding and end the violence. Indeed, the tragedy of *Shalimar* goes even deeper. Rather than inspiring human understanding in the oppressor, the clown himself has lost that understanding. Despite his name, he is no longer a clown.

This loss of the maskhara is part of the loss of Eden, part of Rushdie's own myth—in this case, a myth that has all too great a similarity to the real world. It is part of what makes all the options for Kashmir so terrible and its future so disheartening. Indeed, part of that future is the undoubted loss of the Bhand Pather itself. Raina quotes a master of the Bhand Pather, Ama Kak, saying, "It will all soon die out and no one will ever know that we the *Bhands* had such a rich and developed . . . heritage" ("The *Bhand*"). Here, too, Rushdie shows himself an anticolonial novelist. However despairing he may be about the future of Kashmir, he has set himself the task of trying to preserve the memory of a culture that may soon be destroyed forever.

Notes

1. For a perhaps related point, see Stadtler's discussion of how *Shalimar* "engages with the repressions and exclusions that the postcolonial state imposes on its periphery" (191).
2. Some critics have taken the view that *Shalimar* has significant allegorical components (see, for example, Morton).
3. I take the point to be insightful. For an alternative view, see Eaglestone 21.

Works Cited

Abdullah, Farooq. Foreword. Mathew vii–viii.
Akbar, M. J. *Kashmir: Behind the Vale*. New Delhi: Viking, 1991.
Ali, Agha Shahid. *The Veiled Suite: The Collected Poems*. New York: Norton, 2009.
Amnesty International. "India: Torture and Deaths in Custody in Jammu and Kashmir." Amnesty International, 31 Jan. 1995. Web. 14 Mar. 2012.
Bamzai, Prithivi Nath Kaul. *A History of Kashmir: Political, Social, Cultural, from the Earliest Times to the Present Day*. Delhi: Metropolitan, 1962.
DuPont, Samuel W. "The Art of Resistance: Report from Kashmir." *Commonweal* 23 May 2008: 13–15.

Eaglestone, Robert. "'Age of Reason Is Over . . . an Age of Fury Was Dawning': Contemporary Anglo-American Fiction and Terror." *Wasafiri* 51 (Summer 2007): 19–22.
Gossman, Patricia. *The Human Rights Crisis in Kashmir: A Pattern of Impunity.* New York: Human Rights Watch, 1993.
Malik, Iffat. *Kashmir: Ethnic Conflict, International Dispute.* Karachi: Oxford UP, 2002.
Mathew, George, ed. *Panchayati Raj in Jammu and Kashmir.* New Delhi: Institute of Social Sciences and Concept Publishing Company, 1990.
Morton, Stephen. "'There Were Collisions and Explosions. The World Was No Longer Calm.' Terror and Precarious Life in Salman Rushdie's *Shalimar the Clown*." *Textual Practice* 22.2 (2008): 337–55.
Punjabi, Riyaz. "Panchayati Raj in Kashmir: Yesterday, Today and Tomorrow." Mathew 37–49.
Raina, M. K. "The *Bhand Pather* of Kashmir." *Kashmiri Overseas Association.* Kashmiri Overseas Association, n.d. Web. 14 Mar. 2012.
_____. "Humour, Theatre, Children, Kashmir: Bhand Pather." *Likhati.* Likhati, 10 Jan. 2009. Web. 14 Mar. 2012.
Rushdie, Salman. *Midnight's Children.* New York: Penguin, 1980.
_____. *Shalimar the Clown.* New York: Random, 2005.
Stadtler, Florian. "Terror, Globalization and the Individual in Salman Rushdie's *Shalimar the Clown*." *Journal of Postcolonial Writing* 45.2 (2009): 191–99.
Talbot, Ian, and Gurharpal Singh. *The Partition of India.* Cambridge: Cambridge UP, 2009.
Widmalm, Sten. *Kashmir in Comparative Perspective: Democracy and Violent Separatism in India.* London: Routledge, 2002.

RESOURCES

Chronology of Salman Rushdie

1947	On June 19, Ahmed Salman Rushdie is born in Bombay (now Mumbai), India, to Cambridge-educated businessman Anis Ahmed Rushdie and teacher Negin Bhutt Rushdie. He and his three sisters are raised in the home he will later give to a character in *Midnight's Children*.
1954	Rushdie begins attending Cathedral & John Connon School.
1961	In January, Rushdie enrolls at Rugby School in Warwickshire, England.
1962	Rushdie's family moves to Kensington, England.
1964	The Rushdie family moves to Karachi, Pakistan.
1965	Rushdie enters King's College, Cambridge, where he studies history, reads both Eastern and Western literature, and becomes involved in the college's theater productions.
1968	Rushdie earns his master's degree in history with honors. After graduation, he rejoins his family in Pakistan, where he starts working for Pakistan TV. Facing censorship both from the network and from a magazine to which he submitted an article about his first impressions of Pakistan, he leaves and returns to London.
1968–69	Rushdie acts with Oval House and the Fringe Theatre and works in television, advertising, and publishing.
1970	Rushdie begins a decade as a freelance advertising copywriter, working with firms such as Ogilvy & Mather and Charles Barker in London. He also begins to write two novels, both unpublished.
1975	Rushdie's first novel, *Grimus*, is published by Victor Gollancz. He visits India with Clarissa Luard, a publishing executive, to do research for his next book.

1976	Rushdie marries Clarissa Luard and begins a seven-year period of involvement with the Camden Committee of Community Relations, working on projects to assist immigrants from Bangladesh.
1979	Rushdie's son Zafar is born.
1981	Although its copyright page says 1980, *Midnight's Children* is actually published in March 1981 in the United States and April 1981 in the United Kingdom. It goes on to win the Booker Prize for Fiction, the James Tait Black Memorial Prize, and an award from the English-Speaking Union, and is widely acclaimed as a groundbreaking amalgam of East and West, history and fantasy. The book's success allows Rushdie to quit advertising and become a full-time writer.
1983	Rushdie is named a fellow of the Royal Society for Literature. *Shame* receives the French Prix du Meilleur Livre Étranger and is short-listed for the Booker Prize.
1985	Rushdie narrates the television documentary *The Painter and the Pest*.
1986	Rushdie visits Nicaragua at the invitation of the Sandinista Association of Cultural Workers.
1987	Rushdie recounts his trip to Nicaragua in the nonfiction work *The Jaguar Smile: A Nicaraguan Journey*. He and Clarissa Luard divorce.
1988	Rushdie writes and presents the television documentary *The Riddle of Midnight: India, August 1987*. He marries American novelist Marianne Wiggins. In September, *The Satanic Verses* is published by Viking Penguin. Short-listed for the Booker Prize, it wins the Whitbread Novel Award and the Author of the Year Award in Germany. In October, British Muslims protest in Bradford, and the book is banned in India; bans in Bangladesh, Sri Lanka, Pakistan, Egypt, Indonesia, Singapore, Kenya, Sudan, South Africa, Venezuela, Poland, and elsewhere soon follow. Before the end of the year, protests and riots against the book occur in India, Pakistan, and South Africa, as well as England, leaving dozens dead and hundreds

injured. Several bookstores and publishing houses in England and North America are bombed, and the major book chains announce that they will no longer display or sell the novel, a decision that is eventually reversed when the immediate crisis passes.

1989	On January 14, *The Satanic Verses* and effigies of its author are publicly burned in Bradford, England. On February 14, Ayatollah Ruhollah Khomeini issues a *fatwā* (legal ruling) on Radio Tehran, accusing Rushdie of blasphemy and sentencing him, his publishers, and his translators to death. A price of $5 million is soon placed on his head, and he is forced to go into hiding under the protection of the British government. Marianne Wiggins separates from Rushdie in early August.
1990	*Haroun and the Sea of Stories* is published. In late December, while in hiding, in an effort to make peace, Rushdie issues a statement embracing Islam and announcing that he has agreed to prohibit new translations or a paperback edition of *The Satanic Verses*. The Iranian clerics renew calls for his death.
1991	*Imaginary Homelands: Essays and Criticism, 1981–1991* is published. Rushdie's Italian translator is stabbed in Milan but lives; his Japanese translator is fatally stabbed in Tokyo. Rushdie makes a surprise public appearance at a Columbia University forum on free speech, where he withdraws his earlier decision and asks that an English-language paperback edition be published soon.
1992	Rushdie publishes *The Wizard of Oz* in the British Film Institute's Film Classics series. In March, a consortium of publishers issues a paperback edition of *The Satanic Verses*; no publisher is willing to risk issuing the book on its own. The Penguin group will eventually undertake publication of paperback copies.
1993	*Midnight's Children* wins the Booker of Bookers as the best book to have received the Booker Prize in its first twenty-five years. Rushdie is awarded the Austrian State Prize for European Literature and is named honorary vice president of PEN America and honorary visiting professor at the Massachusetts Institute of Technology (MIT). Rushdie and Marianne Wiggins divorce. His Norwegian publisher survives being shot several times outside his home in Oslo.

1994	*East, West: Stories* is published.
1995	*The Moor's Last Sigh* is published. It wins the Whitbread Award and is short-listed for the Booker Prize for Fiction. Rushdie is named British Book Awards Author of the Year. He makes his first publicized appearance since the *fatwā* for a reading in London and begins to appear regularly at literary and cultural roundtables and conferences.
1996	Rushdie is awarded the European Union's Aristeion Prize for Literature.
1997	Rushdie and Elizabeth West coedit *The Vintage Book of Indian Writing, 1947–1997* (published in the United States as *Mirrorwork: 50 Years of Indian Writing, 1947–1997*). West gives birth to Rushdie's son Milan. Rushdie and West marry.
1998	Rushdie receives the Budapest Grand Prize for Literature. At the UN General Assembly, the Iranian government officially distances itself from the *fatwā*; however, the *fatwā* is not withdrawn by the country's religious authorities. Rushdie nonetheless formally announces that he will no longer live in hiding.
1999	Rushdie publicly promotes his next novel, *The Ground Beneath Her Feet*, with readings and book signings. The Indian government grants him a five-year visa. *The Screenplay of Midnight's Children* is published. The French government names Rushdie a Commandeur de l'Ordre des Arts et des Lettres.
2000	Rushdie travels to India with his son Zafar to attend the Commonwealth Writer's Prize ceremonies. He relocates to New York City.
2001	*Fury: A Novel* is published.
2002	*Step Across This Line: Collected Nonfiction, 1992–2002* is published.
2003	The Royal Shakespeare Company premieres Rushdie's dramatic adaptation of *Midnight's Children* at the Barbican Centre, London.

2004	The New York City Opera premieres an opera based on *Haroun and the Sea of Stories* at Lincoln Center. Rushdie and Elizabeth West divorce. He marries model and television personality Padma Lakshmi. He begins a two-year term as president of PEN American Center.
2005	*Shalimar the Clown* is published. It goes on to receive the Whitbread Award and the Hutch-Crossword Book Award in India.
2007	In June, Rushdie is knighted by Queen Elizabeth II of England for services to literature. Protests erupt in Iran, Pakistan, and other Muslim countries; the Pakistani parliament passes a resolution condemning Rushdie's selection for knighthood; and the leaders of twelve British Muslim groups write a letter describing it as a "deliberate provocation and insult to the 1.5 billion Muslims around the world." Rushdie becomes a Distinguished Writer in Residence at Emory University. He and Padma Lakshmi divorce.
2008	*The Enchantress of Florence* is published. Rushdie is elected to the American Academy of Arts and Letters. *Midnight's Children* is named the Best of the Booker, the best book to have received the award in its first forty years. Rushdie receives the James Joyce Award from the University College Dublin.
2009	*The Best American Stories of 2008*, coedited by Rushdie and Heidi Pitlor, is published.
2010	*Luka and the Fire of Life* is published. Rushdie becomes one of the founding patrons of Ralston College in Savannah, Georgia.

Works by Salman Rushdie

Fiction
Grimus, 1975
Midnight's Children, 1981
Shame, 1983
The Satanic Verses, 1988
Haroun and the Sea of Stories, 1990
East, West: Stories, 1994
The Moor's Last Sigh, 1995
The Ground Beneath Her Feet, 1999
Fury, 2001
Shalimar the Clown, 2005
The Enchantress of Florence, 2008
Luka and the Fire of Life, 2010

Nonfiction
The Jaguar Smile: A Nicaraguan Journey, 1987
Imaginary Homelands: Essays and Criticism, 1981–1991, 1991
The Wizard of Oz, 1992 (Rpt. as "Out of Kansas" in *Step Across This Line*)
The Vintage Book of Indian Writing, 1947–1997, 1997 (coeditor; published in the United States as *Mirrorwork: 50 Years of Indian Writing, 1947–1997*)
Step Across This Line: Collected Nonfiction, 1992–2002, 2002
Best American Short Stories 2008, 2009 (coeditor)

Plays and Screenplays
Salman Rushdie's Haroun and the Sea of Stories, 1998 (adapted with Tim Supple and David Tushingham)
The Screenplay of Midnight's Children, 1999
Salman Rushdie's Midnight's Children, 2003 (adapted with Tim Supple and Simon Reade)

Films
The Painter and the Pest, 1985 (narrator)
The Riddle of Midnight: India, August 1987, 1988 (writer, presenter)

Bibliography

Abdallah, Anouar, et al. *For Rushdie: Essays by Arab and Muslim Writers in Defense of Free Speech.* New York: Braziller, 1994.

Afzal-Khan, Fawzia. *Cultural Imperialism and the Indo-English Novel: Genre and Ideology in R. K. Narayan, Anita Desai, Kamala Markandaya, and Salman Rushdie.* University Park: Pennsylvania State UP, 1993.

Akhtar, Shabbir. *Be Careful with Muhammad! The Salman Rushdie Affair.* London: Bellew, 1989.

Appignanesi, Lisa, and Sara Maitland, eds. *The Rushdie File.* London: Fourth Estate, 1990.

Ball, John Clement. *Satire and the Postcolonial Novel: V. S. Naipaul, Chinua Achebe, Salman Rushdie.* New York: Routledge, 2003.

Banerjee, Mita. *The Chutneyfication of History: Salman Rushdie, Michael Ondaatje, Bharati Mukherjee, and the Postcolonial Debate.* Heidelberg: Winter, 2002.

Blake, Andrew. *Salman Rushdie: A Beginner's Guide.* London: Hodder, 2001.

Bloom, Harold, ed. *Salman Rushdie.* Philadelphia: Chelsea, 2002.

Booker, M. Keith, ed. *Critical Essays on Salman Rushdie.* New York: Hall, 1999.

Brennan, Timothy. *Salman Rushdie and the Third World: Myths of the Nation.* New York: St. Martin's, 1989.

Chauhan, Pradyumna S., ed. *Salman Rushdie Interviews: A Sourcebook of His Ideas.* Westport: Greenwood, 2001.

Clark, Roger Y. *Stranger Gods: Salman Rushdie's Other Worlds.* Montreal: McGill-Queen's UP, 2001.

Cohn-Sherbok, Dan. *The Salman Rushdie Controversy in Interreligious Perspective.* Lewiston: Mellen, 1990.

Cundy, Catherine. *Salman Rushdie.* Manchester: Manchester UP, 1996.

Deszcz, Justyna. *Rushdie in Wonderland: "Fairytaleness" in Salman Rushdie's Fiction.* Frankfurt: Lang, 2004.

Dutheil de la Rochère, Martine Hennard. *Origin and Originality in Rushdie's Fiction.* Bern: Lang, 1999.

Easterman, Daniel. *New Jerusalems: Reflections on Islam, Fundamentalism and the Rushdie Affair.* London: Grafton, 1992.

Fletcher, M. D. *Reading Rushdie: Perspectives on the Fiction of Salman Rushdie.* Amsterdam: Rodopi, 1994.

Goonetilleke, D. C. R. A. *Salman Rushdie.* Basingstoke: Macmillan, 1998.

Gorra, Michael. *After Empire: Scott, Naipaul, Rushdie.* Chicago: U of Chicago P, 1997.

Grant, Damian. *Salman Rushdie.* Plymouth: Northcote, 1999.

Gurnah, Abdulrazak, ed. *The Cambridge Companion to Salman Rushdie*. Cambridge: Cambridge UP, 2007.

Harrison, James. *Salman Rushdie*. New York: Twayne, 1992.

Hassumani, Sabrina. *Salman Rushdie: A Postmodern Reading of His Major Works.* Madison: Fairleigh Dickinson UP, 2002.

Kortenaar, Neil ten. *Self, Nation, Text in Salman Rushdie's* Midnight's Children. Montreal: McGill-Queen's UP, 2004.

Kuortti, Joel. *Fictions to Live In: Narration as an Argument for Fiction in Salman Rushdie's Novels*. Frankfurt: Lang, 1998.

_____. *Place of the Sacred: The Rhetoric of the* Satanic Verses *Affair*. Frankfurt: Lang, 1997.

_____. *The Salman Rushdie Bibliography: A Bibliography of Salman Rushdie's Work and Rushdie Criticism*. Frankfurt: Lang, 1997.

MacDonogh, Steve, ed. *The Rushdie Letters: Freedom to Speak, Freedom to Write*. Lincoln: U of Nebraska P, 1993.

Mittapalli, Rajeshwar, and Joel Kuortti, eds. *Salman Rushdie: New Critical Insights*. 2 vols. New Delhi: Atlantic, 2003.

Mukherjee, Meenakshi, ed. *Rushdie's* Midnight's Children: *A Book of Readings*. Delhi: Pencraft International, 2003.

Parameswaran, Uma. *The Perforated Sheet: Essays on Salman Rushdie's Art*. New Delhi: Affiliated East-West, 1988.

Petersson, Margareta. *Unending Metamorphoses: Myth, Satire and Religion in Salman Rushdie's Novels*. Lund: Lund UP, 1996.

Pipes, Daniel, ed. *The Rushdie Affair: The Novel, the Ayatollah, and the West*. New York: Birch Lane, 1990.

Reder, Michael, ed. *Conversations with Salman Rushdie*. Jackson: UP of Mississippi, 2000.

Reynolds, Margaret, and Jonathan Noakes, eds. *Salman Rushdie: The Essential Guide*. London: Vintage, 2003.

Ruthven, Malise. *A Satanic Affair: Salman Rushdie and the Rage of Islam*. London: Chatto, 1990.

Sanga, Jaina C. *Salman Rushdie's Postcolonial Metaphors: Migration, Translation, Hybridity, Blasphemy, and Globalization*. Westport: Greenwood, 2001.

Sardar, Ziauddin, and Merryl Wyn Davies. *Distorted Imagination: Lessons from the Rushdie Affair*. London: Grey Seal, 1990.

Schürer, Norbert. *Salman Rushdie's* Midnight's Children: *A Reader's Guide*. New York: Continuum, 2004.

Seminck, Hans. *A Novel Visible but Unseen: A Thematic Analysis of Salman Rushdie's* The Satanic Verses. Ghent: Studia Germanica Gandensia, 1993.

Smale, David, ed. *Salman Rushdie* Midnight's Children / The Satanic Verses: *A Reader's Guide to Essential Criticism*. New York: Macmillan, 2001.

Taneja, G. R., and Rajinder Kumar Dhawan, eds. *The Novels of Salman Rushdie*. New Delhi: Indian Society for Commonwealth Studies, 1992.

Teverson, Andrew. *Salman Rushdie*. Manchester: Manchester UP, 2007.

Thiara, Nicole Weickgenannt. *Salman Rushdie and Indian Historiography: Writing the Nation into Being*. Basingstoke: Macmillan, 2009.

Weatherby, W. J. *Salman Rushdie: Sentenced to Death*. New York: Carroll, 1990.

Webster, Richard. *A Brief History of Blasphemy: Liberalism, Censorship and* The Satanic Verses. Southwold: Orwell, 1990.

About the Editor

Bernard F. Rodgers, Jr., is the Emily H. Fisher Professor of Literature at Bard College at Simon's Rock. A member of the National Book Critics Circle and PEN and a consulting editor of the journal *Philip Roth Studies*, he is the author of *Philip Roth: A Bibliography* (1974), *Philip Roth* (1978), and *Voices and Visions: Selected Essays* (2001), and editor of *Critical Insights: John Updike* (2012). His essays and reviews on modern and contemporary American literature and culture—as well as writers such as Salman Rushdie, Milan Kundera, Aharon Appelfeld, Czesław Miłosz, and Ian McEwan—have appeared in numerous publications, including the *Fitzgerald/Hemingway Annual*, *Critique*, *Chicago Review*, *Chicago Tribune*, *Illinois Issues*, *Kwartalnik neofilologiczny* (Warsaw), *MELUS*, *Philip Roth Studies*, *World & I*, and *Berkshire Eagle*. His work has also been published in *Bloom's Modern Critical Interpretations of* Portnoy's Complaint, *Magill's Literary Annual*, *Magill's Survey of World Literature*, *Magill's Book Reviews*, and *Masterplots II* and *IV* and has been broadcast on WBBM-AM and WNIB-FM in Chicago.

Rodgers spent a year as a Fulbright Senior Scholar Lecturer in American literature at Marie Curie-Skłodowska University in Lublin, Poland; served as president of the Massachusetts Foundation for the Humanities; and has been involved as a scholar in projects sponsored by the Chicago Public Library, the Illinois Humanities Council, and the National Endowment for the Humanities. He has also served as special assistant to the chancellor of the City Colleges of Chicago and dean of academic affairs at Simon's Rock. From 1987 to 2004, Rodgers was a vice president of Bard College and the dean of Simon's Rock.

Contributors

Bernard F. Rodgers, Jr., is the Emily H. Fisher Professor of Literature at Bard College at Simon's Rock. He has written on Salman Rushdie for *Magill's Literary Annual* and *Magill's Survey of World Literature*. A member of the National Book Critics Circle, PEN America, and a consulting editor of the journal *Philip Roth Studies*, he is the author of *Philip Roth: A Bibliography* (1974), *Philip Roth* (1978), and *Voices and Visions: Selected Essays* (2001), and editor of *Critical Insights: John Updike* (2012).

R. S. Krishnan is a professor of English and associate vice president for academic affairs and director of summer school at North Dakota State University. He has published on Samuel Johnson, Tobias Smollett, John Locke, Oliver Goldsmith, Tayeb Salih, V. S. Naipaul, Salman Rushdie, Bharathi Mukherjee, and Pico Iyer, among others. His articles and reviews have appeared in *Studies in Scottish Literature, Studies in the Novel, International Fiction Review, Lamar Journal of the Humanities,* and *Atlantic Literary Review*.

Joel Kuortti is a professor of English at the University of Turku and adjunct professor of contemporary culture at the University of Jyväskylä. His research is on postcolonial theory, Indian literature in English, transcultural identity, hybridity, and cultural studies. His publications include *The Salman Rushdie Bibliography* (1997); *Place of the Sacred: The Rhetoric of the Satanic Verses Affair* (1997); *Fictions to Live In: Narration as an Argument for Fiction in Salman Rushdie's Novels* (1998); *Indian Women's Writing in English: A Bibliography* (2002); *Tense Past, Tense Present: Women Writing in English* (2003); and *Writing Imagined Diasporas: South Asian Women Reshaping North American Identity* (2007). He has also coedited *Reconstructing Hybridity: Post-colonial Studies in Transition* (2007) with Jopi Nyman and *Changing Words/Changing Nations: The Concept of Nation in the Transnational Era* (2011) with Om Dwivedi.

Mona Narain is an associate professor of English and women's studies and director of graduate studies at Texas Christian University in Fort Worth, Texas. She has coedited the special issue "Postcolonial Revisions of Early Modern Histories" of the *Journal for Early Modern Culture Studies*, which includes an essay on Salman Rushdie. Other publications on colonialism and postcolonialism include articles on Elizabeth Hamilton's *Translations of the Letters of a Hindoo Rajah* in *Studies in Romanticism*, on South Asian feminists in academia in *Generations: Feminisms in Dialogue*, and on eighteenth-century Indian travelers to Britain and their perceptions in *Literature Compass*. She is working on a book-length study of the latter subject.

Nicole Weickgenannt Thiara is an associate lecturer at the Manchester Metropolitan University in Manchester, England, and author of *Salman Rushdie and Indian Historiography: Writing the Nation into Being* (2009). Her essays on *Midnight's Children*, *The Moor's Last Sigh*, and *The Enchantress of Florence* have appeared in the *Journal of Commonwealth Literature*, the *Journal of Commonwealth and Postcolonial Studies*, and the anthology *(M)Othering the Nation: Constructing and Resisting Regional and National Allegories through the Maternal Body* (2008), edited by Lisa Bernstein. She is working on the book *Narratives of Untouchability: Representations of the Subaltern in Indian Literature and Film* and holds a collaborative fellowship with Annapurna Waughray from the Manchester Metropolitan University to study the emergence of a British Dalit literature.

David J. Zucker lives in Aurora, Colorado, where he recently retired as full-time rabbi/chaplain at Shalom Cares. During his career as a congregational rabbi, visiting professor, and independent scholar, he taught at Regis University, University of Denver, Missouri State University, and Drury College, as well as other colleges and universities. He has written about Philip Roth, Bernard Malamud, and other Jewish American writers in *Studies in Jewish American Literature*, *Midstream*, the *Journal of Ecumenical Studies*, *Jewish Spectator*, *Judaism*, *CCAR Journal*, and the London *Jewish Quarterly*. He is also the author of *Israel's Prophets: An Introduction for Christians and Jews* (1994), *American Rabbis: Facts and Fiction* (1998), and *The Torah: An Introduction for Christians and Jews* (2005), as well as several book chapters and many articles on religion, chaplaincy, and biblical studies.

Roger Y. Clark teaches at Douglas College in New Westminster, British Columbia, and specializes in international literature. He is the author of *Stranger Gods: Salman Rushdie's Other Worlds* (2001) and has contributed nearly two dozen entries to the *Encyclopedia of Literature in Canada*.

Asma Abbas is an associate professor of politics and philosophy at Bard College at Simon's Rock. She is the author of *Liberalism and Human Suffering: Materialist Reflections on Politics, Ethics, and Aesthetics* (2010). Her work has also appeared in the journals *Theory and Event*, *Politics & Culture*, *Journal of Politics*, as well as a volume on pedagogy titled *Educating Outside the Lines* (2011). Abbas is working on a book manuscript titled *Love, Time, and the Anticolonial: Overtures to a Politics of the Unrequited* and a translation and annotation of a political memoir by her father, a founder of the left labor movement in Pakistan.

Harold Branam is a retired professor of English, who taught at Kentucky, La Salle, Pikeville, Temple, and Savannah State universities. A Marshall Scholar and NDEA Fellow, he has written hundreds of critical articles—including numerous articles on multicultural and postcolonial authors, among them Salman Rushdie—mostly for the

Salem Press, where he has contributed to *Magill's Literary Annual* for over twenty-five years. He was also the poetry editor of a literary journal and an assistant editor of the *International Encyclopedia of Communications*. His poetry has appeared in *Now & Then*, *Appalachian Journal*, *Friends Journal*, and other magazines and been read on National Public Radio's *Writer's Almanac*.

Lynn Wells is a professor of English at the University of Regina in Canada. Her areas of specialization include contemporary British fiction, urban fiction, and literature and ethics. She is the author of *Allegories of Telling: Self-Referential Narrative in Contemporary British Fiction* (2003) and *Ian McEwan* (2009). She is the vice president of academics at First Nations University of Canada, a federated college of the University of Regina.

Justyna Deszcz-Tryhubczak is an assistant professor of literature and cofounder of the Center for Young People's Literature and Culture at the Institute of English Studies, University of Wrocław, Poland, where she teaches English literature and a variety of courses related to children's literature. She is the author of *Rushdie in Wonderland: "Fairytaleness" in Salman Rushdie's Fiction* (2004) and has published articles on Salman Rushdie, Angela Carter, fairy tales, and fantasy for young adults in *Folklore* and *Marvel & Tales*. She coedited *Towards or Back to Human Values? Spiritual and Moral Dimensions of Contemporary Fantasy* (2006), *Considering Fantasy: Ethical, Didactic and Therapeutic Aspects of Fantasy in Literature and Film* (2007), and *Relevant across Cultures: Visions of Connectedness and Earth Citizenship in Modern Fantasy for Young Readers* (2009). Her research interests include children's literature and culture, childhood studies, utopianism, ecocriticism, and intermediality.

Lydia Forssander-Song is an assistant professor of English at Trinity Western University in British Columbia, Canada. She was a regular poetry reviewer for the *Canadian Book Review Annual* from 2004 to 2009. Her recent contributions to Salem Press publications include articles on Michael Ondaatje in *Great Lives from History: The 20th Century* (2008), *The English Patient* and *Midnight's Children* in *Masterplots* (2000, 2010), Shirley Geok-lin Lim in *Encyclopedia of American Immigration* (2010), Agha Shahid Ali in *Critical Survey of Poetry: American Poets* (2011), and Chimamanda Ngozi Adichie in *Critical Survey of Short Fiction* (2010).

Dohra Ahmad is an associate professor of English at St. John's University. Her areas of research and teaching interest include world anglophone literature, ethnic American literature, utopian fiction, postcolonial theory, and world literature pedagogy. She is the author of *Landscapes of Hope: Anti-Colonial Utopianism in America* (2009) and the editor of *Rotten English: A Literary Anthology* (2007). Her articles have appeared in the *Journal of Commonwealth Literature*, *Yale Journal of Criticism*, *Social Text*, and *ELH*.

Robert C. Evans is I. B. Young Professor of English at Auburn University at Montgomery. He is the author or editor of more than twenty books and of over two hundred essays, both in print and in online databases. Much of his writing focuses on close reading and critical pluralism. He is the recipient of grants from the National Endowment for the Humanities, the Folger Shakespeare Library, the Newberry Library, the Huntington Library, the American Philosophical Society, the Mellon Foundation, and the Center for Medieval and Renaissance Studies at the University of California, Los Angeles. Much of his recent work has dealt with American literature of the nineteenth and twentieth centuries.

Patrick Colm Hogan is a professor in the English Department of the University of Connecticut, where he is also on the faculty of the India Studies Program. He is the author of over a dozen books, including *Colonialism and Cultural Identity: Crises of Tradition in the Anglophone Literatures of India, Africa, and the Caribbean* (2000), *Empire and Poetic Voice: Cognitive and Cultural Studies of Literary Tradition and Colonialism* (2004), and *Understanding Indian Movies: Culture, Cognition, and Cinematic Imagination* (2008). He has also served as editor for a number of books, including *Literary India: Comparative Studies in Aesthetics, Colonialism, and Culture* (1995) and *Rabindranath Tagore: Universality and Tradition* (2003), both coedited with his wife, literary critic and Kashmiri poet Lalita Pandit.

Index

Abdullah, Sheik, 268, 270
Abu Simbel, Karim (*The Satanic Verses*), 172
Akbar, Emperor, 62–63
Akbar (*The Enchantress of Florence*), 63, 75
Akhtar, Mishal (*The Satanic Verses*), 173
anger, restorative power of, 177
anticolonial nationalism, 264, 276
anticommunalism in *Shalimar the Clown*, 278
Apsara, Vina (*The Ground Beneath Her Feet*), 234, 235, 241
Arab Andalusia
    hydridity in, 57
    religious coexistence in, 225
Arabian Nights, The 110, 185
Arendt, Hannah, 136, 148
art
    hybrid, failure of, 224
    secular faith expressed through, 219
Attâr, Farid ud-Din, 16, 103, 211
Atta ("The Prophet's Hair"), 48, 50
authorial voice. *See* narration
authoritarianism, critique of, 110
Ayesha (*The Satanic Verses*), 173
Aziz, Aadam (*Midnight's Children*), 108, 139

Babri Masjid, 54, 55–56
Babur, Emperor, 55–56
Balich, Drenka (*Sabbath's Theater*), 87
Baum, Frank, 185
Bhand Pather, anticommunalist outlook of, 278
Bhutto, Benazir, fictionalized, 158
Bhutto, Zulfikar Ali, fictionalized, 110, 158

blasphemy. *See* fatwā; Khomeini, Ruhollah; *Satanic Verses* controversy
Boabdil (*The Moor's Last Sigh*), 57
Bombay
    capitalism in, 169
    hybridity in, 71, 226
Brodsky, Joseph, 14
Bulgakov, Mikhail, 112

Cama, Gayomart (*The Ground Beneath Her Feet*), 240
Cama, Lady Spenta (*The Ground Beneath Her Feet*), 240
Cama, Ormus (*The Ground Beneath Her Feet*), 234, 235
Cama, Sir Darius Xerxes (*The Ground Beneath Her Feet*), 236–37
capitalism
    alienation inherent in, 168
    alternative to cultural hybridity, 72
    effects on identity, 181
    oppression commodified by, 176
    rejection of, 178
    religion and, 173
catalogs and lists in *Fury*, 249–62
Celano, Mira (*The Ground Beneath Her Feet*), 245
censorship
    effect on Pakistani media, 16, 157
    Rushdie's view on, 19
    Satanic Verses responses, 3, 17
    World Writers Statement against, 82
Chamcha, Saladin (*The Satanic Verses*), 12, 112, 169, 174–80
Chamchawala, Changez (*The Satanic Verses*), 174
characterization
    lists and catalogs in, 255–57, 259, 262
    otherworlds and, 99

children's literature
  contemporary challenges in, 195
  media and, 195
  Rushdie's books of, 182
Christianity
  law in British India and, 227
  official responses to *Satanic Verses* controversy, 91
  origin of Mahound, 12, 92
clown. *See* jester
colonization
  migrants' experience of, 168
  precursor to later problems, 151
  subversion of, 144
comic device
  embodiment as, 9
  listing and cataloging as, 259
  narratorial tone as, 154
communism
  failure of, 207, 225
  fundamentalism and, 223
compassion, suppression of, 274–75
Cone, Alleluia "Allie" (*The Satanic Verses*), 112–13
Conference of the Birds, The (Attâr), 16, 102, 104, 108–109, 211
contact zones
  definition of, 182
  Rushdie's fiction as, 193, 195
controversy. *See* fatwā; *Satanic Verses* controversy
critical reception, 27–36
cross-cultural exchange, online, 183, 188

Da Gama, Camoens (*The Moor's Last Sigh*), 225
Deggle (*Grimus*), 101
dell'Amore, Mogor (*The Enchantress of Florence*), 63

democracy
  Bombay politics and, 69, 71
  suspension of, 65, 107
  symbols for, 108
demonology, use of, 101
Desai, Anita, 7
diabology, use of, 101
dichotomy in *The Moor's Last Sigh*, 221
disorientation, conception of, 236
Disturbed Areas Act of 1990, 271. *See also* Kashmir conflict
doubles theme, 239–45
Dresang, Eliza, 190
duality in *The Moor's Last Sigh*, 221

East, West: Stories (Rushdie), 20, 46
embodiment
  comic use of, 9
  history, 146
  history, 141–44
emergency rule
  cause of, 117
  democracy and, 65
  fictionalized effects of, 119
  metaphorical depiction of, 117, 124
empathy. *See* compassion
Enchantress of Florence, The (Rushdie), 35, 62, 64
Fakh, Bulbul (*Shalimar the Clown*). *See* Iron Mullah (*Shalimar the Clown*)

fairy tale
  evolution of, 185
  protagonist agency in, 186
  reinforcement of *status quo*, 187
Fall of Man, allusions to, 109, 112
Farishta, Gibreel (*The Satanic Verses*), 12, 112, 169, 171–74, 180
fatwā
  reaffirmation of, 89

response to *The Satanic Verses*, 18, 25, 31, 46, 79, 198, 214
  Rushdie's response, 18–20, 89, 182, 200, 210, 236
feces/theses dichotomy in *The Moor's Last Sigh*, 221
feminism
  resistence to patriarchy, 66
  response to *Shame*, 161
Fielding, Raman (*The Moor's Last Sigh*), 54, 218
Flapping Eagle (*Grimus*), 104, 106
Forster, E. M., 97
Foucault, Michel, 117
Free Islam Convocation, 108
fundamentalism
  construction of, 222, 223
  hybridity versus, 222
  totalizing vision of, 215
Fury (Rushdie), 34–35, 86–88, 247–62
fury theme, 248

Gandhi, Indira
  emergency rule of, 107, 117, 119, 124
  fictionalized, 65, 121
Ganesh (Hindu god), 9
García Márquez, Gabriel, 202
Gegroo brothers (*Shalimar the Clown*), 272, 273
Ghani, Naseem (*Midnight's Children*), 66
globalization
  children's literature in, 189, 195
  effects of, 72, 183
  utopian vision of, 184
"Goodbye, Columbus" (Roth), 83
gossip, history as, 67
Grass, Günter, 5, 10, 202, 203
Greek myth, 241
Grimus (*Grimus*), 105

Grimus (Rushdie), 16, 27–28, 104, 105
Ground Beneath Her Feet, The (Rushdie), 34, 233–45
Guillotine, Madame (*Shame*), 111

Harappa, Rani (*Shame*), 159, 160, 161
"Harmony of the Spheres, The" (Rushdie), 223
Haroun and the Sea of Stories (Rushdie), 106, 182, 184, 188
Harrapa, Iskander (*Shame*), 110, 164–65
Hashim ("The Prophet's Hair"), 48, 50
Hazratbal Mosque riots, 51–53
Hindu deities, 9, 104, 107. *See also individual deities*
Hinduism, 110, 218
historiography
  feminist, 65–66
  Indian nationalist, 63
  Kashmiri nationalist, 72
  subaltern, 69–71
history
  actual events, use of, 45, 64, 124, 154
  allegorical, 64
  alternative, theory of, 46
  art as, 57
  atrophy of, 129
  autobiography conflated with, 117–21, 128
  "chutnification of," 62
  embodiment of, 141–44, 146
  employment of, 267
  fragmented, theory of, 117
  gossip as, 67
  subjectivity of, 125–26, 265
hope, loss of, 138–40, 277
Huma ("The Prophet's Hair"), 48
hybridity
  failure of, 63
  flaws of, 227–28, 228–29

hybridity (*continued*)
  fundamentalism versus, 222
  Hindu nationalist threat to, 68–69
  idealization of, 71–72, 75
  institutionalization of, 229–30
  migrants' experience of, 74
  subversive force of, 74
  valorization of illegitimacy, 226
Hyder, Bilquís (*Shame*), 159, 160
Hyder, Naveed "Good News" (*Shame*), 163
Hyder, Raza (*Shame*), 110, 159, 164–65
Hyder, Sufiya Zinobia (*Shame*), 162–64, 165–66

Iblis, 111. *See also* demonology; diabology; Mahound: origin of name
identity
  concealed, 174
  media effects on, 178
  restored, 177
Imaginary Homelands: Essays and Criticisms, 1981–1991 (Rushdie), 19, 32, 198, 200
Indian English literature
  language choice in, 205
  Rushdie's praise for, 32
  Rushdie's work within, 17, 29
Indian Penal Code 420, 119. *See also* law
Inferno (Dante), 104
Iron Mullah (*Shalimar the Clown*), 274
Islam
  creative expression limited in, 91
  fundamentalist, depiction of, 214
  iconoclasm in, 103
  Rushdie's appeal for change within, 210
  Rushdie's view on, 210
  symbolized in Boabdil, 215

jester, 278–79
Jones, Virgil (*Grimus*), 105
journalism. *See* news reporting
Judaism
  Indian history of, 217
  Indian Islam and, 216
Jussawalla, Feroza, 29
justice versus freedom of speech, 209
Kachhwaha (*Shalimar the Clown*), 273–74, 276
Kālī (Hindu goddess), 110
Kashmir
  history of, 266–67, 270–73
  myth of lost paradise, 265
  sectarianism in, 51–54
  self-rule in, 266–67
Kashmira (*Shalimar the Clown*), 277
Kashmir conflict
  1987 elections, 270
  colonial law in, 271
  depiction in "The Prophet's Hair," 47
  in-fighting, 272–73
  Islamism and, 272
  origins of, 267–69
Kashmiriyat
  idealization of, 72, 264–65, 267
  nationalist historiography and, 72
Kathāsaritsāgara (Somadeva), 184–85
Kaul, Boonyi (*Shalimar the Clown*), 276
Kemal, Mahmoud (*Shame*), 113
Khalifa, Haroun (*Haroun and the Sea of Stories*), 186
Khalifa, Haroun (*Luka and the Fire of Life*), 192
Khalifa, Luka (*Luka and the Fire of Life*), 191–92
Khalifa, Rashid (*Luka and the Fire of Life*), 194
Khamanei, Ali (ayatollah of Iran), 89
Khattam-Shud (*Haroun and the Sea of Stories*), 213

Khomeini, Ruhollah (ayatollah of Iran)
fictionalized, 13, 213
response to *The Satanic Verses*, 18,
 25, 31, 46, 79, 198, 214
Kissing of Abbas Ali Baig, The, 228
Kosík, Karel, 135

language
 choice of, 205
 hybridity of, 8–9
law
 British colonial, 227, 271
 miscegenation and, 226
 mythologized, 119
 state terror through, 271
literature
 political engagement of, 134
 politics' intrusion into, 135
 reader participation in, 133
 sacred versus secular, 13, 208
Little Brain (*Fury*), 247
Loki (Norse god), 107
London, Thatcherism in, 168
Luka and the Fire of Life (Rushdie),
 182, 183, 184, 191–95

magic realism
 inspiration for Rushdie's fiction, 14
 mode for discussing Pakistan, 156
 newness through, 147
 political consciousness in South
  America and, 202
 profit motive of, 230
 Rushdie's work as, 8, 44, 99
Mahendra, Neela (*Fury*), 92, 255
Mahound (*The Satanic Verses*), 82
 origin of name, 12, 92
Mahound (*The Satanic Verses*), 172–73
Maria (*The Ground Beneath Her Feet*),
 243

Márquez, Gabriel García. *See* García
 Márquez, Gabriel.
Master and Margarita, The (Bulgakov),
 112
Maulana Dawood (*Shame*), 164
Media (*Grimus*), 107
Merchant of Venice, The (Shakespeare),
 216
Merchant, Umeed "Rai" (*The Ground
 Beneath Her Feet*), 234, 240
Methwold, William (*The Ground Beneath Her Feet*), 236
Midnight's Children (Rushdie), 16–17,
 28–30, 64–66, 107–10, 115–29
migrancy theme, 4, 6, 204–206
Milo, Mila (*Fury*), 87, 255
Miłosz, Czesław, 7
mimicry, 144
Miranda, Vasco (*The Moor's Last Sigh*),
 224, 229, 230
*Mirrorwork: 50 Years of Indian Writing,
 1947–1997* (Rushdie), 32
miscegenation
 1830 Petition of Grievances, 226
 illegitimacy and, 226
 racial purity versus, 222
Moi-e-Muqqadas, theft of, 48, 51–53. *See
 also* Kashmir conflict; sectarianism
Moor's Last Sigh, The (Rushdie), 33, 44,
 54–58, 68, 72, 213, 231
Muhammad (prophet), fictionalized, 81
Mumbai's Axis, 70, 218

naming
 doubling in, 240
 multiplicity of, 6
Nandy, Ashis, 46
narration
 authorial commentary, 154
 authorial voice in, 238–39, 255–56

narration (*continued*)
  Indian storytelling as, 118
  lists and catalogs in, 250
  polyphony in, 121–22
  satanic, 112
  skaz, 154
  tone set by, 154
  unreliable, 122–23, 127
Nehru, Jawaharlal
  fictionalized, 115
  Indian nationalism and, 61, 63
  vision for independent India, 65, 71
news reporting
  justice versus sensationalism, 209
  similarity with fiction, 208–209
Noman, Abdullah (*Shalimar the Clown*), 268, 272
Noman, Anees (*Shalimar the Clown*), 272
Noman, Firdaus (*Shalimar the Clown*), 272
Noman, Noman Sher (*Shalimar the Clown*). *See* Shalimar (*Shalimar the Clown*)
Norse myth, 104, 107. *See also* individual deities; Ragnarök

Odin (Norse god), 107
online gaming, 183, 189, 191–93
orality, written, 182
Orientalism, subversion of, 185
origins, exploration of, 223
Orpheus myth, 241
Othello (Shakespeare), 112
otherworldly realism, 99
otherworlds
  narrative structure and, 99
  parallel to reality, 242–44
outsideness
  norm of, 244–45
  synonym for disorientation, 237

Padma (*Midnight's Children*), 109, 118
Pakistan
  allegorical representation of, 155–57
  Islamization program in, 158
  secularism and, 99
panchayat system in Kashmir, 266–67
Parameswaran, Uma, 26, 27
parentage, uncertain, 6, 10, 216
Parvati (Hindu goddess), 104
Parvati-the-witch (*Midnight's Children*), 117, 119
political literature
  modern fairy tales as, 186
  revisionism in, 183
  status quo in classic fairy tales, 187
  subaltern characters in, 142
  vilification technique in, 267
politics
  archetypal contests in, 253
  community building as, 136, 148
  crisis of, 135
  intrusion into literature, 135
  plebeianization in India, 69
  power struggle in, 270
  subjectivity in, 136
polyphony. *See* narration
pop cosmopolitanism, 183
  effects of, 183–84
  global youth culture and, 188
Portnoy's Complaint (Roth), 83–85
postcolonial colonialism, 264, 269
postcolonial emancipation myth, 264
postcolonial literature
  English language in, 205
  Rushdie's influence on, 17
postmodern identity
  acting in, 169
  rejection of, 179
postmodernism, 168
"Prophet's Hair, The" (Rushdie), 47–51

Qara Köz, Princess (*The Enchantress of Florence*), 62, 64

racial purity, miscegenation versus, 223
racism
  restitution for, 177
  transmuting power of, 175
radical change theory, 190
Ragnarök, allusions to, 104, 107
Rancière, Jacques, 136
realism
  actual events referenced, 45, 64, 154
  actual persons referenced, 31, 86, 267
  lists and catalogs' support of, 250, 251, 259
religion
  coexistence in Moorish Spain, 225
  difference with literature, 207–208
  fundamentalism in, 221
  iconoclasm and mysticism in, 103
  misuse of, 53, 106
  resemblances between, 219
  role in Rushdie's fiction, 97
  substitutions of, 218
  truths or objects, use of, 105
repetition
  American literary tradition of, 261
  metrical emphasis, 251
  Rushdie's use of, 248
rock music
  "The Ground Beneath Her Feet" (song), 34
  influence on Rushdie's fiction, 233
Roth, Philip, 77–78, 214

Sabbath, Mickey (*Sabbath's Theater*), 85, 87–88
Sabbath's Theater (Roth), 85, 86–88
Salman the Persian (*The Satanic Verses*), 12, 81

Saravati, Uma (*The Moor's Last Sigh*), 220
Satanic Verses historical episode, 12, 111
Satanic Verses controversy
  critical analysis and, 31
  influence on later writing, 235–36
  initial fallout, 11, 17–18, 79–83
  non-Muslim response to, 80, 91
  Rushdie's defense, 11, 13
  violence in, 3, 18, 77
Satanic Verses, The (Rushdie), 12, 17, 31, 32, 73–75, 78–83, 103, 111–13, 168–81
Scheherazade (*The Arabian Nights*), 110
science fiction, Rushdie's work as, 27
sectarianism
  early modern Kashmir and, 265
  Kashmiriyat opposed to, 264
  postindependence India threatened by, 120
  violence and, 51–54
secularism
  Babri Masjid destruction and, 56
  expression through art, 57, 219
  Islam and, 210
  Pakistan and, 99
  Rushdie's promotion of, 98–99
  Rushdie's upbringing and, 16
selfhood
  fluidity of, 170
  inability to unify, 180
  Lucretian concept of, 171
  Ovidian concept of, 171
  unified, 179
sensationalism, journalism versus, 209
September 11, 2001, terrorist attacks
  Fury publication, 247
  Rushdie's response to, 210, 211–12
Shakespeare, William, 112, 216
Shakil, Omar Khayyam (*Shame*), 152, 153–54, 161, 163

Shalimar (*Shalimar the Clown*), 275, 277
Shalimar the Clown (Rushdie), 35, 72–73, 264–79
Shame (Rushdie), 30–31, 67, 68, 110–11, 150, 166
sharam, 153
Shiva (Hindu god), 104, 107
Shiva (*Midnight's Children*), 110, 119
Shiv Sena
    administration of, 55
    fictionalized, 70, 218
    goals of, 218
Sín ("The Prophet's Hair"), 49, 51
Sinai, Ahmed (*Midnight's Children*), 109
Sinai, Saleem (*Midnight's Children*), 9, 64, 109, 115, 146
Singer, Jamila (*Midnight's Children*), 108, 113
Singh, Gulab, 266
Singh, Hari, 267–68
Sisodia, Whisky (*The Satanic Verses*), 178
Solanka, Malik (*Fury*), 86, 87–88, 247–48
Somadeva, 106, 184
Song of Myself (Whitman), 104, 261
Sontag, Susan, 3
Special Powers Act of 1990, 271. *See also* Kashmir conflict
Step Across This Line: Collected Nonfiction, 1992–2002 (Rushdie), 19, 32, 200
storytelling
    blending Eastern and Western, 182
    fable form of, 201
    utopia preserved through, 187
Sufism, 103, 105, 106
Sufyan, Mishal (*The Satanic Verses*), 176
Sufyan, Muhammad (*The Satanic Verses*), 113

Tai Bibi (*Midnight's Children*), 143
Tai (*Midnight's Children*), 117, 143
technology, impact on parent-child dynamic, 190
terrorism
    religion and, 101
    Rushdie's response to, 210, 211–12
    theme of, 34
Thackeray, Bal, fictionalized, 33, 55, 218
Thatcherism
    acceptance of, 170
    cultural imperialism and, 176
    depiction of, 168, 175
    theses/feces dichotomy in *The Moor's Last Sigh*, 221
twins, 240–41

U2, 34
unreliable narrator. *See* narration
urban center, 168, 226
utopia
    failure of, 223
    institutionalization of, 187
    preservation of, 188
    reality institutionalized in, 223

Vakil, Zeenat (*The Moor's Last Sigh*), 218, 222
Vakil, Zeenat (*The Satanic Verses*), 73, 179
Valence, Hal (*The Satanic Verses*), 176
Vintage Book of Indian Writing, 1947–1997, The (Rushdie), 32
violence
    cycle of, 269
    Kashmiri sectarianism and, 51–54
    personal motivation for, 275
    retribution through, 272
    societal legitimation of, 273, 275

Whitman, Walt, 104, 261
Widow, the (*Midnight's Children*), 65, 110, 121
Wonderful Wizard of Oz, The (Baum), 185–88

Zain-ul-Abidin, Sultan, 265
Zia-ul-Haq, Muhammad, fictionalized, 110, 158
Zogoiby, Abraham (*The Moor's Last Sigh*), 215, 222
Zogoiby, Aurora (*The Moor's Last Sigh*), 54, 215, 220
Zogoiby, Flory (*The Moor's Last Sigh*), 215, 222
Zogoiby, Moraes (*The Moor's Last Sigh*), 56, 215